cook's library

One Pot

cook's library

One Pot

p

This is a Parragon Book
This edition published in 2003

Parragon
Queen Street House
4 Queen Street
Bath BA1 1HE, UK

ISBN: 0-75258-751-X

Printed in China

NOTE

This book uses metric and imperial measurements. Follow the same units of measurement throughout; do not mix metric and imperial. All spoon measurements are level: teaspoons are assumed to be 5 ml, and tablespoons are assumed to be 15 ml. Unless otherwise stated, milk is assumed to be full fat, eggs and individual vegetables such as potatoes are medium, and pepper is freshly ground black pepper.

The times given for each recipe are an approximate guide only because the preparation times may differ according to the techniques used by different people and the cooking times may vary as a result of the type of oven used. The preparation times include chilling and marinating times, where appropriate.

Recipes using raw or very lightly cooked eggs should be avoided by infants, the elderly, pregnant women, convalescents, and anyone suffering from an illness.

Contents

Introduction

Cooking one-pot meals has many advantages, the most obvious of which is damage limitation – in other words, you don't have to spend time juggling numerous pans on your stove, only to follow an enjoyable meal with having to wash them all up. There are other, more subtle benefits, too. If there is only one pan to keep your eye on or, occasionally, when a second pan is required to prepare rice or pasta to accompany the one-pot meal – and many one-pot dishes require little attention during cooking anyway – there is less chance of something spoiling, boiling over or burning when your back is turned. Slow-cooked dishes in a casserole or covered pan lose fewer nutrients and the flavours of their ingredients are wonderfully enhanced and intermingled. At the opposite end of the spectrum, fast-cook, stir-fry dishes retain the colour, texture and flavour of their ingredients, plus much of their nutritional value. Last, but by no means least, using only one pot cuts down the amount of fuel required, assisting the family budget and the environment at the same time. All in all, it is difficult to understand why anyone still bothers with meat and two veg.

When you look through the collection of recipes in this book, you may be surprised to discover how versatile one-pot cooking is. Probably the first dishes that spring to mind are hearty and satisfying stews and there are certainly plenty of these, ranging from richly flavoured Beef and Potato Goulash (see page 32) to spicy and exotic Thai Green Fish Curry (see page 154). These sorts of dishes are perfect for the busy cook with a hungry family as, once the initial preparation is completed, you can just leave the pot to bubble gently, emitting its appetizing aroma, while you get on with something else. Slow cooking is the best way with inexpensive cuts of meat, as it transforms them into melt-in-the-mouth tenderness, creating an economical, as well as delicious meal. As most stews taste even better on reheating, you can even prepare them the day before.

Lighter stews and meal-in-bowl soups are just made for those in-between occasions. When the weather lets you down and sunshine turns to miserable rain, what could be more cheering than a colourful Rich Chicken Casserole (see page 88)? Weekends are meant for relaxing, but, with a family, they often seem to be one long dash to complete the chores, do the shopping and chauffeur the kids around. Solve the problem of Saturday lunch with a bowl of Tuscan Onion Soup (see page 96) or Fish and Crab Chowder (see page 142) and a loaf of fresh, crusty bread.

Pot roasts bring a welcome change to the family menu. They have all the advantages of a traditional roast – and are often much more succulent – with none of the bother and mess. As timing is not critical, they are also excellent for informal entertaining, allowing you to relax with your guests and not worry about late arrivals.

Bakes are always popular, whether family favourites, such as Macaroni Cheese and Tomato (see page 133), or more adventurous dishes, such as Seafood Lasagne (see page 164). As a rule, they cook more quickly than stews and casseroles, so they are a good choice for midweek suppers when less time is available.

Of course, when time is really short, reach for the wok. Stir-fried dishes are the original fast food. After all, the technique was invented to cope with a chronic fuel shortage – the ingredients all go into one pan and are cooked in minutes. Preparation takes a little longer, as it is important to make sure that everything is ready before you start cooking and that ingredients are chopped or sliced to about the same size so that they cook evenly. Even so, these are dishes that can take less than 10 minutes from kitchen to table. Pan-fried dishes are not usually quite so fast and, like stir-fries, do require quite a lot of attention during cooking. However, the results are worth it.

For those who love to cook, but can't stand the washing up, the king of one-pot dishes must be the risotto, a glorious rice-based combination. For good results, you must use the highest-quality ingredients – never leftovers – and you can't hurry a risotto. Once the rice starts cooking, you must stir assiduously and keep a sharp eye out for the precise moment to add more stock. The uniquely creamy result is worth the bother, whether delicate Minted Green Risotto (see page 112) or luxurious Rich Lobster Risotto (see page 171) – and you've still used only one pot. Other rice dishes, such as pilaus, may be less demanding, although no less delicious. While thinking about grains, don't overlook the ingenious Moroccan tagine. While a fabulous stew cooks in the pan below, couscous steams gently in a basket on top, so that they are ready to be served together.

Equipment

Everything you require for satisfactory one-pot cooking is probably already in your kitchen, but if you are considering buying replacements or want to drop hints about presents to family and friends, there are one or two things worth considering.

A set of good saucepans really is worth having. First, you do need a set because it is important to have the right size pan for the quantity of food you are cooking and this will vary depending on the particular recipe and the number of servings. The pan must be large enough to contain all the ingredients and to allow you to stir them without sloshing them all over the hob, but not so big that the liquid evaporates and the food scorches or, worse, burns into a kind of welded mass on the base. Secondly, you need the best quality you can afford. Cheap, flimsy pans do not distribute the heat evenly, so look for those with a heavy base. A tight-fitting lid is essential and, if it is made of heatproof glass, you can check on progress without having to lift it. However, glass lids are more vulnerable to damage than metal ones – never run cold water straight on to a hot lid. If you have a dishwasher, make sure the pans are suitable. Some people prefer non-stick linings and modern ones are much more resilient than older linings. They are particularly useful if you are concerned about fat intake, as you can cook with less fat or oil than in a conventional pan.

Flameproof casseroles are one of humankind's greatest achievements. They can be used on the hob for softening onions and browning meat, then transferred straight to the oven or they can be used to cook the whole dish on the hob. Most of them are attractively designed, so they can also be transferred straight to the table without the need for extra serving dishes. Again, a range of sizes is useful.

A wok is also well worth having. It can be used for any number of cooking techniques in addition to stir-frying, including deep-frying and steaming. If you are going to buy only one, choose a wok that is bigger than you think you will need. They are available in a range of materials and, like saucepans, a heavy one is better than a flimsy one. Non-stick woks are available, but they cannot be heated to the high temperatures required for perfect stir-frying. Non-stick woks will almost certainly require seasoning before use: follow the manufacturer's instructions. Some woks are sold with a dome-shaped lid, while others will require you to buy this separately. It is not essential, but is useful.

A heavy-based frying pan is a worthwhile investment. Many professional cooks prefer cast-iron, although this will need seasoning, and heavy-gauge steel is also a good choice. A frying pan with a metal handle can also be used under the grill to brown the tops of dishes, such as frittata. However, this can be a safety hazard for careless cooks, so if you fall into this category, make sure you have a well-secured wooden handle (you can always cover it in foil to put it under the grill). Whether the pan has a non-stick lining is a matter of personal choice.

In a strict definition of one-pot cooking, steamers could be seen as cheating, but they are invaluable. Extra vegetables, grains or even desserts can be steamed above the main dish, using no extra fuel and creating very little more washing up. Chinese stacking bamboo steamers are inexpensive and easy to use with a wok, while collapsible metal ones are convenient if storage space is limited.

Preparation is an integral part of cooking and, again, time and effort are saved if you have the right tools. Sharp knives are essential, as they speed up slicing and chopping, ensure even-sized and neatly shaped pieces and are safer – it's the blunt knives that slip and cut fingers. You will need a minimum of two. A cook's knife is used for chopping or slicing vegetables, herbs and meat. Choose one with a heavy, wide blade, about 18–20 cm/7–8 inches long. A small paring knife, about 8–10 cm/3¼–4 inches long, is the best size for peeling and trimming vegetables. There are many other sorts of knives – bread, utility, cheese, grapefruit, ham and tomato, for example – and the bigger the selection you have, the more likely you will be able to match the right tool to the job.

A swivel-blade vegetable peeler is inexpensive and easier to use than a knife. As the nutrients in many vegetables, such as potatoes, are concentrated directly beneath the skin, peeling them thinly makes sense. You can also use a vegetable peeler for shaving Parmesan or other hard cheese for garnishes.

Chopping boards are necessary and you should use separate boards for raw meat, poultry and fish and for vegetables to avoid cross contamination. Materials vary from wood to plastic and even glass and all have both advantages and disadvantages. Traditional wooden blocks, at least 4 cm/1½ inches thick, are the most popular and practical, but they cannot be sterilized. Plastic boards are less appealing, but can be bleached or washed with boiling water and are dishwasher safe. Laminated chopping boards are best kept for decoration, as they are dangerously slippery and, as the laminate chips easily and lifts with time, they may be unhygienic.

Measuring spoons and jugs and kitchen scales take the guesswork out of cooking. However, precise measurements are not usually so critical with one-pot cooking as they are with, say, baking. In all recipes, spoon measurements are level, rather than heaped.

There are, of course, masses of other kitchen tools and all have their uses – some more frequently than others. Small items, such as a can opener, slotted and wooden spoons and a lemon squeezer or reamer, can be acquired over time. Larger, more expensive equipment, such as a food processor, make life easier, but they are a major investment. If you don't have one, don't despair – a box grater is adequate for cheese and breadcrumbs, you can push a mixture through a wire sieve to purée it and a pestle and heavy mortar is just as good for grinding. As with equipment for any activity, from carpentry to cooking, whatever you are buying, it is worth paying for the best quality that you can afford.

Little Extras

All the recipes in this book are designed to stand alone as an adequate, tasty and nutritious meal, but with little extra effort or cost, you can turn an ordinary supper into a special occasion. A judicious use of ready-prepared accompaniments and garnishes also makes entertaining easy.

Nowadays, supermarket shelves are stacked with a marvellous selection of breads and rolls, from the ever-popular French baguette to Italian focaccia and ciabatta and from Indian naan to Lebanese flatbreads. Serve them with risottos, curries and bakes, as well as soups and stews. Packs of prepared mixed salad leaves make an easy and refreshing accompaniment to almost any dish. You don't even have to make your own dressing, as a vast range, from thousand island to simple vinaigrette, is on sale. Pasta salads, coleslaw, tabbouleh and many other salads can be found on the delicatessen counter in the supermarket, where you can also buy olives, gherkins and other pickles.

Many of the recipes suggest a suitable garnish and almost every dish looks more attractive sprinkled with chopped fresh herbs. Other easy garnishes include chopped nuts and seeds. Ready-made croûtons are an inexpensive and useful store-cupboard item.

When you are shopping, it is worth keeping your eyes open for these little extras that will give your one-pot meals that finishing touch.

Basic Recipes

These recipes form the basis of several of the dishes contained throughout this book. Many of these basic recipes can be made in advance and stored in the refrigerator until required.

Fresh Chicken Stock

MAKES
1.75 LITRES/3 PINTS

1 kg/2 lb 4 oz chicken, skinned
2 sticks celery, chopped
1 onion, sliced
2 carrots, chopped
1 garlic clove
few sprigs of fresh parsley
2 litres/3½ pints water
salt and pepper

1 Place all the ingredients in a large saucepan and bring to the boil.

2 Skim away any surface scum using a large flat spoon. Reduce the heat to a gentle simmer, partially cover, and cook for 2 hours. Leave to cool.

3 Line a sieve with clean muslin and place over a large jug or bowl. Pour the stock through the sieve. The cooked chicken can be used in another recipe. Discard the other solids. Cover the stock and chill.

4 Skim off any surface fat before using. Store in the refrigerator for up to 3 days, or freeze in small batches until required.

Fresh Vegetable Stock

MAKES
1.75 LITRES/3 PINTS

1 large onion, sliced
1 large carrot, diced
1 stick celery, chopped
2 garlic cloves
1 dried bay leaf
few sprigs of fresh parsley
pinch of grated nutmeg
2 litres/3½ pints water
salt and pepper

1 Place all the ingredients in a large saucepan and bring to the boil.

2 Skim away any surface scum using a large flat spoon. Reduce the heat to a gentle simmer, partially cover, and cook for 45 minutes. Leave to cool.

3 Line a sieve with clean muslin and place over a large jug or bowl. Pour the stock through the sieve. Discard the solids.

4 Cover the stock and store in the refrigerator for up to 3 days, or freeze in small portions.

Fresh Fish Stock

MAKES
1.75 LITRES/3 PINTS

1 kg/2 lb 4 oz white fish bones, heads and scraps
1 large onion, chopped
2 carrots, chopped
2 celery sticks, chopped
½ tsp black peppercorns
½ tsp grated lemon rind
few sprigs of fresh parsley
2 litres/3½ pints water
salt and pepper

1 Rinse all the fish trimmings thoroughly in cold water and place in a large saucepan with the other ingredients. Bring to the boil.

2 Skim away any surface scum using a large flat spoon.

3 Reduce the heat to a gentle simmer and cook, partially covered, for 30 minutes. Leave to cool.

4 Line a sieve with clean muslin and place over a large jug or bowl. Pour the stock through the sieve. Discard the solids. Cover the stock and store in the refrigerator for up to 3 days until required, or freeze in small batches.

Fresh Beef Stock

MAKES
1.75 LITRES/3 PINTS

about 1 kg/2 lb 4 oz bones from a cooked joint or raw chopped beef
2 onions, studded with 6 cloves, or sliced or chopped coarsely
2 carrots, sliced
1 leek, sliced
1–2 celery sticks, sliced
1 Bouquet Garni
about 2.25 litres/4 pints water

1 Use chopped marrow bones with a few strips of shin of beef, if possible. Put in a roasting tin and cook in a preheated oven, 230°C/450°F/Gas Mark 8, for 30–50 minutes, until browned.

2 Transfer to a large saucepan with the other ingredients. Bring the stock to the boil and remove any scum from the surface with a large flat spoon.

3 Cover and simmer gently for 3–4 hours. Strain the stock and leave to cool. Remove any fat from the surface and chill. If stored for more than 24 hours the stock must be boiled every day, cooled quickly and chilled again.

4 The stock may be frozen for up to 2 months; place in a large plastic bag and seal, leaving at least 2.5 cm/1 inch of headspace to allow for expansion.

Chinese Stock

MAKES
2.5 LITRES/4½ PINTS

750 g/1 lb 10 oz chicken pieces, trimmed and chopped
750 g/1 lb 10 oz pork spare ribs
3.75 litres/6 pints cold water
3–4 pieces of fresh root ginger, chopped
3–4 spring onions, each tied into a knot
3–4 tbsp Chinese rice wine or dry sherry

1 Place the chicken and pork in a large saucepan with the water. Add the ginger and spring onions.

2 Bring to the boil, and skim away any surface scum using a large flat spoon. Reduce the heat and simmer the stock, uncovered, for at least 2–3 hours.

3 Strain the stock, discarding the chicken, pork, ginger and spring onions. Add the Chinese rice wine and return to the boil, then reduce the heat and simmer for 2–3 minutes. Leave to cool.

4 Refrigerate the stock when cool. It will keep for up to 4–5 days. Alternatively, it can be frozen in small batches and defrosted as required.

Cornflour Paste

Mix 1 part cornflour with about 1.5 parts of cold water. Stir until smooth. The paste can be used to thicken sauces.

Fresh Bouquet Garni

1 fresh or dried bay leaf
few sprigs of fresh parsley
few sprigs of fresh thyme

Tie the herbs together with a length of string or cotton.

Dried Bouquet Garni

1 dried bay leaf
good pinch of dried mixed herbs or any one herb
good pinch of dried parsley
8–10 black peppercorns
2–4 cloves
1 garlic clove (optional)

Put all the ingredients in a small square of muslin and secure with string or cotton, leaving a long tail so it can be tied to the handle of the pan for easy removal.

How to Use This Book

Each recipe contains a wealth of useful information, including a breakdown of nutritional quantities, preparation and cooking times, and level of difficulty. All of this information is explained in detail below.

A full-colour photograph of the finished dish.

The ingredients for each recipe are listed in the order that they are used.

The nutritional information provided for each recipe is per serving or per portion. Optional ingredients, variations or serving suggestions have not been included in the calculations.

17

ONE POT

This is a quick and tasty way to use leftover roast chicken. The sauce can also be used for any cooked poultry, lamb or beef.

Fragrant Chicken *and* Broad Beans

SERVES 4

1 tsp mustard oil
3 tbsp vegetable oil
1 large onion, chopped finely
3 garlic cloves, crushed
1 tbsp tomato purée
2 tomatoes, peeled and chopped
1 tsp ground turmeric
½ tsp cumin seeds, ground
½ tsp coriander seeds, ground
½ tsp chilli powder
½ tsp garam masala
1 tsp red wine vinegar
1 small red pepper, chopped
125 g/4 oz frozen broad beans
500 g/1 lb cooked chicken breasts, cut into bite-sized pieces
salt
fresh coriander sprigs, to garnish

1 Heat the mustard oil in a large, frying pan set over a high heat for about 1 minute until it begins to smoke. Add the vegetable oil, reduce the heat and then add the onion and the garlic. Fry until they are golden.

2 Add the tomato purée, chopped tomatoes, ground turmeric, cumin and coriander seeds, chilli powder, garam masala and red wine vinegar to the frying pan. Stir the mixture until fragrant.

3 Add the red pepper and broad beans and stir for 2 minutes until the pepper is softened. Stir in the chicken, and salt to taste. Leave to simmer gently for 6–8 minutes until the chicken is heated through and the beans are tender.

4 Serve garnished with coriander leaves.

NUTRITION
Calories *270*; Sugars 3 *g*; Protein *36 g*; Carbohydrate *7 g*; Fat *11 g*; Saturates *2 g*

easy
25 mins
15 mins

COOK'S TIP
This dish is an ideal way of making use of any type of leftover poultry. Any variety of beans works well, but vegetables are just as useful, especially courgettes, potatoes or broccoli.

The method is clearly explained with step-by-step instructions that are easy to follow.

Cook's tips provide useful information regarding ingredients or cooking techniques.

The number of stars represents the difficulty of each recipe, ranging from very easy (1 star) to challenging (4 stars).

This amount of time represents the preparation of ingredients, including cooling, chilling and soaking times.

This represents the cooking time.

Meat

From ham to sausages and from beef to pork, you are sure to find an easy-to-prepare midweek supper or something special to serve guests. This chapter is packed with great ideas for meaty soups, succulent stews, spicy curries and almost instant stir-fries. It includes familiar favourites, such as Scotch Broth (see page 20) and Chilli con Carne (see page 33), and classic dishes, such as Pork Stroganoff (see page 40) and Lamb Biryani (see page 49). Adventurous cooks will enjoy experimenting with more unusual meats, trying out such recipes as Sweet and Sour Venison Stir-fry (see page 50). There are meals with child appeal, luxurious special occasion dishes, hearty winter-warmers, tasty light lunches, hot or aromatic curries and recipes from countries as far apart as China, Mexico and Italy. In fact, something to suit all tastes – just popped into the pot.

POT

ıditional winter
full of goodness,
with lots of tasty golden vegetables along with tender barley and lamb.

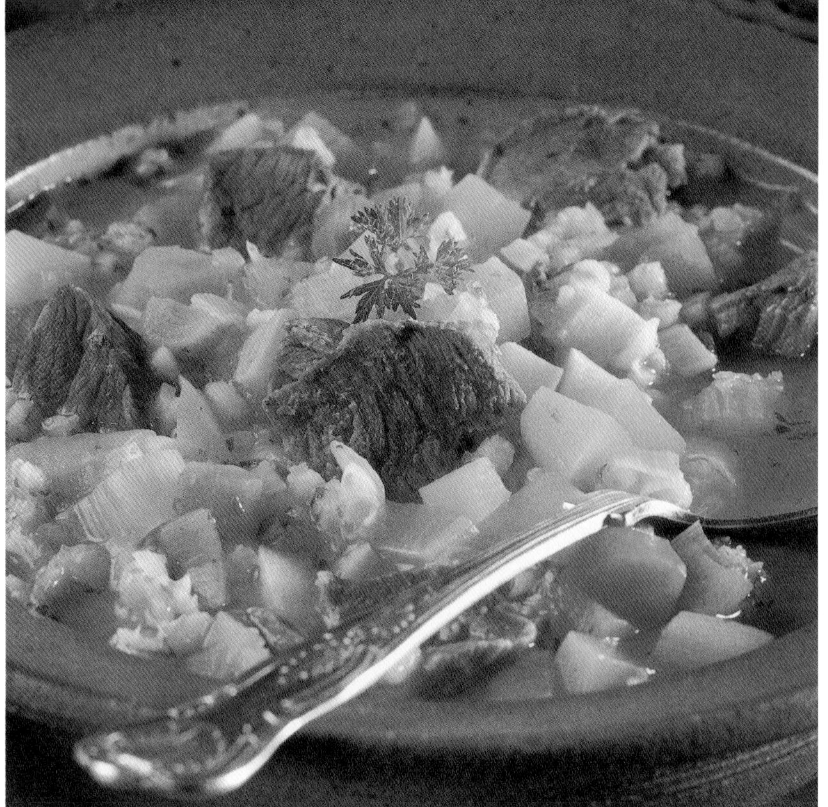

Scotch Broth

SERVES 4 – 6

- 55 g/2 oz pearl barley
- 300 g/10½ oz lean boneless lamb, such as shoulder or neck fillet, trimmed of fat and cut into 1-cm/½-inch cubes
- 700 ml/1¼ pints water
- 2 garlic cloves, chopped finely or crushed
- 1 litre/1¾ pints chicken or meat stock
- 1 onion, chopped finely
- 1 bay leaf
- 1 large leek, quartered lengthways and sliced
- 2 large carrots, diced finely
- 1 parsnip, diced finely
- 125 g/4½ oz swede, diced
- 2 tbsp chopped fresh parsley
- salt and pepper

1 Rinse the barley under cold running water. Put in a pan and add water to cover generously. Bring to the boil over a medium heat and boil for 3 minutes, skimming off the foam from the surface. Remove the pan from the heat, cover and set aside.

2 Put the lamb in another large pan with the measured water and bring to the boil. Skim off the foam that rises to the surface.

3 Stir in the garlic, stock, onion and bay leaf. Reduce the heat, partially cover and simmer for 15 minutes.

4 Drain the barley and add to the soup. Add the leek, carrots, parsnip and swede. Simmer, stirring occasionally, for about 1 hour or until the lamb and vegetables are tender.

5 Season to taste with salt and pepper, stir in the parsley and serve.

NUTRITION

Calories *186*; Sugars *6 g*; Protein *13 g*; Carbohydrate *23 g*; Fat *5 g*; Saturates *2 g*

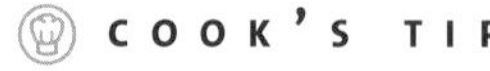

moderate

10–15 mins

1 hr 30 mins

COOK'S TIP

This soup is lean when the lamb is trimmed. By making it beforehand and chilling in the refrigerator, you can remove any hardened fat before reheating.

Packed with tomatoes, chickpeas and vegetables, this thick and hearty main course soup is bursting with exotic flavours and aromas.

Spicy Lamb Soup

1 Heat the oil in a large pan or flameproof casserole over a medium-high heat. Add the lamb, in batches if necessary, and cook, stirring occasionally, until evenly browned on all sides, adding a little more oil if needed. Remove the meat, with a slotted spoon.

2 Reduce the heat and add the onion and garlic to the pan. Cook, stirring frequently, for 1–2 minutes.

3 Add the water and return all the meat to the pan. Bring just to the boil and skim off any foam that rises to the surface. Reduce the heat and stir in the tomatoes, bay leaf, thyme, oregano, cinnamon, cumin, turmeric and harissa. Simmer for about 1 hour or until the meat is very tender.

4 Discard the bay leaf. Stir in the chickpeas, carrot and potato and simmer for 15 minutes. Add the courgette and peas and simmer for a further 15–20 minutes or until all the vegetables are tender.

5 Season to taste with salt and pepper and add more harissa if desired. Ladle the soup into warmed bowls, garnish with chopped fresh mint or coriander and serve immediately.

SERVES 4

1–2 tbsp olive oil
450 g/1 lb lean boneless lamb, such as shoulder or neck fillet, trimmed of fat and cut into 1-cm/½-inch cubes
1 onion, chopped finely
2–3 garlic cloves, crushed
1.2 litres/2 pints water
400 g/14 oz canned chopped tomatoes in juice
1 bay leaf
½ tsp dried thyme
½ tsp dried oregano
pinch of ground cinnamon
¼ tsp ground cumin
¼ tsp ground turmeric
1 tsp harissa
400 g/14 oz canned chickpeas, rinsed and drained
1 carrot, diced
1 potato, diced
1 courgette, quartered lengthways and sliced
100 g/3½ oz fresh or frozen green peas
salt and pepper
chopped fresh mint or coriander, to garnish

NUTRITION

Calories *323*; Sugars *6 g*; Protein *27 g*; Carbohydrate *25 g*; Fat *13 g*; Saturates *4 g*

moderate

10 mins

1 hr 45 mins

Strips of tender lean beef are combined with crisp water chestnuts and cooked rice in a tasty beef broth with a tang of orange.

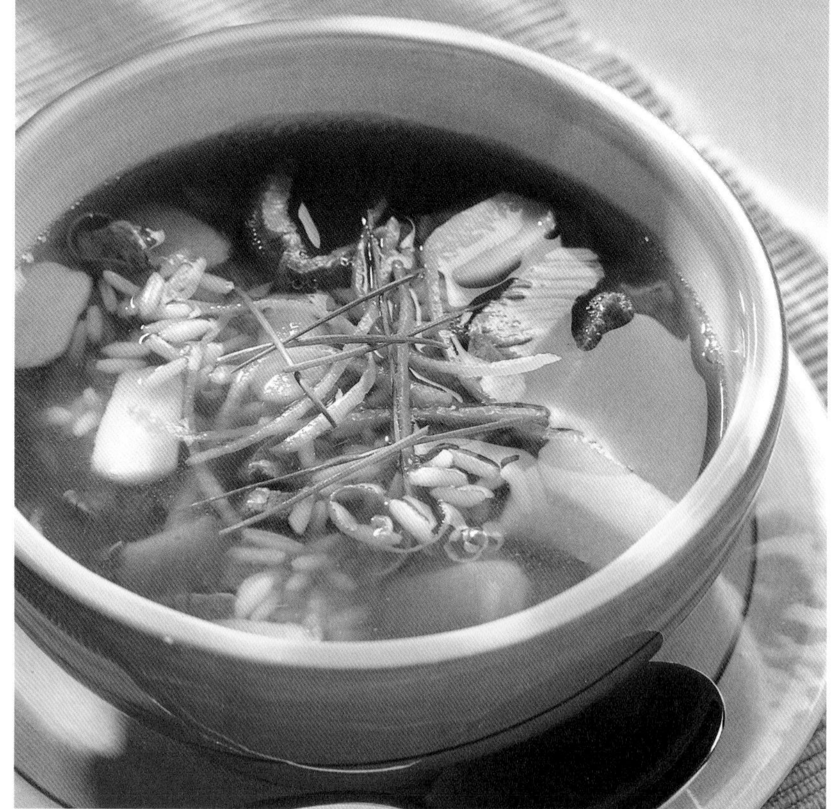

Beef, Water Chestnut *and* Rice Soup

SERVES 4

- 350 g/12 oz lean beef (such as rump or sirloin)
- 1 litre/1¾ pints Fresh Beef Stock
- cinnamon stick, broken
- 2 star anise
- 2 tbsp dark soy sauce
- 2 tbsp dry sherry
- 3 tbsp tomato purée
- 115 g/4 oz canned water chestnuts, drained and sliced
- 175 g/6 oz cooked white rice
- 1 tsp grated orange rind
- 6 tbsp orange juice
- salt and pepper

to garnish

- strips of orange rind
- 2 tbsp snipped chives

1 Carefully trim away any fat from the beef. Cut the beef into thin strips and then place into a large saucepan.

2 Pour over the stock and add the cinnamon, star anise, soy sauce, sherry, tomato purée and water chestnuts. Bring to the boil, skimming away any surface scum with a flat ladle. Cover the pan and simmer gently for about 20 minutes or until the beef is tender.

3 Skim the soup with a flat ladle again to remove any scum. Remove and discard the cinnamon and star anise and blot the surface with kitchen paper to remove any fat.

4 Stir in the rice, orange rind and juice. Adjust the seasoning if necessary. Heat through for 2–3 minutes before ladling into warm bowls. Serve garnished with strips of orange rind and snipped chives.

NUTRITION

Calories *219*; Sugars *5 g*; Protein *27 g*; Carbohydrate *20 g*; Fat *8 g*; Saturates *2 g*

 easy

 15 mins

 25 mins

COOK'S TIP

Omit the rice for a lighter soup that is an ideal starter for an Oriental meal of many courses. For a more substantial soup that would be a meal in its own right, add diced vegetables such as carrot, pepper or courgette.

A wonderful meal-in-a-bowl, this soup is ideal for a winter supper or lunch. The beefy flavour, enhanced with spices, is very warming.

Beef *and* Vegetable Soup

1 To peel the tomatoes, place them in a heatproof bowl, pour in enough boiling water to cover and stand for 30 seconds. Drain and plunge into cold water. The skins will then slide off easily. Chop the tomatoes.

2 Using a large knife, cut the corn cobs into 2.5-cm/1-inch pieces.

3 Place the stock in a pan with the tomatoes, carrot, onion, potatoes and cabbage. Bring to the boil, then reduce the heat and simmer for 10–15 minutes or until the vegetables are tender.

4 Add the corn cob pieces, the cumin, chilli powder, paprika and beef pieces. Bring back to the boil over a medium heat and cook until heated through.

5 Ladle into warmed soup bowls and serve sprinkled with fresh coriander, if using, with a salsa of your choice handed round separately.

SERVES 4–6

225 g/8 oz tomatoes
2 corn cobs
1 litre/1¾ pints beef stock
1 carrot, sliced thinly
1 onion, chopped
1–2 small waxy potatoes, diced
¼ cabbage, sliced thinly
¼ tsp ground cumin
¼ tsp mild chilli powder
¼ tsp paprika
225 g/8 oz cooked beef, cut into bite-sized pieces
3–4 tbsp chopped fresh coriander (optional)
hot salsa of your choice, to serve

NUTRITION

Calories *167*; Sugars *7 g*; Protein *16 g*; Carbohydrate *17 g*; Fat *5 g*; Saturates *2 g*

easy

 15 mins

 20 mins

COOK'S TIP

To thicken the soup and give it a flavour of the popular Mexican steamed dumplings known as a tamale, stir in a few tablespoons of masa harina, mixed into a thinnish paste with a little water, at Step 4. Cook until thick.

Veal plays an important role in Italian cuisine and there are dozens of recipes for all cuts of this meat.

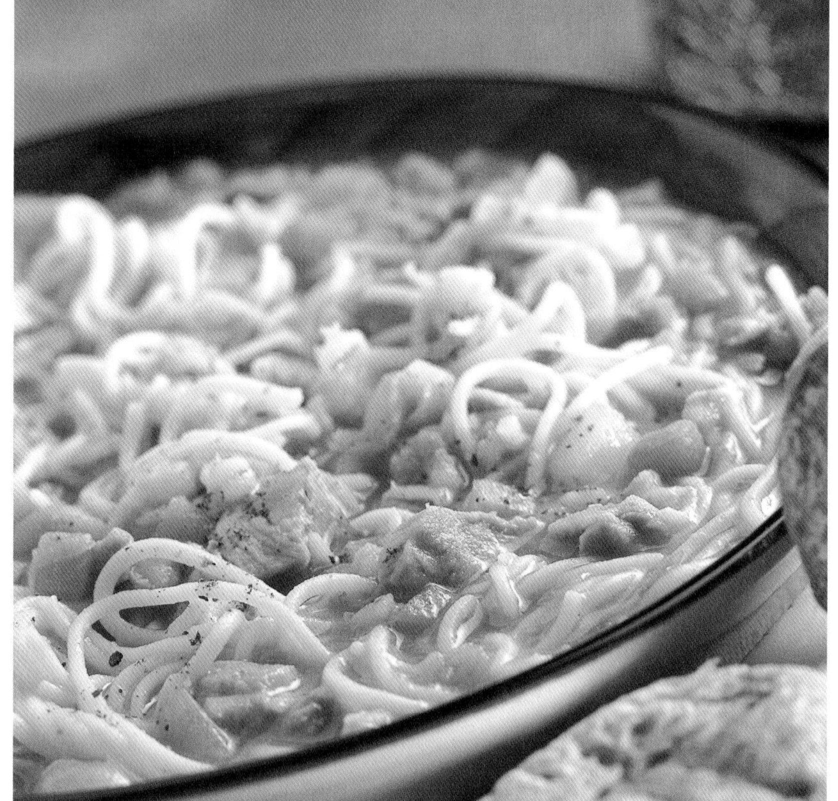

Tuscan Veal Broth

SERVES 4

55 g/2 oz dried peas, soaked for 2 hours and drained
900 g/2 lb boned neck of veal, diced
1.2 litres/2 pints Fresh Beef Stock (see page 15)
600 ml/1 pint water
55 g/2 oz pearl barley, washed
1 large carrot, diced
1 small turnip (about 175 g/6 oz), diced
1 large leek, sliced thinly
1 red onion, chopped finely
100 g/3½ oz chopped tomatoes
1 fresh basil sprig
100 g/3½ oz dried vermicelli
salt and white pepper

1 Put the peas, veal, stock and water into a large saucepan and bring to the boil over a low heat. Using a slotted spoon, skim off any scum that rises to the surface of the liquid.

2 When all of the scum has been removed, add the pearl barley and a pinch of salt to the mixture. Simmer gently over a low heat for 25 minutes.

3 Add the carrot, turnip, leek, onion, tomatoes and basil to the pan and season with salt and pepper to taste. Leave to simmer for about 2 hours, skimming the surface, using a slotted spoon, from time to time. Remove the pan from the heat and then set aside for 2 hours.

4 Set the pan over a medium heat and bring to the boil. Add the vermicelli and cook for 12 minutes. Season with salt and pepper to taste and remove and discard the basil. Ladle into soup bowls and serve immediately.

NUTRITION

Calories *420*; Sugars *5 g*; Protein *54 g*; Carbohydrate *37 g*; Fat *7 g*; Saturates *2 g*

 challenging

 2 hrs 15 mins

4 hrs 45 mins

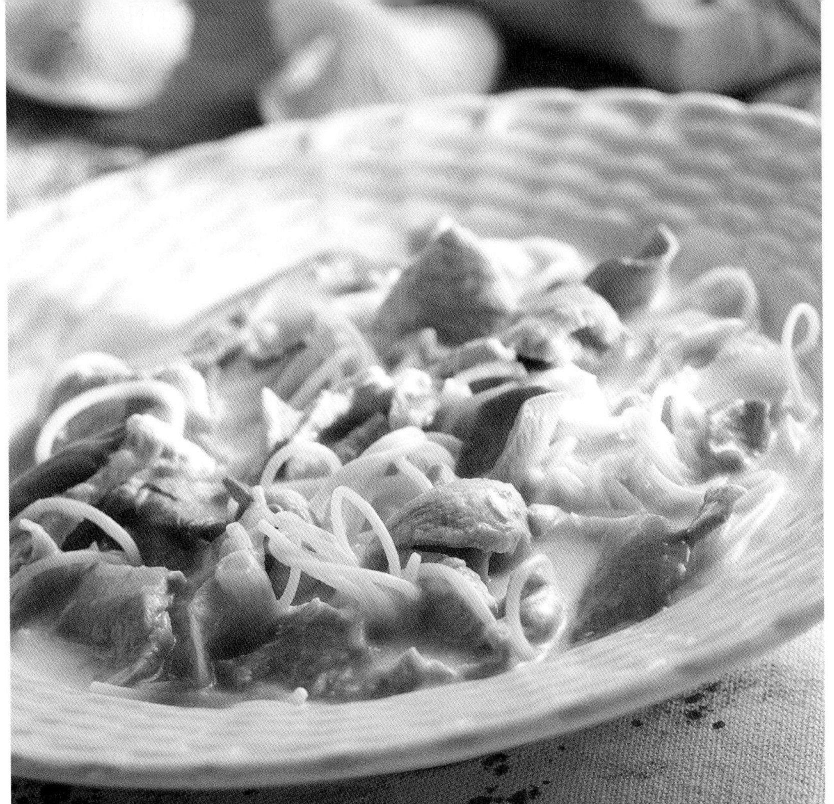

Wild mushrooms are available commercially and an increasing range of cultivated varieties is now to be found in many supermarkets.

Veal *and* Wild Mushroom Soup

SERVES 4

450 g/1 lb veal, sliced thinly
450 g/1 lb veal bones
1.2 litres/2 pints water
1 small onion
6 peppercorns
1 tsp cloves
pinch of mace
140 g/5 oz oyster and shiitake mushrooms, chopped roughly
150 ml/ ¼ pint double cream
100 g/3 ½ oz dried vermicelli
1 tbsp cornflour
3 tbsp milk
salt and pepper

1 Put the veal, bones and water into a large saucepan. Bring to the boil and lower the heat. Add the onion, peppercorns, cloves and mace and simmer for about 3 hours, until the veal stock is reduced by one third.

2 Strain the stock, skim off any fat on the surface with a slotted spoon, and pour the stock into a clean saucepan. Add the veal meat to the pan.

3 Add the mushrooms and cream, bring to the boil over a low heat and then leave to simmer for 12 minutes, stirring occasionally.

4 Meanwhile, cook the vermicelli in lightly salted boiling water for 10 minutes or until tender, but still firm to the bite. Drain and keep warm.

5 Mix the cornflour and milk to form a smooth paste. Stir into the soup to thicken. Season to taste with salt and pepper and, just before serving, add the vermicelli. Transfer the soup to a warm tureen and serve immediately.

NUTRITION

Calories *413*; Sugars *3 g*; Protein *28 g*; Carbohydrate *28 g*; Fat *22 g*; Saturates *12 g*

easy

5 mins

3 hrs 15 mins

COOK'S TIP

You can make this soup with the more inexpensive cuts of veal, such as breast or neck slices. The long cooking time ensures that the meat is tender.

Spicy or smoky sausages add substance to this soup, which makes a hearty and warming supper, served with crusty bread and green salad.

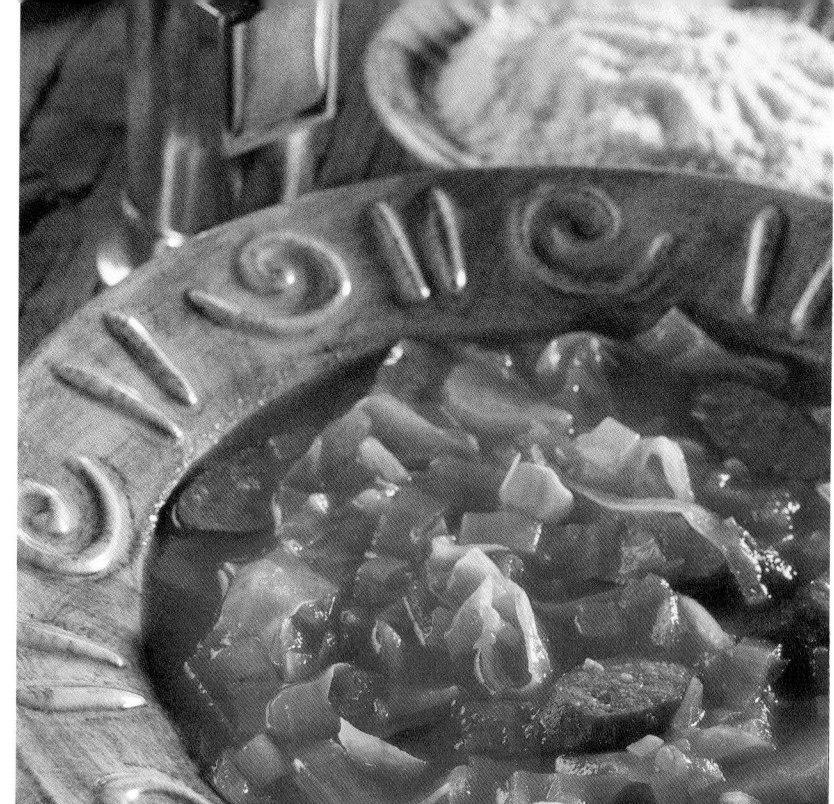

Cabbage Soup *with* Sausage

SERVES 6

350 g/12 oz lean sausages, preferably highly seasoned
2 tsp oil
1 onion, chopped finely
1 leek, halved lengthways and sliced thinly
2 carrots, halved and sliced thinly
400 g/14 oz canned chopped tomatoes
350 g/12 oz young green cabbage, cored and shredded coarsely
1–2 garlic cloves, chopped finely
pinch dried thyme
1.5 litres/2¾ pints chicken or meat stock
salt and pepper
freshly grated Parmesan cheese, to serve

1 Put the sausages in water to cover generously and bring to the boil. Reduce the heat and simmer until firm. Drain the sausages and, when cool enough to handle, remove the skin, if you wish, and slice thinly.

2 Heat the oil in a large saucepan over a medium heat, add the onion, leek and carrots and cook for 3–4 minutes, stirring until the onion starts to soften.

3 Add the tomatoes, cabbage, garlic, thyme, stock and sausages. Bring to the boil, reduce the heat to low and cook gently, partially covered, for about 40 minutes until the vegetables are tender.

4 Taste the soup and adjust the seasoning, if necessary. Ladle into warm bowls and serve with Parmesan cheese.

NUTRITION
Calories *246*; Sugars *13 g*; Protein *15 g*; Carbohydrate *21 g*; Fat *12 g*; Saturates *4 g*

 easy
 15 mins
 1 hr 15 mins

COOK'S TIP

If you don't have fresh stock, use water, with 1 stock cube dissolved in it. Add a little more onion and garlic, plus a bouquet garni (remove it before serving).

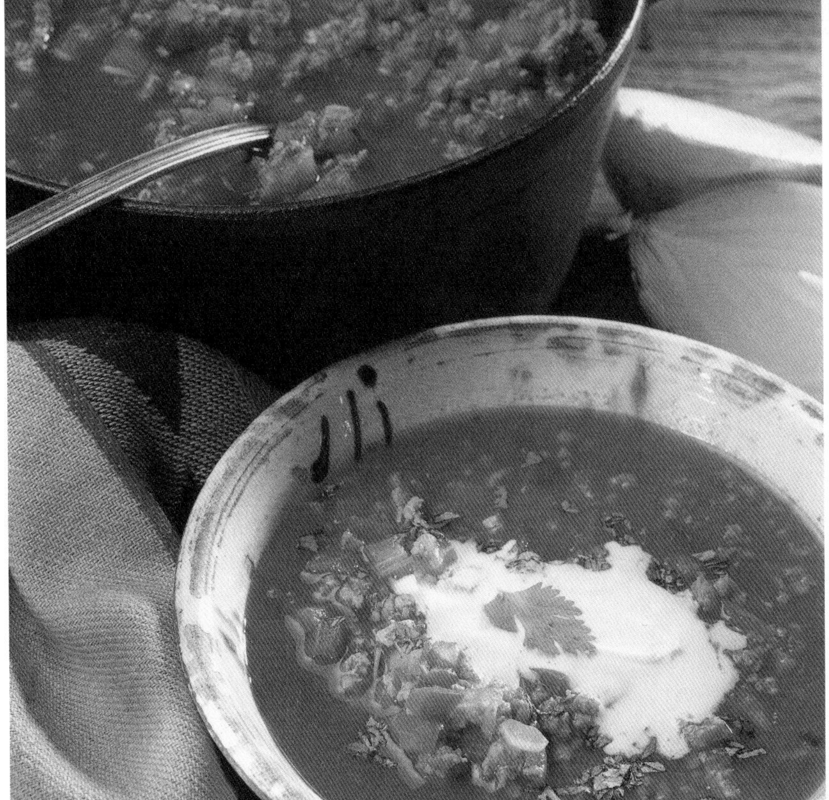

This meaty chilli soup tastes lighter than one made with beef. Good for informal entertaining, the recipe is easily doubled.

Pork Chilli Soup

1 Heat the oil in a large pan over a medium-high heat. Add the pork, season with salt and pepper, and cook, stirring frequently, until no longer pink. Reduce the heat to medium and add the onion, celery, pepper and garlic. Cover and cook, stirring occasionally, for a further 5 minutes until the onion is softened.

2 Add the tomatoes, tomato purée and the stock. Stir in the coriander, cumin, oregano and chilli powder. Season with salt and pepper to taste.

3 Bring just to the boil, then reduce the heat to low, cover and simmer for about 30–40 minutes until all the vegetables are very tender. Taste and adjust the seasoning, adding more chilli powder if you like it hotter.

4 Ladle the chilli soup into warm bowls and sprinkle with chopped coriander or parsley. You can either hand the soured cream separately or top each serving with a spoonful.

SERVES 3

2 tsp olive oil
500 g/1 lb 2 oz lean minced pork
1 onion, chopped finely
1 celery stick, chopped finely
1 pepper, deseeded and chopped finely
2–3 garlic cloves, chopped finely
400 g/14 oz canned chopped tomatoes in juice
3 tbsp tomato purée
450 ml/16 fl oz chicken or meat stock
¼ tsp ground coriander
¼ tsp ground cumin
¼ tsp dried oregano
1 tsp mild chilli powder
salt and pepper
chopped fresh coriander leaves or parsley, to garnish
soured cream, to serve

NUTRITION

Calories *308*; Sugars *13 g*; Protein *40 g*; Carbohydrate *15 g*; Fat *10 g*; Saturates *3 g*

 easy

 10 mins

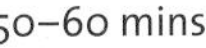 50–60 mins

Prosciutto is a cured ham, which is air- and salt-dried for up to 1 year. Parma ham is said to be the best of the many different varieties available.

Chickpeas *and* Parma Ham

SERVES 4

1 tbsp olive oil
1 medium onion, sliced thinly
1 garlic clove, chopped
1 small red pepper, deseeded and cut into thin strips
200 g/7 oz Parma ham, cut into strips
400g/14 oz canned chickpeas, drained and rinsed
1 tbsp chopped fresh parsley, to garnish
crusty bread, to serve

1 Heat the oil in a frying pan. Add the onion, garlic and pepper and cook over a medium heat, stirring occasionally, for 3–4 minutes or until the vegetables have softened. Add the Parma ham and fry for 5 minutes or until the ham is just beginning to brown.

2 Add the chickpeas to the pan and cook, stirring constantly, for about 2–3 minutes until warmed through.

3 Sprinkle with chopped parsley and transfer to warm serving plates. Serve with lots of fresh crusty bread.

NUTRITION

Calories *180*; Sugars *2 g*; Protein *12 g*; Carbohydrate *18 g*; Fat *7 g*; Saturates *1 g*

moderate
10 mins
15 mins

COOK'S TIP

Whenever possible, use fresh herbs. They are becoming more readily available, especially since the introduction of 'growing' herbs, small pots of herbs which you can buy from the supermarket or greengrocer and grow at home.

If you can get fresh peas – and willing helpers to shell them – do use them: you will need 1 kg/2 lb 4 oz. Add them to the pan with the stock.

Rice *and* Peas

1 Heat the olive oil and half of the butter in a heavy-based pan. Add the pancetta or bacon and onion and cook over a low heat, stirring occasionally, for 5 minutes until the onion is softened and translucent, but not browned.

2 Add the stock and fresh peas, if using, to the pan and bring to the boil. Stir in the rice and season to taste with pepper. Bring to the boil, lower the heat and simmer, stirring occasionally, for 20–30 minutes until the rice is tender.

3 Add the parsley and frozen or canned petits pois, if using these instead of fresh peas, and cook for about 8 minutes until the peas are heated through. Stir in the remaining butter and the Parmesan.

4 Transfer to a warmed serving dish and serve immediately with freshly ground black pepper.

SERVES 4

1 tbsp olive oil
4 tbsp butter
55 g/2 oz pancetta or streaky bacon, chopped
1 small onion, chopped
1.4 litres/2½ pints hot chicken stock
200 g/7 oz risotto rice
3 tbsp chopped fresh parsley
225 g/8 oz fresh, frozen or canned petits pois
55 g/2 oz Parmesan cheese, grated
pepper

NUTRITION

Calories *409*; Sugars *2 g*; Protein *15 g*; Carbohydrate *38 g*; Fat *23 g*; Saturates *12 g*

 easy

 10 mins

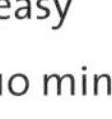 50 mins

A satisfying bake of lean minced beef, courgettes and tomatoes cooked in a low-fat 'custard' with a cheesy crust.

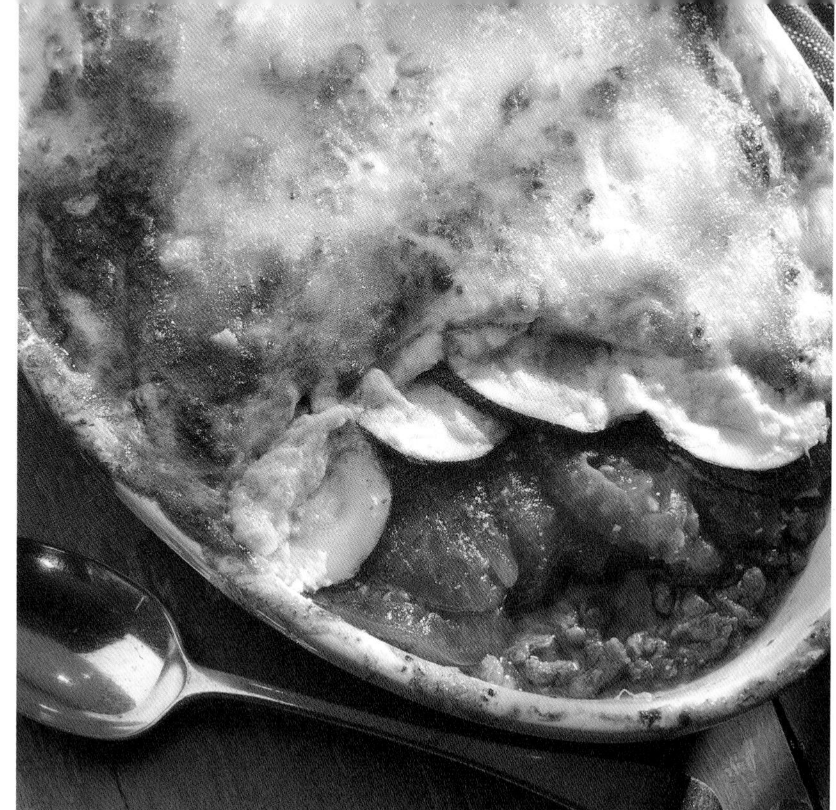

Beef *and* Tomato Gratin

SERVES 4

350 g/12 oz lean beef, minced
1 large onion, chopped finely
1 tsp dried mixed herbs
1 tbsp plain flour
300 ml/½ pint beef stock
1 tbsp tomato purée
2 large tomatoes, sliced thinly
4 medium courgettes, sliced thinly
2 tbsp cornflour
300 ml/½ pint skimmed milk
150 ml/5 fl oz low-fat natural fromage frais
1 medium egg yolk
4 tbsp freshly grated Parmesan cheese
salt and pepper

to serve
crusty bread
steamed vegetables

1 Preheat the oven to 190°C/375°F/Gas Mark 5. In a large frying pan, dry-fry the beef and onion for 4–5 minutes until browned.

2 Stir in the dried mixed herbs, flour, beef stock and tomato purée, and season. Bring to the boil and simmer for 30 minutes until thickened.

3 Transfer the beef mixture to an ovenproof gratin dish. Cover with a layer of the sliced tomatoes and then add a layer of sliced courgettes. Blend the cornflour with a little milk. Pour the remaining milk into a saucepan and bring to the boil. Add the cornflour mixture and cook, stirring, for 1–2 minutes until thickened. Remove from the heat and beat in the fromage frais and egg yolk. Season well.

4 Spread the white sauce over the layer of courgettes. Place the dish onto a baking sheet and sprinkle with grated Parmesan. Bake in the oven for 25–30 minutes until golden-brown. Serve with crusty bread and vegetables.

NUTRITION
Calories *278*; Sugars *10 g*; Protein *29 g*; Carbohydrate *20 g*; Fat *10 g*; Saturates *5 g*

 moderate

 10 mins

1 hr 15 mins

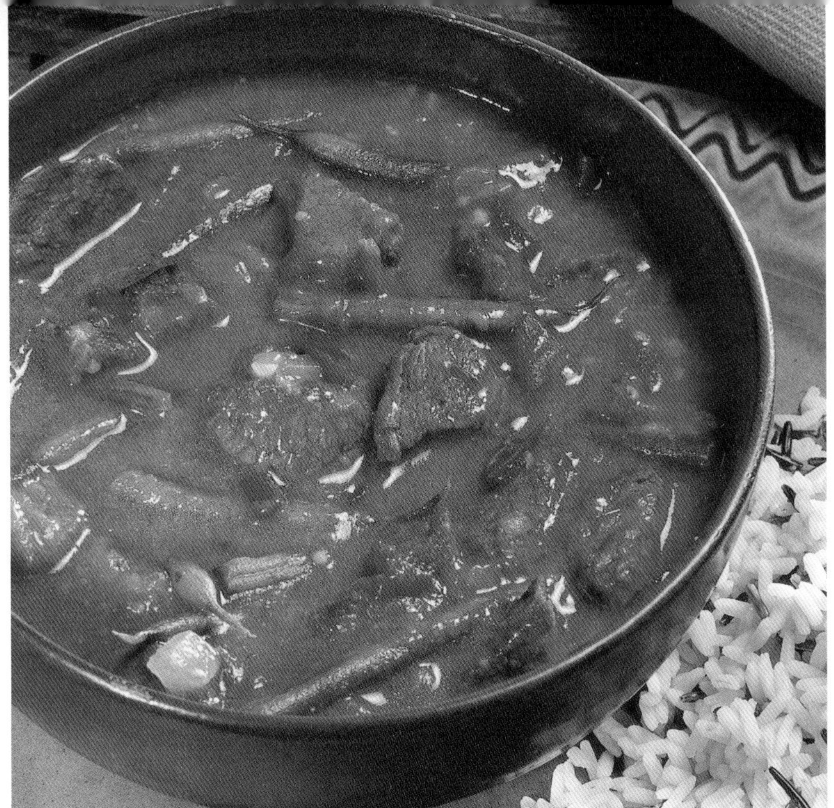

This rich, smoky-flavoured Mexican stew is delicious; leftovers make a great filling for tacos, too!

Michoacan Beef

1 Place the flour in a large bowl and season with salt and pepper. Add the beef and toss to coat well. Remove from the bowl, shaking off the excess flour.

2 Heat the oil in a frying pan and brown the meat briefly over a high heat. Reduce the heat to medium, add the onions and garlic and cook for 2 minutes, stirring occasionally.

3 Add the tomatoes, pinch of sugar, chillies and stock, cover and simmer over a low heat for 1½ hours or until the meat is very tender, adding the French beans 15 minutes before the end of the cooking time. Skim off any fat that rises to the surface.

4 Transfer to individual bowls and serve with simmered beans and rice.

SERVES 4–6

about 3 tbsp plain flour
1 kg/2 lb 4 oz stewing beef, cut into large bite-sized pieces
2 tbsp vegetable oil
2 onions, chopped
5 garlic cloves, chopped
400 g/14 oz tomatoes, diced
1½ dried chipotle chillies, reconstituted, deseeded and cut into thin strips, or a few shakes of bottled chipotle salsa
1.5 litres/2¾ pints beef stock
350 g/12 oz French beans
pinch of sugar
salt and pepper

to serve
simmered beans
cooked rice

COOK'S TIP

This is traditionally made with nopales, edible cacti, which give the dish a distinctive flavour. Look for them in specialist shops. For this recipe you need 350–400 g/12–14 oz canned or fresh nopales.

NUTRITION

Calories *315*; Sugars *6 g*; Protein *41 g*; Carbohydrate *16 g*; Fat *10 g*; Saturates *3 g*

 easy

 10 mins

 2 hrs

In this recipe, the potatoes are actually cooked in the goulash. For a change, you may prefer to substitute small, scrubbed new potatoes.

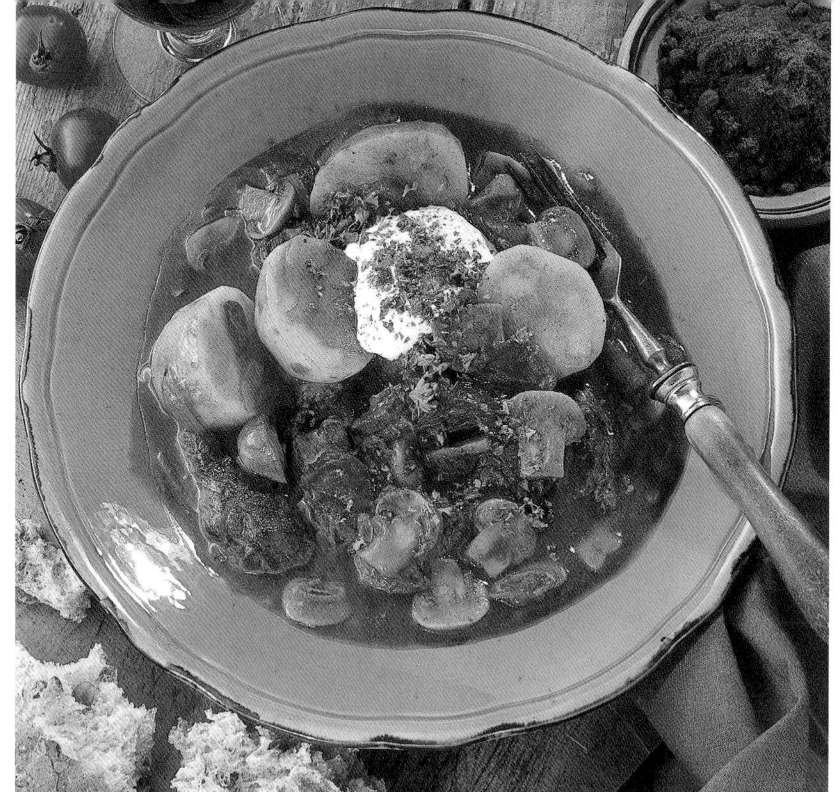

Beef *and* Potato Goulash

SERVES 4

2 tbsp vegetable oil
1 large onion, sliced
2 garlic cloves, crushed
750 g/1 lb 10 oz lean stewing steak
2 tbsp paprika
400 g/14 oz canned chopped tomatoes
2 tbsp tomato purée
1 large red pepper, deseeded and chopped
175 g/6 oz mushrooms, sliced
600 ml/1 pint beef stock
500 g/1 lb 2 oz potatoes, cut into large chunks
1 tbsp cornflour
salt and pepper

to garnish
4 tbsp low-fat natural yogurt
paprika
chopped fresh parsley

1 Heat the oil in a large pan. Add the onion and garlic and cook over a medium heat, stirring occasionally, for 3–4 minutes until softened.

2 Cut the steak into chunks, add to the pan and cook over a high heat for about 3 minutes until browned all over.

3 Lower the heat to medium and stir in the paprika. Add the tomatoes, tomato purée, red pepper and mushrooms. Cook the mixture, stirring constantly, for 2 minutes.

4 Pour in the beef stock. Bring to the boil, stirring occasionally, then reduce the heat to low. Cover and simmer gently for about 1½ hours until the meat is cooked through and tender.

5 Add the potatoes, cover and cook for a further 20–30 minutes until tender.

6 Blend the cornflour with a little water and add to the pan, stirring until thickened and blended. Cook for 1 minute then season with salt and pepper to taste. Top with the yogurt, sprinkle over the paprika and chopped fresh parsley and serve immediately.

NUTRITION
Calories *477*; Sugars *11 g*; Protein *47 g*; Carbohydrate *39 g*; Fat *16 g*; Saturates *5 g*

 easy
15 mins
2 hrs 15 mins

Probably the best known Mexican dish and one that is a great favourite with all. The chilli content can be increased to suit your taste.

Chilli con Carne

1 Cut the beef into 2-cm/¾-inch cubes. Heat the oil in a flameproof casserole and fry the beef until well sealed. Remove from the casserole.

2 Add the onion and garlic to the casserole and cook until lightly browned. Stir in the flour and cook for 1–2 minutes. Stir in the tomato juice and tomatoes and bring to the boil. Replace the beef and add the chilli sauce, cumin and seasoning. Cover and place in a preheated oven, 160°C/325°F/Gas Mark 3, for 1½ hours or until almost tender.

3 Stir in the beans, oregano and parsley and adjust the seasoning to taste. Cover the casserole and return to the oven for 45 minutes. Sprinkle with herbs and serve with boiled rice and tortillas.

SERVES 4

750 g/1 lb 10 oz lean braising or stewing steak
2 tbsp vegetable oil
1 large onion, sliced
2–4 garlic cloves, crushed
1 tbsp plain flour
425 ml/15 fl oz tomato juice
400 g/14 oz canned tomatoes
1–2 tbsp sweet chilli sauce
1 tsp ground cumin
425 g/15 oz canned red kidney beans, drained
½ teaspoon dried oregano
1–2 tbsp chopped fresh parsley
salt and pepper
chopped fresh herbs, to garnish
boiled rice and tortillas, to serve

NUTRITION

Calories *443*; Sugars *11 g*; Protein *48 g*; Carbohydrate *30 g*; Fat *15 g*; Saturates *4 g*

easy

 5 mins

 2 hrs 30 mins

COOK'S TIP

Because chilli con carne requires quite a lengthy cooking time, it saves time and fuel to prepare double the quantity you need and freeze half of it to serve on another occasion. Thaw and use within 3–4 weeks.

The spicy peanut sauce in this recipe will complement almost any meat; the dish is just as delicious made with chicken or pork.

Potato, Beef *and* Peanut Pot

SERVES 4

1 tbsp vegetable oil
5 tbsp butter
450 g/1 lb lean steak, cut into thin strips
1 onion, halved and sliced
2 garlic cloves, crushed
600 g/1 lb 5 oz waxy potatoes, cubed
½ tsp paprika
4 tbsp crunchy peanut butter
600 ml/1 pint beef stock
4 tbsp unsalted peanuts
2 tsp light soy sauce
55 g/2 oz sugar snap peas
1 red pepper, deseeded and cut into strips
sprigs fresh parsley, to garnish (optional)

1 Heat the oil and butter in a flameproof casserole.

2 Add the steak strips and fry them gently for about 3–4 minutes, stirring and turning the meat until it is sealed on all sides.

3 Add the onion and garlic to the meat and cook gently for a further 2 minutes, stirring constantly.

4 Add the potato cubes and cook for 3–4 minutes or until they begin to brown.

5 Stir in the paprika and peanut butter, then gradually stir in the beef stock. Bring the mixture to the boil, stirring frequently.

6 Finally, add the peanuts, soy sauce, sugar snap peas and red pepper.

7 Cover the casserole and cook over a low heat for 45 minutes or until the beef is cooked right through.

8 Garnish the dish with parsley sprigs, if desired, and serve immediately.

NUTRITION

Calories *559*; Sugars *5 g*; Protein *35 g*; Carbohydrate *24 g*; Fat *37 g*; Saturates *13 g*

easy
5 mins
1 hr

COOK'S TIP

Serve this dish with plain boiled rice or noodles, if you wish.

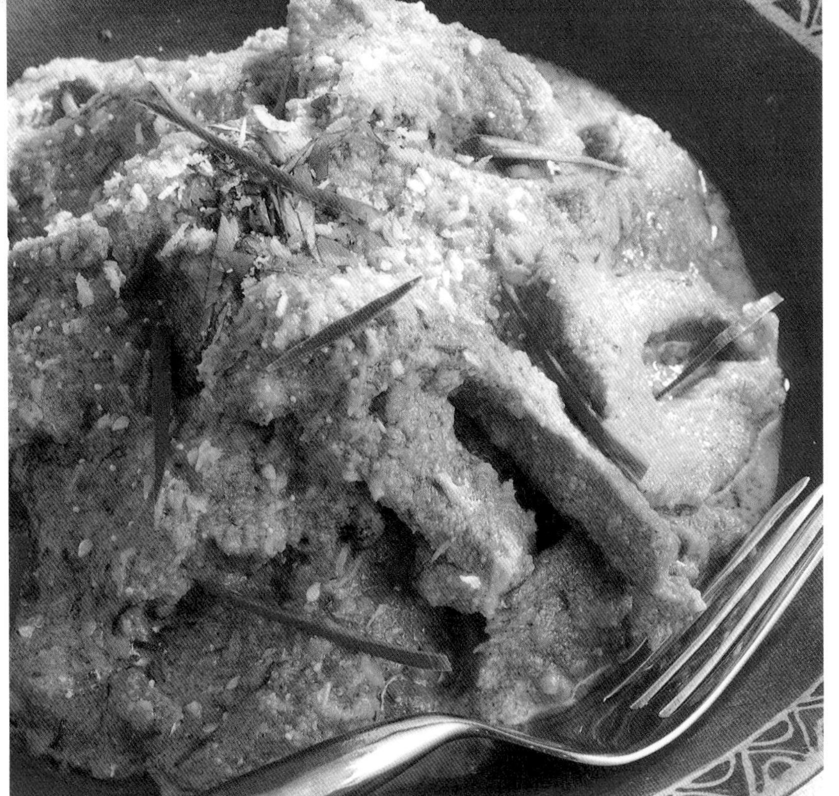

Roasting the spices for this dish gives it a nice dark colour and a richer flavour. Serve with chapatis and white lentils for a substantial meal.

Sliced Beef *with* Yogurt

1 Place the beef in a large bowl. Combine with the yogurt, ginger, garlic, chilli powder, turmeric, garam masala, salt, cardamoms and black cumin seeds and set aside until required.

2 Dry-fry the ground almonds, desiccated coconut, poppy seeds and sesame seeds in a heavy frying pan until golden, shaking the pan occasionally.

3 Transfer the spice mixture to a food processor and process until finely ground. (Add 1 tablespoon water to blend, if necessary.) Add the ground spice mixture to the meat mixture and combine.

4 Heat a little oil in a large pan and cook the onions until golden brown. Remove the onions from the pan. Stir-fry the meat in the remaining oil for about 5 minutes, then return the onions to the pan and stir-fry for a further 5–7 minutes. Add the water, cover and simmer over a low heat, stirring occasionally, for 25–30 minutes. Add the chillies and coriander and serve hot.

SERVES 4

450 g/1 lb lean beef slices, cut into 2.5-cm/1-inch slices
5 tbsp natural yogurt
1 tsp finely chopped fresh root ginger
1 tsp crushed garlic
1 tsp chilli powder
pinch of ground turmeric
2 tsp garam masala
1 tsp salt
2 cardamoms
1 tsp black cumin seeds
55 g/2 oz ground almonds
1 tbsp desiccated coconut
1 tbsp poppy seeds
1 tbsp sesame seeds
300 ml/10 fl oz vegetable oil
2 medium onions, chopped finely
300 ml/10 fl oz water
2 fresh red chillies
few fresh coriander leaves, chopped

NUTRITION

Calories *981*; Sugars *5 g*; Protein *33 g*; Carbohydrate *6 g*; Fat *94 g*; Saturates *14 g*

easy

 20 mins

 45 mins

If tomatillos are not available, use fresh tomatoes and bottled green salsa instead, and add a good hit of lime juice at the end.

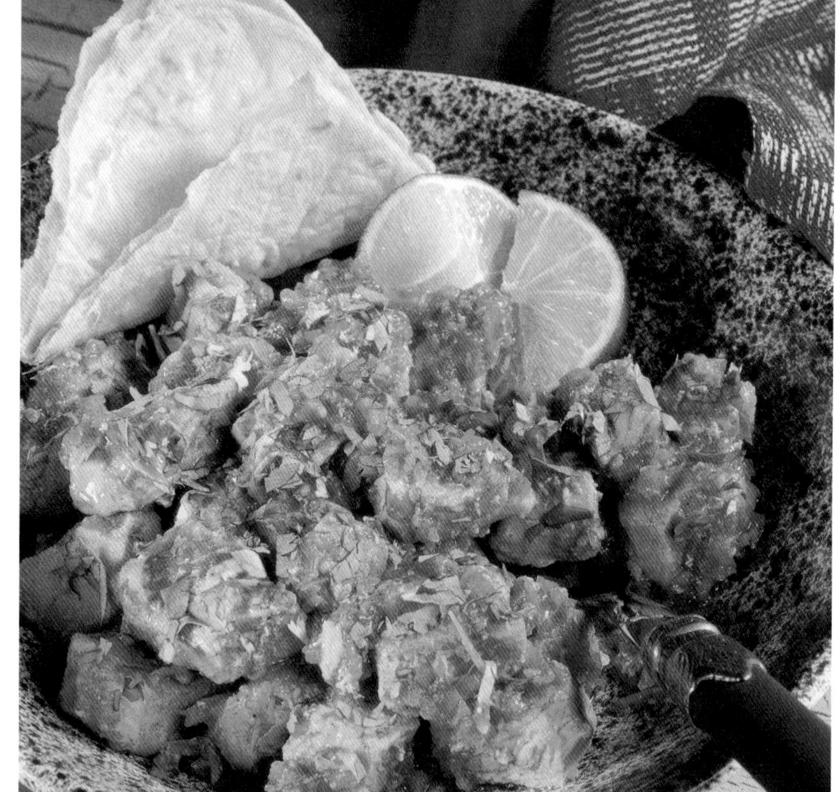

Chilli Verde

SERVES 4

1 kg/2 lb 4 oz pork, cut into bite-sized chunks
1 onion, chopped
2 bay leaves
1 garlic bulb, cut in half
1 stock cube
2 garlic cloves, chopped
450 g/1 lb fresh tomatillos, husks removed, cooked in a small amount of water until just tender, then chopped or 450 g/1 lb canned tomatillos
2 large fresh mild green chillies, such as anaheim, or a combination of 1 green pepper and 2 jalapeño chillies, deseeded and chopped
3 tbsp vegetable oil
225 ml/8 fl oz pork or chicken stock
½ tsp mild chilli powder
½ tsp cumin
4–6 tbsp chopped fresh coriander, to garnish

to serve
warmed flour tortillas
lime wedges

NUTRITION
Calories *433*; Sugars *6 g*; Protein *56 g*; Carbohydrate *9 g*; Fat *19 g*; Saturates *4 g*

moderate

10 mins
1 hr 30 mins

1. Place the pork in a large pan with the onion, bay leaves and garlic bulb. Add water to cover and bring to the boil. Skim off the scum from the surface and add the stock cube, stirring well to mix and dissolve. Reduce the heat to very low and simmer gently for about 1½ hours or until the meat is very tender.
2. Meanwhile, put the chopped garlic in a blender or food processor with the tomatillos and green chillies and pepper, if using. Process to a purée.
3. Heat the oil in a pan, add the tomatillo mixture and cook over a medium-high heat for about 10 minutes or until thickened. Add the stock, chilli powder and cumin.
4. When the meat is tender, remove from the pan and add to the sauce. Simmer gently to combine the flavours.
5. Garnish with the chopped coriander and serve with warmed tortillas and lime wedges.

This khorma, a traditional recipe from northern India, has a thick, richly flavoured and creamy-textured sauce and is quite simple to cook.

Beef Khorma *with* Almonds

1 Heat the oil in a pan. Add the onions and stir-fry until golden brown. Remove half of the onions from the pan, set aside and reserve.

2 Add the meat to the remaining onions in the pan and stir-fry for about 5 minutes. Remove the pan from the heat.

3 Combine the garam masala, ground coriander, ginger, garlic, salt and yogurt in a bowl. Gradually add the meat to the spice mixture and mix to coat well. Return the meat mixture to the pan. Cook, stirring constantly, for 5–7 minutes or until the mixture is golden.

4 Add the cloves, cardamoms and peppercorns. Add the water, lower the heat, cover the pan and then simmer for approximately 45–60 minutes. If necessary, add another 300 ml/10 fl oz water and cook for a further 10–15 minutes, stirring occasionally.

5 Just before serving, garnish with the reserved onions, chopped almonds, green chillies and the fresh coriander leaves. Serve with chapatis.

SERVES 4

300 ml/10 fl oz vegetable oil
3 medium onions, chopped finely
1 kg/2 lb 4 oz lean beef, cubed
1½ tsp garam masala
1½ tsp ground coriander
1½ tsp finely chopped fresh root ginger
1½ tsp crushed garlic
1 tsp salt
150 ml/5 fl oz natural yogurt
2 cloves
3 green cardamoms
4 black peppercorns
600 ml/1 pint water
chapatis, to serve

to garnish

6 almonds, soaked, peeled and chopped
2 fresh green chillies, chopped
few fresh coriander leaves

NUTRITION

Calories *735*; Sugars *6 g*; Protein *41 g*; Carbohydrate *9 g*; Fat *60 g*; Saturates *9 g*

easy

 20 mins

 1 hr 30 mins

Thai food has become so popular in recent years that most ingredients can be found in your local supermarket.

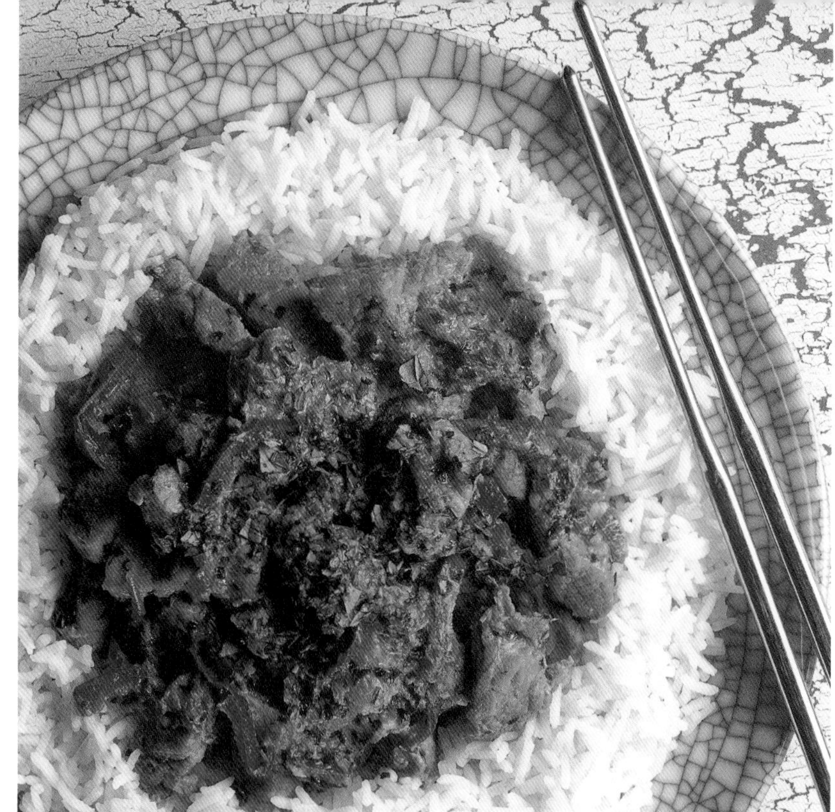

Red Pork Curry

SERVES 4 – 6

900 g/2 lb boned pork shoulder, sliced
700 ml/1¼ pints coconut milk
2 fresh red chillies, deseeded and sliced
2 tbsp Thai fish sauce
2 tsp brown sugar
1 large red pepper, deseeded and sliced
6 kaffir lime leaves, shredded
½ bunch fresh mint leaves, shredded
½ bunch Thai basil leaves, shredded

red curry paste

1 tbsp coriander seeds
2 tsp cumin seeds
2 tsp black or white peppercorns
1 tsp salt
5–8 dried hot red chillies
3–4 shallots, chopped
6–8 garlic cloves
5-cm/2-inch piece of root ginger, chopped
2 tsp kaffir grated lime rind or 2 lime leaves
1 tbsp ground red chilli powder
1 tbsp shrimp paste
2 lemon grass stalks, sliced thinly

NUTRITION

Calories *398*; Sugars *12 g*; Protein *38 g*; Carbohydrate *47 g*; Fat *9 g*; Saturates *3 g*

 moderate

 15 mins

 45 mins

1 To make the red curry paste, grind the coriander seeds, cumin seeds, peppercorns and salt to a fine powder in a mortar with a pestle. Add the chillies, one at a time, according to taste, until ground.

2 Put the shallots, garlic, ginger, kaffir lime rind or leaves, chilli powder and shrimp paste in a food processor. Process for about 1 minute. Add the ground spices and process again. Adding water, a few drops at a time, continue to process until a thick paste forms. Scrape the mixture into a bowl and stir in the lemon grass.

3 Put about half the red curry paste in a large deep heavy-based frying pan with the pork. Cook over a medium heat, stirring gently, for 2–3 minutes until the pork is evenly coated and begins to brown.

4 Stir in the coconut milk and bring to the boil. Cook, stirring frequently, for about 10 minutes. Reduce the heat, stir in the chillies, Thai fish sauce and brown sugar and simmer for about 20 minutes. Add the red pepper and simmer for a further 10 minutes.

5 Chop the lime leaves and add to the curry with half the mint and basil. Transfer to a serving dish, sprinkle with the remaining mint and basil and serve the curry with rice.

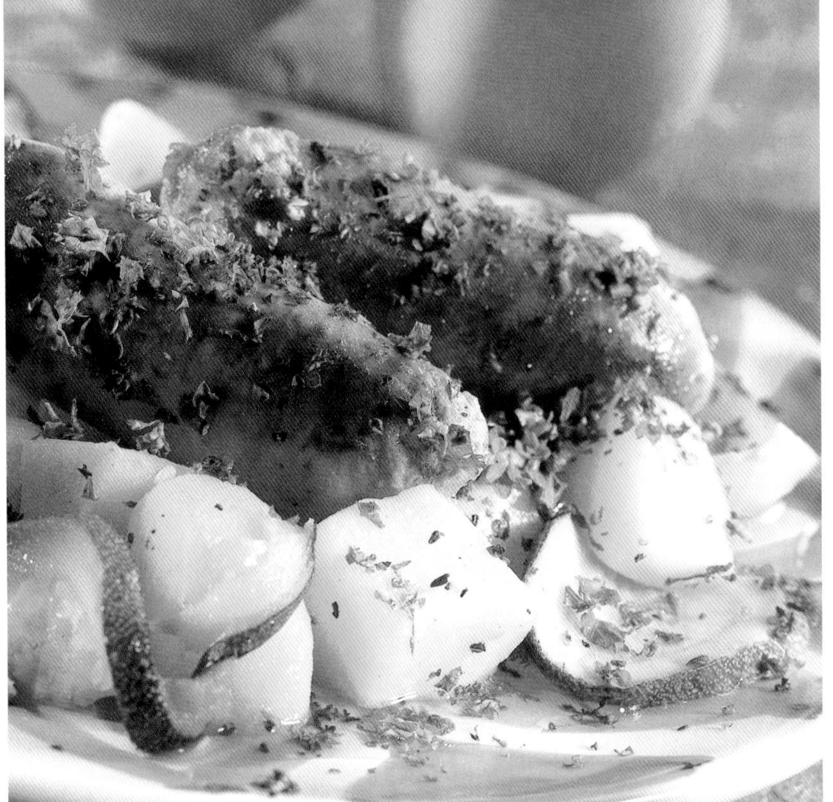

This dish is a meal in itself, containing both meat and potatoes cooked in a herby wine gravy. A selection of fresh vegetables may be served with the dish, if wished.

Potato *and* Sausage Pan-fry

1 Cook the cubed potatoes in a saucepan of boiling water for 10 minutes or until softened. Drain thoroughly and set aside.

2 Meanwhile, melt the butter in a large frying pan. Add the herb sausages and cook for 5 minutes, turning them frequently to ensure that they brown evenly on all sides.

3 Add the bacon rashers, onion, courgette and potatoes to the pan. Cook for a further 10 minutes, stirring, and turning the sausages frequently.

4 Stir in the white wine, stock, Worcestershire sauce and chopped mixed herbs. Season with salt and pepper to taste and cook the mixture over a gentle heat for 10 minutes. Add more salt and pepper, if necessary.

5 Transfer the potato and sausage pan-fry to warm serving plates, garnish with chopped fresh herbs and serve at once.

SERVES 4

675 g/1½ lb waxy potatoes, cubed
25 g/1 oz butter
8 large herb sausages
4 smoked bacon rashers
1 onion, quartered
1 courgette, sliced
150 ml/¼ pint dry white wine
300 ml/½ pint vegetable stock
1 tsp Worcestershire sauce
2 tbsp chopped mixed fresh herbs
salt and pepper
chopped fresh herbs, to garnish

NUTRITION

Calories *774*; Sugars *9 g*; Protein *31 g*; Carbohydrate *50 g*; Fat *48 g*; Saturates *15 g*

easy

15 mins

35 mins

COOK'S TIP

Use different flavours of sausage to vary the dish – there are many different varieties available, such as leek and mustard.

Tender, lean pork, cooked in a tasty, rich tomato sauce is flavoured with the extra tang of natural yogurt.

Pork Stroganoff

SERVES 4

350 g/12 oz lean pork fillet
1 tbsp vegetable oil
1 medium onion, chopped
2 garlic cloves, crushed
25 g/1 oz plain flour
2 tbsp tomato purée
425 ml/15 fl oz Fresh Chicken or Fresh Vegetable Stock (see page 14)
125 g/4½ oz button mushrooms, sliced
1 large green pepper, deseeded and diced
½ tsp ground nutmeg
4 tbsp low-fat natural yogurt, plus extra to serve
salt and pepper
white rice, freshly boiled, to serve
ground nutmeg, to garnish

1 Trim away any excess fat and membrane from the pork, then cut the meat into slices 1 cm/½ inch thick.

2 Heat the oil in a large saucepan and gently fry the pork, onion and garlic for 4–5 minutes until they are lightly browned.

3 Stir in the flour and tomato purée, pour in the chicken or vegetable stock and stir to mix thoroughly.

4 Add the mushrooms, green pepper, seasoning and nutmeg. Bring to the boil, cover and simmer for 20 minutes until the pork is cooked through.

5 Remove the saucepan from the heat, cool slightly and stir in the yogurt.

6 Serve the pork and sauce on a bed of rice with an extra spoonful of yogurt, and garnish with a dusting of ground nutmeg.

NUTRITION

Calories *223*; Sugars *7 g*; Protein *22 g*; Carbohydrate *12 g*; Fat *10 g*; Saturates *3 g*

easy
2 hrs 15 mins
30 mins

COOK'S TIP

You can buy ready-made stock from leading supermarkets. Although more expensive, they are more nutritious than stock cubes, which are high in salt and artificial flavourings.

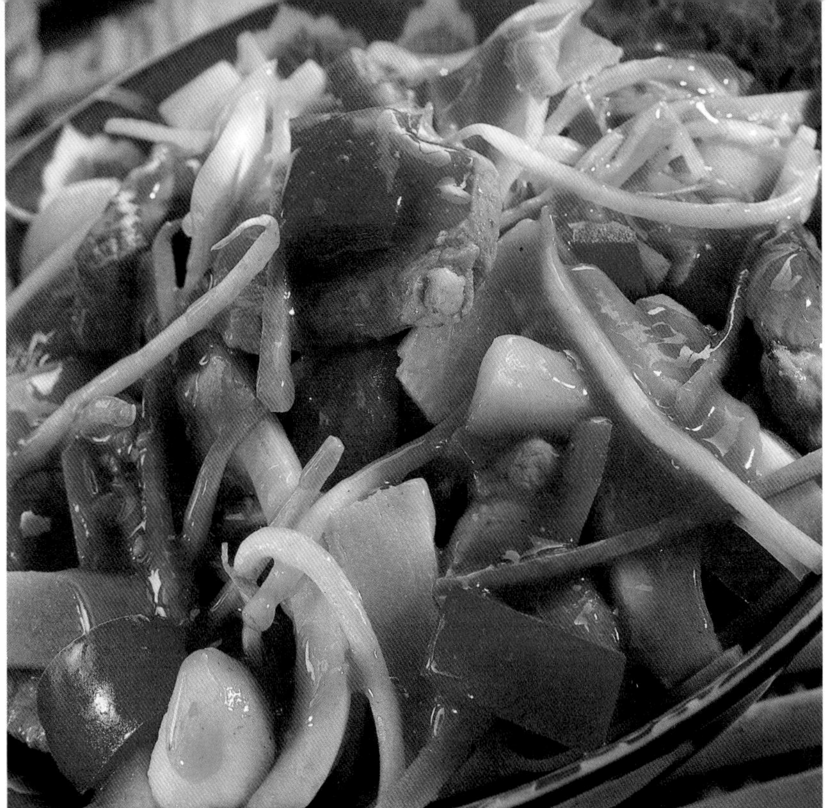

This is a very simple dish which lends itself to almost any combination of vegetables that you have to hand.

Pork Stir-fry *with* Vegetables

SERVES 4

350 g/12 oz lean pork fillet, sliced thinly
2 tbsp vegetable oil
2 garlic cloves, crushed
1-cm/½-inch piece of fresh root ginger, cut into slivers
1 carrot, cut into thin strips
1 red pepper, deseeded and diced
1 fennel bulb, sliced
25 g/1 oz water chestnuts, halved
85 g/3 oz beansprouts
2 tbsp Chinese rice wine
300 m/10 fl oz pork or chicken stock
pinch of dark brown sugar
1 tsp cornflour
2 tsp water

1 Heat the oil in a preheated wok. Add the garlic, ginger and pork. Stir-fry for 1–2 minutes until the meat is sealed.

2 Add the carrot, pepper, fennel and water chestnuts to the wok and stir-fry for about 2–3 minutes.

3 Add the beansprouts and stir-fry for 1 minute. Remove the pork and vegetables, set aside and keep warm.

4 Add the Chinese rice wine, pork or chicken stock and sugar to the wok. Blend the cornflour to a smooth paste with the water and stir it into the sauce. Bring to the boil, stirring constantly until thickened and clear.

5 Return the meat and vegetables to the wok and cook for 1–2 minutes until heated through and coated with the sauce. Serve immediately.

NUTRITION

Calories *216*; Sugars *3 g*; Protein *19 g*; Carbohydrate *5 g*; Fat *12 g*; Saturates *3 g*

 moderate

 5 mins

15 mins

COOK'S TIP

Use dry sherry instead of the Chinese rice wine if you have difficulty obtaining it.

Prunes add an earthy, wine flavour to this spicy stew. Serve with tortillas or crusty bread to dip into the rich sauce.

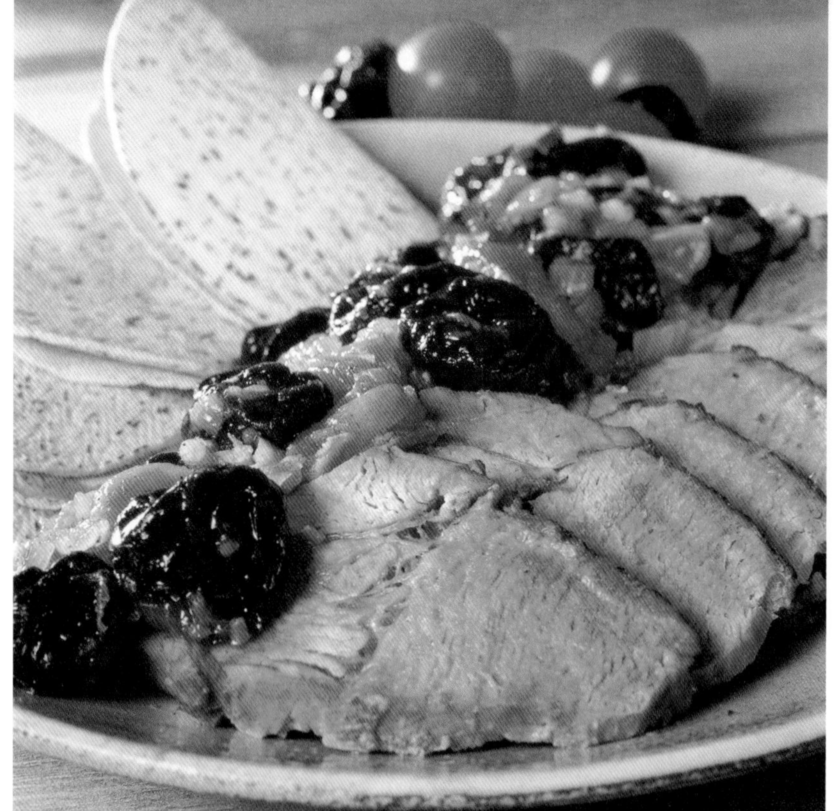

Pork *with* Vegetables

SERVES 4

- 1.5 kg/3 lb 5 oz pork joint, such as leg or shoulder
- juice of 2–3 limes
- 10 garlic cloves, chopped
- 3–4 tbsp mild chilli powder
- 4 tbsp vegetable oil
- 2 onions, chopped
- 500 ml/18 fl oz chicken stock
- 25 small tart tomatoes, chopped roughly
- 25 prunes, stoned
- 1–2 tsp sugar
- pinch of ground cinnamon
- pinch of ground allspice
- pinch of ground cumin
- salt
- warmed corn tortillas, to serve

1. Combine the pork with the lime juice, garlic, chilli powder, 2 tablespoons of oil, and salt. Set aside to marinate in the refrigerator overnight.
2. Remove the pork from the marinade. Wipe the pork dry with kitchen paper and reserve the marinade. Heat the remaining oil in a flameproof casserole and brown the pork evenly until just golden. Add the onions, the reserved marinade and stock. Cover and cook in a preheated oven, 180°C/350°F/Gas Mark 4, for about 2–3 hours until tender.
3. Spoon off the fat from the surface of the cooking liquid and add the tomatoes. Continue to cook for about 20 minutes until the tomatoes are tender. Mash the tomatoes into a coarse purée. Add the prunes and sugar, then adjust the seasoning, adding cinnamon, allspice and cumin to taste, as well as extra chilli powder, if wished.
4. Increase the oven temperature to 200°C/400°F/Gas Mark 6 and return the meat and sauce to the oven for a further 20–30 minutes or until the meat has browned on top and the juices have thickened.
5. Remove the meat from the pan and set aside for a few minutes. Carefully carve it into thin slices and spoon the sauce over the top. Serve the pork warm with corn tortillas.

NUTRITION

Calories *352*; Sugars *1 g*; Protein *39 g*; Carbohydrate *24 g*; Fat *12 g*; Saturates *2 g*

 moderate

8 hrs 15 mins

3–4 hrs

Dried cannellini beans feature in many Italian, Spanish, French and Greek stews and casseroles, especially during the winter months.

Basque Pork *and* Beans

1 Drain the cannellini beans and put in a large pan with fresh water to cover. Bring to the boil and boil rapidly for 10 minutes. Lower the heat and simmer for 20 minutes. Drain and set aside.

2 Add enough oil to cover the base of a frying pan in a very thin layer. Heat the oil over medium heat, add a few pieces of the pork and fry on all sides until brown. Remove from the pan and set aside. Repeat with the remaining pork.

3 Add 1 tablespoon oil to the frying pan, if necessary, then add the onion and cook for 3 minutes. Stir in the garlic and cook for a further 2 minutes. Return the pork to the pan.

4 Add the tomatoes and bring to the boil. Lower the heat, then stir in the pepper slices, orange rind and the drained beans. Season with salt and pepper to taste.

5 Transfer the contents of the pan to a casserole. Cover the casserole and cook in a preheated oven, 180°C/350°F/Gas Mark 4, for 45 minutes until the beans and pork are tender. Sprinkle with chopped parsley and serve immediately, straight from the casserole.

SERVES 4

- 200 g/7 oz dried cannellini beans, soaked in cold water overnight
- olive oil, for frying
- 600 g/1 lb 4 oz boneless leg of pork, cut into 5-cm/2-inch chunks
- 1 large onion, sliced
- 3 large garlic cloves, crushed
- 400 g/14 oz canned chopped tomatoes
- 2 green peppers, deseeded and sliced
- finely grated rind of 1 large orange
- salt and pepper
- finely chopped fresh parsley, to garnish

NUTRITION

Calories *352*; Sugars *1 g*; Protein *39 g*; Carbohydrate *24 g*; Fat *12 g*; Saturates *2 g*

easy

 8 hrs 15 mins

 1 hr 30 mins

Served with vegetable rice or potatoes with spices and onions, this dish is a great success at dinner parties.

Lamb Pot Roast

SERVES 4

2.5 kg/5 lb 8 oz leg of lamb
2 tsp fresh root ginger, chopped finely
2 tsp fresh garlic, crushed
2 tsp garam masala
1 tsp salt
2 tsp black cumin seeds
4 black peppercorns
3 cloves
1 tsp chilli powder
3 tbsp lemon juice
300 ml/½ pint oil
1 large onion, peeled
about 2 litres/4 pints water

1 Remove the fat from the lamb. Prick the lamb all over with a fork.

2 In a bowl, mix the ginger, garlic, garam masala, salt, black cumin seeds, peppercorns, cloves and chilli powder until well combined. Stir in the lemon juice and mix well. Rub the mixture all over the leg of lamb and set aside.

3 Heat the oil in a pan. Place the meat in the pan and place the onion alongside.

4 Add enough water to cover the meat and cook over a low heat for 2½–3 hours, turning occasionally. (If, after a while, the water has evaporated and the meat is not tender, add a little extra water.) Once the water has completely evaporated, turn the roast over to brown it on all sides.

5 Remove the roast from the pan and transfer to a serving dish. Cut the roast into slices or serve it whole to be carved at the table. Serve hot or cold.

NUTRITION

Calories *661*; Sugars *14 g*; Protein *47 g*; Carbohydrate *20 g*; Fat *53 g*; Saturates *10 g*

easy

20 mins
3 hrs

COOK'S TIP

Traditionally, a pan called a *degchi* is used for pot-roasting in India. It is set over hot ashes and contains hot coals in its lid.

The sweet spicy blend of cinnamon, coriander and cumin is the perfect foil for the tender lamb and apricots in this warming casserole.

Fruity Lamb Casserole

1 Place the meat in a mixing bowl and add the cinnamon, coriander, cumin and oil. Mix thoroughly so that the lamb is well coated in the spices.

2 Heat a non-stick frying pan for a few seconds until it is hot, then add the spiced lamb. Reduce the heat and cook for 4–5 minutes, stirring, until browned all over. Using a slotted spoon, remove the lamb and transfer to a large ovenproof casserole.

3 Add the onion, garlic, tomatoes and tomato purée to the frying pan and cook, stirring occasionally, for 5 minutes. Season to taste with salt and pepper. Stir in the apricots and sugar, add the stock and bring to the boil.

4 Spoon the sauce over the lamb and mix well. Cover and cook in a preheated oven, 180°C/350°F/Gas Mark 4, for 1 hour, removing the lid of the casserole for the last 10 minutes.

5 Roughly chop the coriander and sprinkle over the casserole to garnish. Serve with brown rice, steamed couscous or bulgar wheat.

SERVES 4

450 g/1 lb lean lamb, trimmed and cut into 2.5-cm/1-inch cubes
1 tsp ground cinnamon
1 tsp ground coriander
1 tsp ground cumin
2 tsp olive oil
1 red onion, chopped finely
1 garlic clove, crushed
400 g/14 oz canned chopped tomatoes
2 tbsp tomato purée
125 g/4½ oz ready-to-eat dried apricots
1 tsp caster sugar
300 ml/10 fl oz vegetable stock
salt and pepper
1 small bunch of fresh coriander, to garnish
brown rice, steamed couscous or bulgar wheat, to serve

NUTRITION

Calories *384*; Sugars *16 g*; Protein *32 g*; Carbohydrate *17 g*; Fat *22 g*; Saturates *9 g*

easy

 5 mins

 1 hr 15 mins

A big pot of 'cocido' is warming on a cold day, great for a family meal. Serve with a selection of several salsas and a stack of corn tortillas.

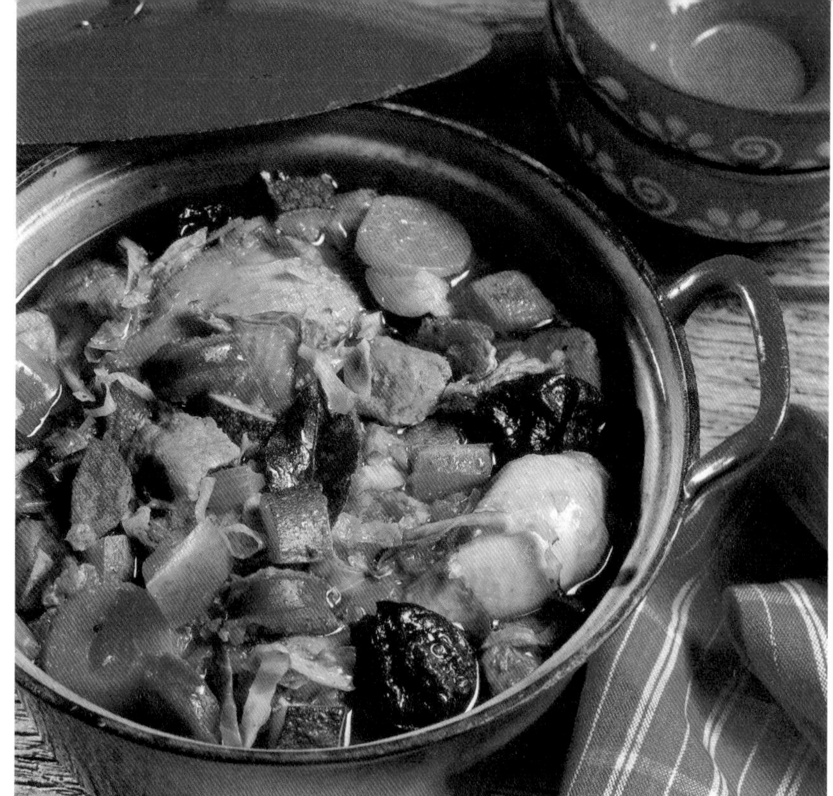

Simmered Medley

SERVES 6 – 8

900 g/2 lb boneless pork
2 bay leaves
1 onion, chopped
8 garlic cloves, chopped finely
2 tbsp chopped fresh coriander
1 carrot, sliced thinly
2 celery sticks, diced
2 chicken stock cubes
½ chicken, cut into portions
4–5 ripe tomatoes, diced
½ tsp mild chilli powder
grated rind of ¼ orange
¼ tsp ground cumin
juice of 3 oranges
1 courgette, cut into bite-sized pieces
¼ cabbage, sliced thinly and blanched
1 apple, cut into bite-sized pieces
about 10 prunes, stoned
¼ tsp ground cinnamon
pinch of ground ginger
2 hard chorizo sausages, about 350 g/12 oz in total, cut into bite-sized pieces
salt and pepper

NUTRITION

Calories *555*; Sugars *17 g*; Protein *47 g*; Carbohydrate *19 g*; Fat *33 g*; Saturates *12 g*

moderate

20 mins

2 hrs 5 mins

1 Combine the pork, bay leaves, onion, garlic, coriander, carrot and celery in a large pan and fill with cold water. Bring to the boil, skim off the scum on the surface. Reduce the heat and simmer gently for 1 hour.

2 Add the stock cubes to the pan, with the chicken, tomatoes, chilli powder, orange rind and cumin. Cook for a further 45 minutes or until the chicken is tender. Spoon off the fat that forms on the top.

3 Add the orange juice, courgette, cabbage, apple, prunes, cinnamon, ginger and chorizo. Simmer for a further 20 minutes or until the courgette is soft and tender and the chorizo is completely cooked through.

4 Season with salt and pepper to taste. Serve with rice, tortillas and salsa.

This type of dish
in the Balkans, th
Russia to the Mi(
The saffron and
pomegranate juice give
it an exotic flavour.

Azerbaijani Lamb Pilaf

1 Heat the oil in a large flameproof casserole or wide pan over a high heat. Add the lamb, in batches, and cook stirring and turning frequently, for about 7 minutes until lightly browned.

2 Add the onions, reduce the heat to medium-high and cook for about 2 minutes until beginning to soften. Add the cumin and rice and cook, stirring to coat, for about 2 minutes until the rice is translucent. Stir in the tomato purée and the saffron threads.

3 Add the pomegranate juice and stock and bring to the boil, stirring. Stir in the apricots or prunes and raisins. Reduce the heat to low, cover, and simmer for 20–25 minutes until the lamb and rice are tender and the liquid has been absorbed.

4 Season to taste, sprinkle the chopped mint and watercress over the pilaf and serve from the casserole.

SERVES 4 – 6

2–3 tbsp vegetable oil
650 g/1 lb 7 oz boneless lamb shoulder, cut into 2.5-cm/1-inch cubes
2 onions, chopped coarsely
1 tsp ground cumin
200 g/7 oz arborio, long-grain or basmati rice
1 tbsp tomato purée
1 tsp saffron threads
100 ml/3½ fl oz pomegranate juice (see Cook's Tip)
850 ml/1½ pints lamb or chicken stock or water
115 g/4 oz dried apricots or prunes, ready soaked and halved
2 tbsp raisins
salt and pepper

to serve

2 tbsp chopped fresh mint
2 tbsp chopped fresh watercress

NUTRITION

Calories *399*; Sugars *19 g*; Protein *25 g*; Carbohydrate *45 g*; Fat *13 g*; Saturates *4 g*

 easy
 15 mins
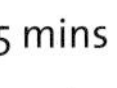 50 mins

COOK'S TIP

Pomegranate juice is available from Middle Eastern grocery shops. If you cannot find it, substitute unsweetened grape or apple juice.

This curry uses the typically hot chilli flavour of Thai red curry paste, made with dried red chillies, which gives it a warm, russet-red colour.

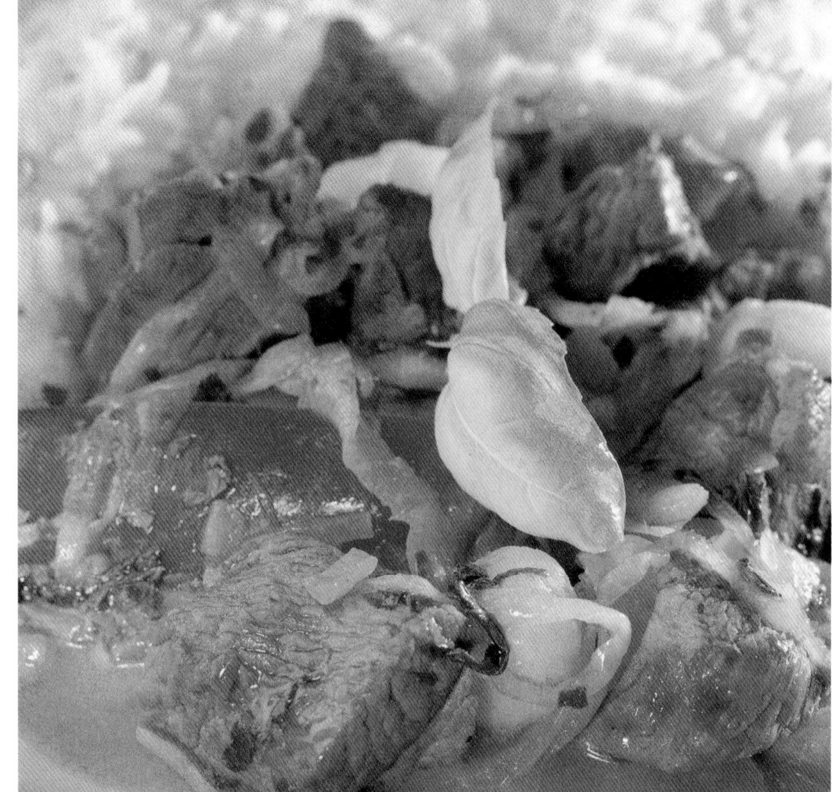

Red Lamb Curry

SERVES 4

- 2 tbsp vegetable oil
- 1 large onion, sliced
- 2 garlic cloves, crushed
- 500 g/1 lb 2 oz boneless lean leg of lamb, cut into 3-cm/1¼-inch cubes
- 2 tbsp Thai red curry paste
- 150 ml/5 fl oz coconut milk
- 1 tbsp soft light brown sugar
- 1 large red pepper, deseeded and sliced thickly
- 120 ml/4 fl oz lamb or beef stock
- 1 tbsp fish sauce
- 2 tbsp lime juice
- 225 g/8 oz canned water chestnuts, drained
- 2 tbsp chopped fresh coriander
- 2 tbsp chopped fresh basil
- salt and pepper
- boiled jasmine rice, to serve
- fresh basil leaves, to garnish

NUTRITION
Calories *363*; Sugars *11 g*; Protein *29 g*; Carbohydrate *21 g*; Fat *19 g*; Saturates *6 g*

 moderate

10 mins

40 mins

1 Heat the oil in a preheated wok or large, heavy-based frying pan over a high heat and stir-fry the onion and garlic for 2–3 minutes, until softened. Add the lamb and fry the mixture quickly until lightly browned.

2 Stir in the curry paste and cook for a few seconds, then add the coconut milk and sugar and bring to the boil. Reduce the heat and simmer the lamb for 15 minutes, stirring occasionally.

3 Stir in the red pepper, stock, fish sauce and lime juice, cover and simmer for a further 15 minutes, or until the meat is tender.

4 Add the water chestnuts, coriander and basil, and season with salt and pepper to taste. Garnish with fresh basil leaves and serve with jasmine rice.

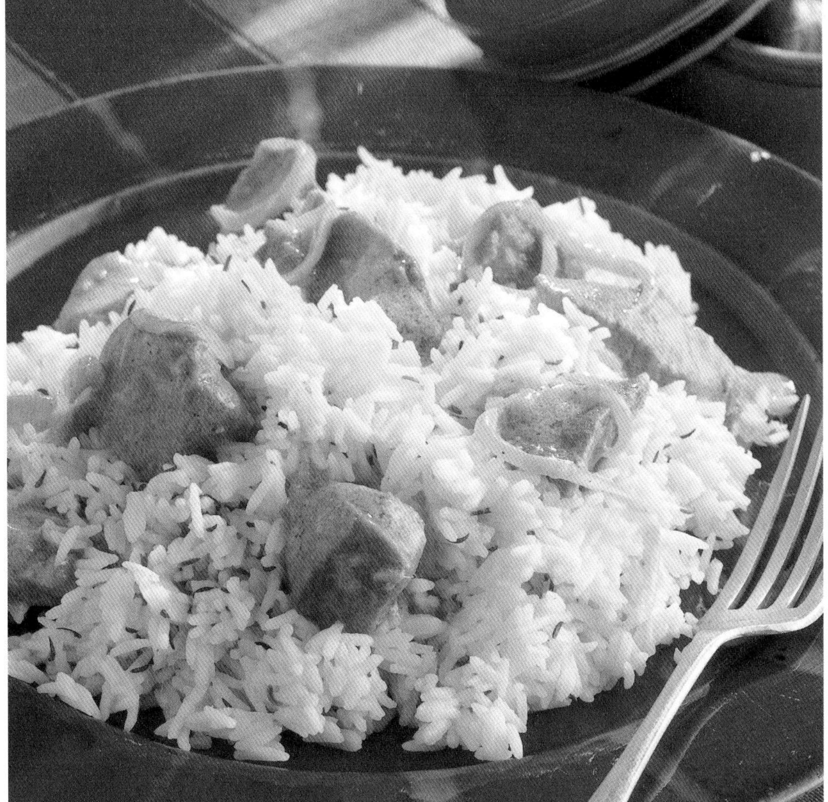

Cooked on festive occasions, especially for weddings, lamb biryani is amongst the most popular dishes in India. The meat can be cooked in advance and added to the rice on the day of the party.

Lamb Biryani

SERVES 4 – 6

- 150 ml/¼ pint milk
- 1 tsp saffron
- 5 tbsp ghee
- 3 medium onions, sliced
- 1 kg/2 lb 5 oz lean lamb, cubed
- 7 tbsp natural yogurt
- 1½ tsp fresh root ginger, chopped finely
- 1½ tsp crushed garlic
- 2 tsp garam masala
- 2 tsp salt
- ¼ tsp turmeric
- 600 ml/1 pint water
- 450 g/1 lb basmati rice
- 2 tsp black cumin seeds
- 3 cardamoms
- 4 tbsp lemon juice
- 2 fresh green chillies
- ¼ bunch of fresh coriander

1 Boil the milk in a pan with the saffron and set aside. Heat the ghee in a pan and fry the onions until golden. Remove half of the onions and ghee from the pan and set aside in a bowl.

2 Combine the meat, yogurt, ginger, garlic, garam masala, 1 tsp salt and turmeric in a large bowl and mix well.

3 Return the pan with the ghee and onions to the heat, add the meat mixture, stir for about 3 minutes and add the water. Cook over a low heat for 45 minutes, stirring occasionally. Check to see whether the meat is tender: if not, add 150 ml/¼ pint water and cook for 15 minutes. Once all the water has evaporated, stir-fry for about 2 minutes and set aside.

4 Meanwhile, place the rice in a pan. Add the cumin seeds, cardamoms, salt and enough water for cooking, and cook over a medium heat until the rice is half-cooked. Drain. Remove half of the rice and place in a bowl.

5 Spoon the meat mixture on top of the rice in the pan. Add half each of the saffron mixture, lemon juice, chillies and coriander. Add the other half of the rice, saffron, lemon juice, chillies and coriander. Cover and cook over a low heat for 15–20 minutes or until the rice is cooked. Stir well and serve hot.

NUTRITION

Calories *1073*; Sugars *14 g*; Protein *66 g*; Carbohydrate *108 g*; Fat *42 g*; Saturates *23 g*

easy

 15 mins

 1 hr 45 mins

Venison is super-lean and low in fat, so it's the perfect choice for a healthy diet. Cooked quickly with crisp vegetables, it's ideal in a stir-fry.

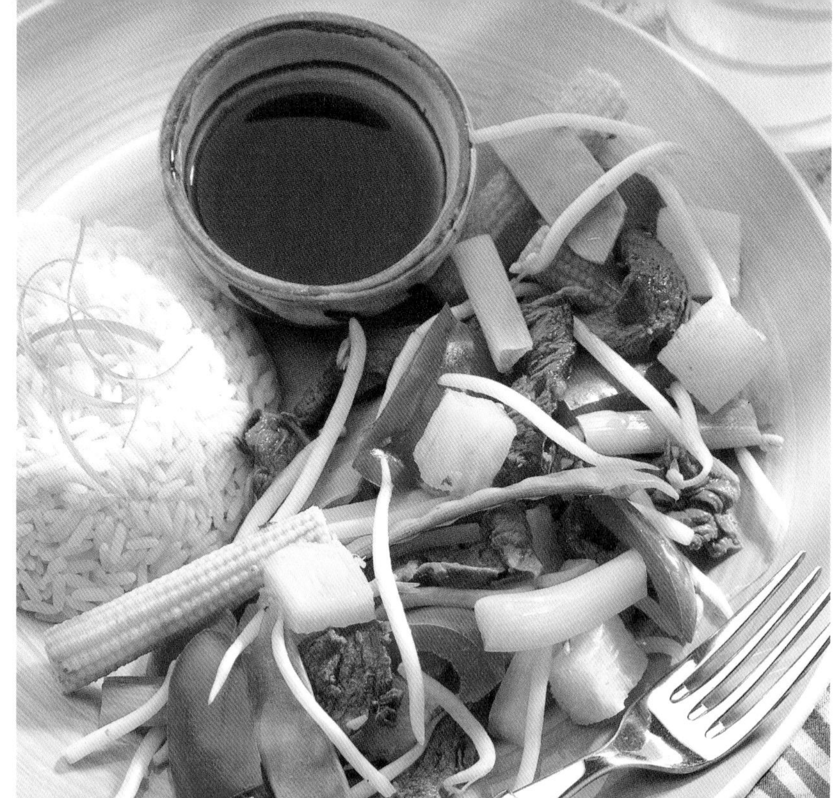

Sweet *and* Sour Venison Stir-fry

SERVES 4

- 1 bunch spring onions
- 1 red pepper
- 100 g/3½ oz mangetout
- 100 g/3½ oz baby corn cobs
- 350 g/12 oz lean venison steak
- 1 tbsp vegetable oil
- 1 garlic clove, crushed
- 2.5-cm/1-inch piece of fresh root ginger, chopped finely
- 3 tbsp light soy sauce, plus extra for serving
- 1 tbsp white wine vinegar
- 2 tbsp dry sherry
- 2 tsp clear honey
- 225 g/8 oz canned pineapple pieces in natural juice, drained
- 25 g/1 oz beansprouts
- freshly cooked rice, to serve

1 Cut the spring onions into 2.5-cm/1-inch pieces. Halve and deseed the red pepper and cut it into 2.5-cm/1-inch pieces. Trim the mangetout and baby corn cobs. Set aside.

2 Trim the meat and cut it into thin strips. Heat the oil in a large frying pan or wok until hot and stir-fry the meat, garlic and ginger for 5 minutes.

3 Add the spring onions, red pepper, mangetout and baby corn cobs, then stir in the soy sauce, vinegar, sherry and honey. Stir-fry for a further 5 minutes.

4 Carefully stir in the pineapple pieces and beansprouts and cook for a further 1–2 minutes to heat through. Serve the stir-fry with freshly cooked rice and extra soy sauce for dipping.

NUTRITION

Calories *219*; Sugars *18 g*; Protein *23 g*; Carbohydrate *20 g*; Fat *5 g*; Saturates *1 g*

very easy

15 mins

15 mins

COOK'S TIP

For a nutritious meal-in-one, cook 225 g/8 oz egg noodles in boiling water for 3–4 minutes. Drain and add to the pan at Step 4, with the pineapple and beansprouts, plus an extra 2 tablespoons soy sauce.

Polenta can be served fresh, as in this dish, or it can be cooled, then sliced and grilled or fried.

Polenta *with* Rabbit Stew

1 Grease a large ovenproof dish with a little butter. Mix the polenta, salt and water in a large pan, whisking well to prevent lumps from forming. Bring to the boil and boil for 10 minutes, stirring vigorously and constantly. Turn the polenta into the prepared dish and bake in a preheated oven, 190°C/375°F/Gas Mark 5, for 40 minutes.

2 Meanwhile, heat the oil in a large pan and add the rabbit pieces, garlic and shallots. Fry for 10 minutes until browned.

3 Stir in the wine and cook for a further 5 minutes.

4 Add the carrot, celery, bay leaves, rosemary, tomatoes, olives and 300 ml/10 fl oz water. Cover the pan and simmer for about 45 minutes or until the rabbit is tender. Season with salt and pepper to taste.

5 To serve, spoon or cut a portion of polenta and place on each serving plate. Top with a ladleful of rabbit stew. Serve immediately.

SERVES 4

butter, for greasing
300 g/10½ oz polenta or cornmeal
1 tbsp coarse sea salt
1.2 litres/2 pints water
4 tbsp olive oil
2 kg/4 lb 8 oz rabbit joints
3 garlic cloves, peeled
3 shallots, sliced
150 ml/5 fl oz red wine
1 carrot, sliced
1 celery stick, sliced
2 bay leaves
1 fresh rosemary sprig
3 tomatoes, peeled and diced
85 g/3 oz stoned black olives
salt and pepper

NUTRITION

Calories *726*; Sugars *2 g*; Protein *61 g*; Carbohydrate *55 g*; Fat *25 g*; Saturates *6 g*

moderate

20 mins

1 hr 45 mins

Poultry

Chicken is the perfect choice for one-pot cooking, as there are so many different cuts, from inexpensive thighs to delicate breast meat, as well as the whole bird. In addition, as it is often rather bland in flavour, it benefits from being combined with vegetables, fruit, herbs and aromatics. Almost everyone loves chicken and the recipes in this chapter reflect its universal popularity with dishes from Mexico, India, Thailand, Spain, Italy and the Middle East, among other countries. It is a versatile meat and can be cooked in any number of ways from casseroles to stir-fries and from risottos to curries. There are recipes for all occasions and every time of year from Sunday lunch with the family to an al fresco dinner party. Hot and spicy, rich and creamy, filling and flavoursome, subtle and delicate – there is a one-pot chicken dish that is sure to please.

This hearty and nourishing soup, combining chickpeas and chicken, is an ideal starter for a family supper.

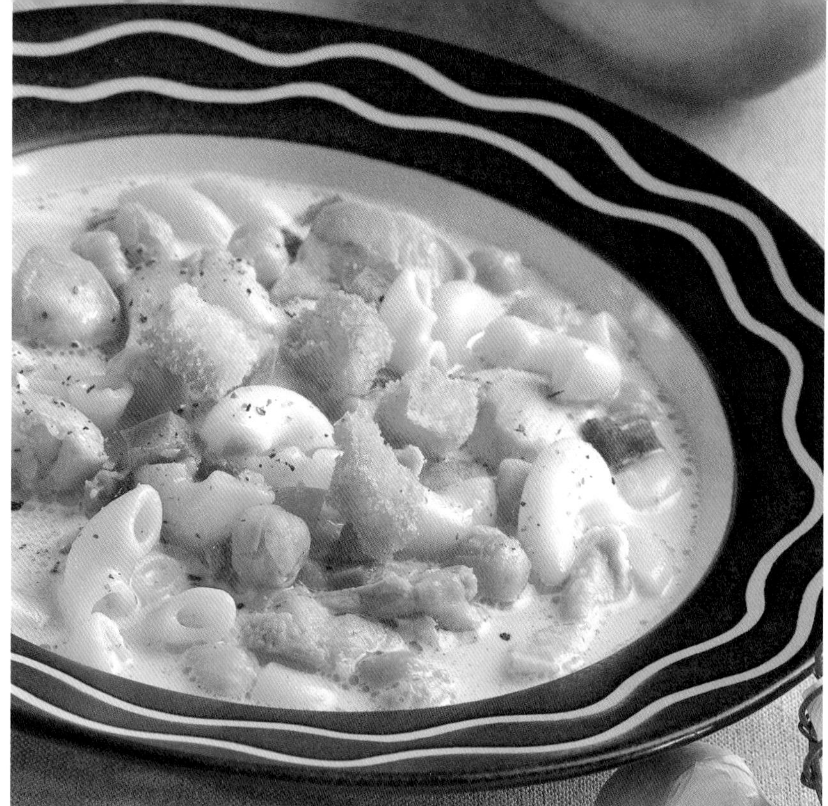

Chicken *and* Chickpea Soup

SERVES 4

25 g/1 oz butter
3 spring onions, chopped
2 garlic cloves, crushed
1 fresh marjoram sprig, chopped finely
350 g/12 oz boned chicken breasts, diced
1.2 litres/2 pints/5 cups chicken stock
350 g/12 oz canned chickpeas, drained
1 bouquet garni
salt and white pepper
1 red pepper, diced
1 green pepper, diced
115 g/4 oz small dried pasta shapes, such as elbow macaroni
croûtons, to serve

1 Melt the butter in a large saucepan. Add the spring onions, garlic, sprig of fresh marjoram and the diced chicken and cook, stirring frequently, over a medium heat for 5 minutes.

2 Add the chicken stock, chickpeas and bouquet garni and season to taste with salt and white pepper.

3 Bring the soup to the boil, lower the heat and simmer for about 2 hours.

4 Add the diced peppers and pasta to the pan, then simmer the soup for a further 20 minutes.

5 Transfer the soup to a warm tureen. To serve, ladle the soup into individual serving bowls and serve immediately, garnished with croûtons.

NUTRITION

Calories *347*; Sugars *2 g*; Protein *28 g*; Carbohydrate *37 g*; Fat *11 g*; Saturates *4 g*

moderate
15 mins
2 hr 25 mins

COOK'S TIP

If you prefer, you can use dried chickpeas. Cover with cold water and set aside to soak for 5–8 hours. Drain and add the beans to the soup, according to the recipe, and allow an additional 30 minutes–1 hour cooking time.

This soup evolved from the foodstalls that line the streets of Tlalpan, a suburb of Mexico City: avocado, chicken and chillies provide a typically Mexican flavour.

Chicken *and* Chipotle Soup

SERVES 4

1.5 litres/2¾ pints chicken stock
2–3 garlic cloves, chopped finely
1–2 chipotle chillies, cut into very thin strips (see Cook's Tip)
1 avocado
lime or lemon juice, for tossing
3–5 spring onions, sliced thinly
350–400 g/12–14 oz skinless boneless cooked chicken breast, torn or cut into shreds or thin strips
2 tbsp chopped fresh coriander

to serve
1 lime, cut into wedges
handful of tortilla chips (optional)

1 Place the stock, garlic and chipotle chillies in a pan and bring to the boil.

2 Meanwhile, cut the avocado in half around the stone. Twist apart, then remove the stone with a knife. Carefully peel off the skin, dice the flesh and toss in lime or lemon juice to prevent the flesh from turning brown.

3 Arrange the spring onions, chicken, avocado and fresh coriander in the base of 4 individual soup bowls or in a large tureen.

4 Ladle the hot stock into the bowls and serve with lime wedges and a handful of tortilla chips if using.

COOK'S TIP

Chipotle chillies are smoked and are available canned or dried. They add a distinctive smoky flavour to dishes and are very hot. Canned chipotles must be drained and dried chipotles reconstituted before using.

NUTRITION

Calories *216*; Sugars *1 g*; Protein *28 g*; Carbohydrate *2 g*; Fat *11 g*; Saturates *2 g*

very easy

10 mins

5 mins

The vermicelli gives this Chinese-style soup an Italian twist. Use egg noodles if you prefer.

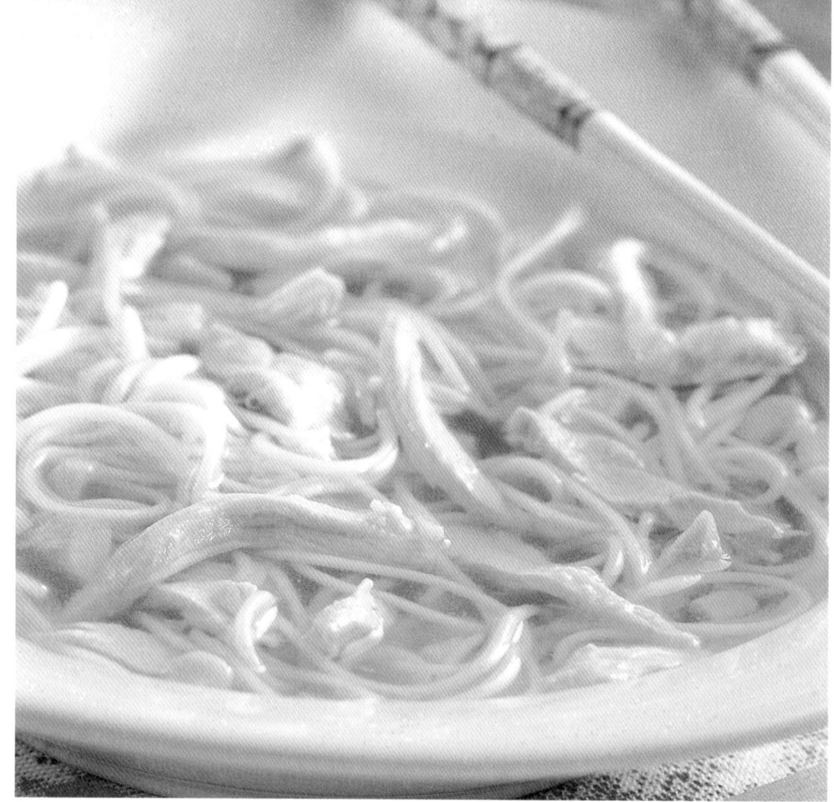

Chicken, Noodle *and* Corn Soup

SERVES 4

450 g/1 lb skinless, boneless chicken breasts, cut into strips
1.2 litres/2 pints chicken stock
150 ml/¼ pint double cream
salt and pepper
100 g/3½ oz dried vermicelli
1 tbsp cornflour
3 tbsp milk
175 g/6 oz sweetcorn

1 Put the chicken, stock and cream into a large saucepan and bring to the boil over a low heat. Reduce the heat slightly and simmer for about 20 minutes. Season the soup with salt and black pepper to taste.

2 Meanwhile, cook the vermicelli in lightly salted boiling water for 10–12 minutes, until just tender. Drain the pasta and keep warm.

3 In a small bowl, mix together the cornflour and milk to make a smooth paste. Stir the cornflour into the soup until thickened.

4 Add the sweetcorn and vermicelli to the pan and heat through.

5 Transfer the soup to a warm tureen or individual soup bowls and serve.

NUTRITION

Calories *401*; Sugars *6 g*; Protein *31 g*; Carbohydrate *17 g*; Fat *24 g*; Saturates *13 g*

easy
5 mins
30 mins

COOK'S TIP

For crab and sweetcorn soup, substitute 450 g/1 lb cooked crab meat for the chicken breasts. Flake the crab meat well before adding it to the saucepan and reduce the cooking time by 10 minutes.

This delicately flavoured summer soup is surprisingly easy to make, and tastes delicious.

Lemon *and* Chicken Soup

1 Melt the butter in a large saucepan. Add the shallots, carrots, celery and chicken and cook over a low heat, stirring occasionally, for 8 minutes.

2 Thinly pare the lemons and blanch the lemon rind in boiling water for 3 minutes. Squeeze the juice from the lemons.

3 Add the lemon rind and juice to the pan, together with the chicken stock. Bring the soup slowly to the boil over a low heat and simmer for 40 minutes, stirring occasionally.

4 Add the spaghetti to the pan and cook for 15 minutes. Season to taste with salt and white pepper and add the cream. Heat through, but do not allow the soup to boil or it will curdle.

5 Pour the soup into a tureen or individual bowls, garnish with parsley and half slices of lemon and serve immediately.

SERVES 4

4 tbsp butter
8 shallots, sliced thinly
2 carrots, sliced thinly
2 celery sticks, sliced thinly
225 g/8 oz chicken breasts, chopped finely
3 lemons, thinly pared and juiced, with slices reserved for garnish
1.2 litres/2 pints chicken stock
225 g/8 oz dried spaghetti, broken into small pieces
salt and white pepper
150 ml/5 fl oz double cream

to garnish

1 sprig of fresh parsley
3 lemon slices, halved

COOK'S TIP

You can prepare this soup in advance up to the end of Step 3, so that all you need do before serving is heat it through very gently before adding the pasta and the finishing touches.

NUTRITION

Calories *506*; Sugars *4 g*; Protein *19 g*; Carbohydrate *41 g*; Fat *31 g*; Saturates *19 g*

easy

 10 mins

 1 hr 10 mins

This soup is a good way of using up leftover cooked chicken and rice. Any kind of rice is suitable, from white or brown long-grain rice to wild rice.

Chicken *and* Rice Soup

SERVES 4

- 1.5 litres/2¾ pints chicken stock (see Cook's Tip)
- 2 small carrots, sliced very thinly
- 1 celery stick, diced finely
- 1 baby leek, halved lengthways and sliced thinly
- 115 g/4 oz petit pois, defrosted if frozen
- 175 g/6 oz cooked rice
- 150 g/5½ oz cooked chicken, sliced
- 2 tsp chopped fresh tarragon
- 1 tbsp chopped fresh parsley
- salt and pepper
- fresh parsley sprigs, to garnish

1 Put the stock in a large saucepan and add the carrots, celery and leek. Bring the stock to the boil, reduce the heat to low and simmer gently, partially covered, for 10 minutes.

2 Stir in the peas, rice and chicken and continue cooking for a further 10–15 minutes, or until the vegetables are tender.

3 Add the chopped tarragon and parsley to the soup, then taste and season with salt and pepper as needed.

4 Ladle the soup into warm bowls, garnish with parsley and serve immediately with crusty bread.

NUTRITION

Calories *165*; Sugars *3 g*; Protein *14 g*; Carbohydrate *19 g*; Fat *4 g*; Saturates *1 g*

very easy

25 mins

30 mins

COOK'S TIP

If the stock you are using is a little weak, or if you have used a stock cube, add the herbs at the beginning, so that they can flavour the stock for a longer time.

Make this soup when you want a change from traditional chicken soup. It is nicely spicy. Use a generous amount of fresh coriander leaves to garnish.

Thai-style Chicken *and* Coconut Soup

1 Put the stock in a pan with the chicken, chilli, lemon grass, lime leaves and ginger. Bring almost to the boil, reduce the heat, cover and simmer for 20–25 minutes, or until the chicken is cooked through and firm to the touch.

2 Remove the chicken from the pan and strain the stock. When the chicken is cool, slice thinly or shred into bite-sized pieces.

3 Return the stock to the saucepan and heat to simmering. Stir in the coconut milk and spring onions. Add the chicken and continue simmering for about 10 minutes, or until the soup is heated through and all the different flavours have mingled.

4 Stir in the chilli purée. Season to taste with salt and, if wished, add a little more chilli purée.

5 Ladle into warm bowls and float fresh coriander leaves on top to serve.

SERVES 4

1.2 litres/2 pints chicken stock
200 g/7 oz skinless, boneless chicken
1 fresh chilli, split lengthways and deseeded
7.5-cm/3-inch piece of lemon grass, split lengthways
3–4 lime leaves
2.5-cm/1-inch piece of fresh root ginger, peeled and sliced
120 ml/4 fl oz coconut milk
6–8 spring onions, sliced diagonally
¼ tsp chilli purée, or to taste
salt
fresh coriander leaves, to garnish

NUTRITION

Calories *76*; Sugars *2 g*; Protein *13 g*; Carbohydrate *3 g*; Fat *1 g*; Saturates *0.25 g*

easy

5 mins

40 mins

COOK'S TIP

Once the stock is flavoured and the chicken cooked, this soup is very quick to finish. If you wish, poach the chicken and strain the stock ahead of time. Store in the refrigerator separately.

This simple, Japanese style of cooking is ideal for thinly sliced breast of chicken. Mirin is a rich, sweet rice wine which is available from Oriental shops.

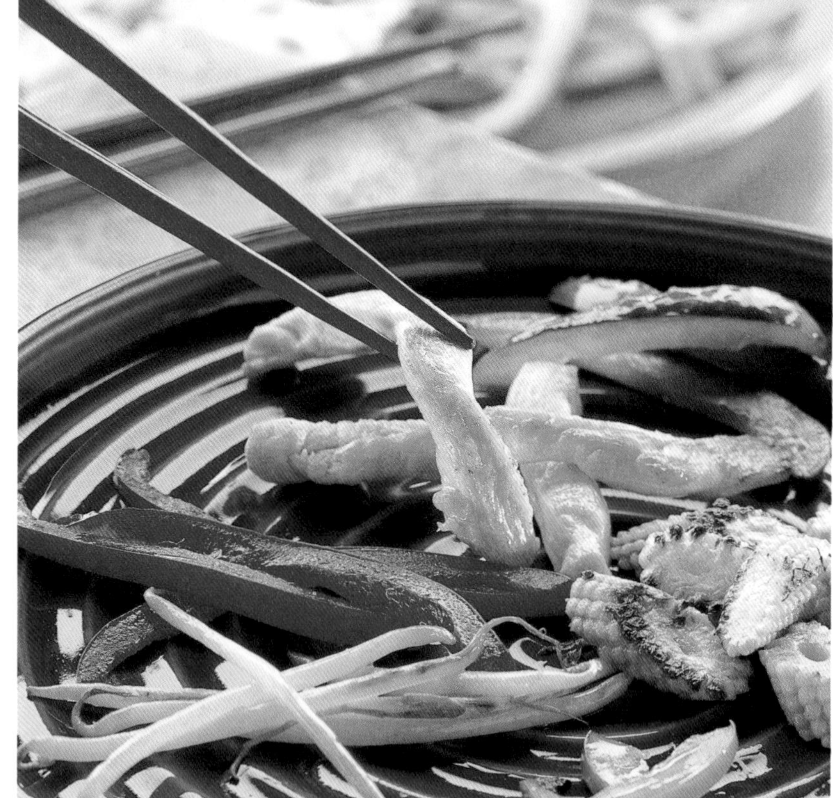

Teppanyaki

SERVES 4

4 boneless chicken breasts
1 red pepper
1 green pepper
4 spring onions
8 baby corn cobs
100 g/3½ oz beansprouts
1 tbsp sesame or sunflower oil
4 tbsp soy sauce
4 tbsp mirin
1 tbsp grated fresh root ginger

1 Remove the skin from the chicken and slice at a slight angle, to a thickness of about 5 mm/¼ inch.

2 Deseed and thinly slice the peppers and trim and slice the spring onions and baby corn cobs. Arrange the peppers, spring onions, corn cobs and beansprouts on a plate with the sliced chicken.

3 Heat a large griddle or heavy frying pan then lightly brush with oil. Add the vegetables and chicken slices in small batches, allowing space between them so that they cook thoroughly.

4 In a small bowl, mix together the soy sauce, mirin and ginger and serve as a dip with the chicken and vegetables.

NUTRITION

Calories *206*; Sugars *4 g*; Protein *30 g*; Carbohydrate *6 g*; Fat *7 g*; Saturates *2 g*

easy
5 mins
10 mins

COOK'S TIP

Mirin is a rich, sweet rice wine from Japan. You can buy it in Oriental supermarkets, but if it is not available, add 1 tablespoon soft light brown sugar to the sauce instead.

Even plain potato cakes are a great favourite. In this recipe, the potatoes are combined with minced chicken and mashed banana.

Chicken *and* Banana Cakes

1 Cook the diced potatoes in a saucepan of boiling water for about 10 minutes until tender. Drain well and mash until smooth. Stir in the minced chicken.

2 Mash the banana and add it to the potato with the flour, lemon juice, onion and half of the chopped sage. Season to taste with salt and pepper and stir the mixture together thoroughly.

3 Divide the mixture into 8 equal portions. With lightly floured hands, shape each portion into a round patty.

4 Heat the butter and oil in a frying pan, add the potato cakes and cook for 12–15 minutes or until cooked through, turning once. Remove from the pan and keep warm.

5 Stir the cream and stock into the pan with the remaining chopped sage. Cook over a low heat for 2–3 minutes.

6 Arrange the potato cakes on a warmed serving plate, garnish with fresh sage leaves and serve immediately with the cream and sage sauce.

SERVES 4

450 g/1 lb floury potatoes, diced
225 g/8 oz minced chicken
1 large banana
2 tbsp plain flour
1 tsp lemon juice
1 onion, chopped finely
2 tbsp chopped fresh sage
2 tbsp butter
2 tbsp vegetable oil
150 ml/5 fl oz single cream
150 ml/5 fl oz chicken stock
salt and pepper
fresh sage leaves, to garnish

NUTRITION

Calories *439*; Sugars *11 g*; Protein *22 g*; Carbohydrate *39 g*; Fat *23 g*; Saturates *10 g*

moderate
 5–10 mins
 25–30 mins

COOK'S TIP

Do not boil the sauce once the cream has been added, or it will curdle. Cook it gently over a very low heat.

This is a quick and tasty way to use leftover roast chicken. The sauce can also be used for any cooked poultry, lamb or beef.

Fragrant Chicken *and* Broad Beans

SERVES 4

1 tsp mustard oil
3 tbsp vegetable oil
1 large onion, chopped finely
3 garlic cloves, crushed
1 tbsp tomato purée
2 tomatoes, peeled and chopped
1 tsp ground turmeric
½ tsp cumin seeds, ground
½ tsp coriander seeds, ground
½ tsp chilli powder
½ tsp garam masala
1 tsp red wine vinegar
1 small red pepper, chopped
125 g/4 oz frozen broad beans
500 g/1 lb cooked chicken breasts, cut into bite-sized pieces
salt
fresh coriander sprigs, to garnish

1 Heat the mustard oil in a large, frying pan set over a high heat for about 1 minute until it begins to smoke. Add the vegetable oil, reduce the heat and then add the onion and the garlic. Fry until they are golden.

2 Add the tomato purée, chopped tomatoes, ground turmeric, cumin and coriander seeds, chilli powder, garam masala and red wine vinegar to the frying pan. Stir the mixture until fragrant.

3 Add the red pepper and broad beans and stir for 2 minutes until the pepper is softened. Stir in the chicken, and salt to taste. Leave to simmer gently for 6–8 minutes until the chicken is heated through and the beans are tender.

4 Serve garnished with coriander leaves.

NUTRITION

Calories *270*; Sugars *3 g*; Protein *36 g*; Carbohydrate *7 g*; Fat *11 g*;Saturates *2 g*

 easy
25 mins
15 mins

COOK'S TIP

This dish is an ideal way of making use of any type of leftover poultry. Any variety of beans works well, but vegetables are just as useful, especially courgettes, potatoes or broccoli.

Spices, herbs, fruit, nuts and vegetables are combined to make an appealing casserole with lots of flavour.

Spiced Chicken Casserole

1 Heat the olive oil in a large saucepan and fry the chicken, shallots or pickling onions, and carrots for about 6 minutes or until browned.

2 Add the remaining ingredients, except the grapes, and simmer over a low heat for 2 hours until the meat is very tender. Stir the casserole occasionally.

3 Add the grapes just before serving. Garnish with herbs and serve with wild rice or puréed potato.

SERVES 4 – 6

3 tbsp olive oil
900 g/2 lb chicken meat, sliced
10 shallots or pickling onions
3 carrots, chopped
60 g/2 oz chestnuts, sliced
60 g/2 oz flaked almonds, toasted
1 tsp freshly grated nutmeg
3 tsp ground cinnamon
300 ml/½ pint white wine
300 ml/½ pint chicken stock
175 ml/6 fl oz white wine vinegar
1 tbsp chopped fresh tarragon
1 tbsp chopped fresh flat-leaved parsley
1 tbsp chopped fresh thyme
grated rind of 1 orange
1 tbsp dark muscovado sugar
sea salt and pepper
125 g/4½ oz seedless black grapes, halved
fresh herbs, to garnish
wild rice or puréed potato, to serve

NUTRITION

Calories *385*; Sugars *14 g*; Protein *37 g*; Carbohydrate *19 g*; Fat *15 g*; Saturates *2 g*

easy
10 mins
2 hrs 15 mins

COOK'S TIP

This casserole would also be delicious served with thick slices of crusty wholemeal bread to soak up the sauce.

All the sunshine colours and flavours of the Mediterranean are combined in this easy dish.

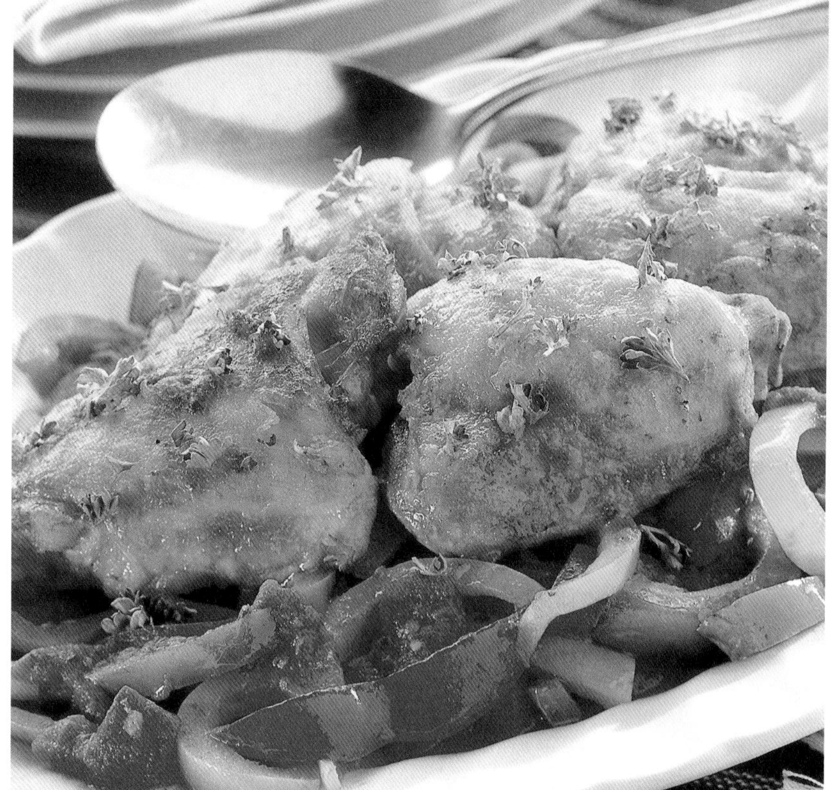

Chicken Peperonata

SERVES 4

- 8 skinless chicken thighs
- 2 tbsp wholemeal flour
- 2 tbsp olive oil
- 1 small onion, sliced thinly
- 1 garlic clove, crushed
- 1 each large red, yellow and green peppers, sliced thinly
- 400 g/14 oz canned chopped tomatoes
- 1 tbsp chopped oregano
- salt and pepper
- fresh oregano, to garnish
- crusty wholemeal bread, to serve

1. Remove the skin from the chicken thighs and toss in the flour.
2. Heat the oil in a wide pan and fry the chicken quickly until sealed and lightly browned, then remove from the pan. Add the onion to the pan and gently fry until soft. Add the garlic, peppers, tomatoes and oregano, then bring the mixture to the boil, stirring.
3. Arrange the chicken over the vegetables, season well with salt and pepper, then cover the pan tightly and simmer for 20–25 minutes or until the chicken is completely cooked and tender.
4. Season, garnish with oregano and serve with crusty wholemeal bread.

NUTRITION
Calories *328*; Sugars *7 g*; Protein *35 g*; Carbohydrate *13 g*; Fat *15 g*; Saturates *4 g*

easy
15 mins
40 mins

COOK'S TIP

For extra flavour, halve the peppers and grill under a preheated grill until the skins are charred. Leave to cool then remove the skins and seeds. Slice the peppers thinly and use in the recipe.

A karahi is a versatile two-handled metal pan, similar to a wok. Food is always cooked over a high heat in a karahi.

Karahi Chicken

1 Heat the ghee in a karahi, wok or a large, heavy-based frying pan. Add the garlic and onion. Stir-fry for about 4 minutes until the onion is golden.

2 Stir in the garam masala, ground coriander, mint and bay leaf.

3 Add the diced chicken and cook over a high heat, stirring occasionally, for about 5 minutes. Add the stock, lower the heat and simmer for 10 minutes until the sauce has thickened and the chicken juices run clear when the meat is tested with a sharp knife.

4 Stir in the chopped fresh coriander and season with salt to taste, mix well and serve immediately with warm naan bread or chapatis.

SERVES 4

2 tbsp ghee
3 garlic cloves, crushed
1 onion, chopped finely
2 tbsp garam masala
1 tsp coriander seeds, ground
½ tsp dried mint
1 bay leaf
750 g/1 lb 10 oz lean boneless chicken, diced
200 ml/7 fl oz chicken stock
1 tbsp chopped fresh coriander
salt
warm naan bread or chapatis, to serve

COOK'S TIP

It is important always to heat a karahi or wok before you add the oil to help maintain the high temperature.

NUTRITION

Calories *270*; Sugars *1 g*; Protein *41 g*; Carbohydrate *1 g*; Fat *11 g*; Saturates *2 g*

easy

5 mins

20 mins

Fresh spring vegetables are the basis of this colourful casserole, which is topped with hearty wholemeal dumplings.

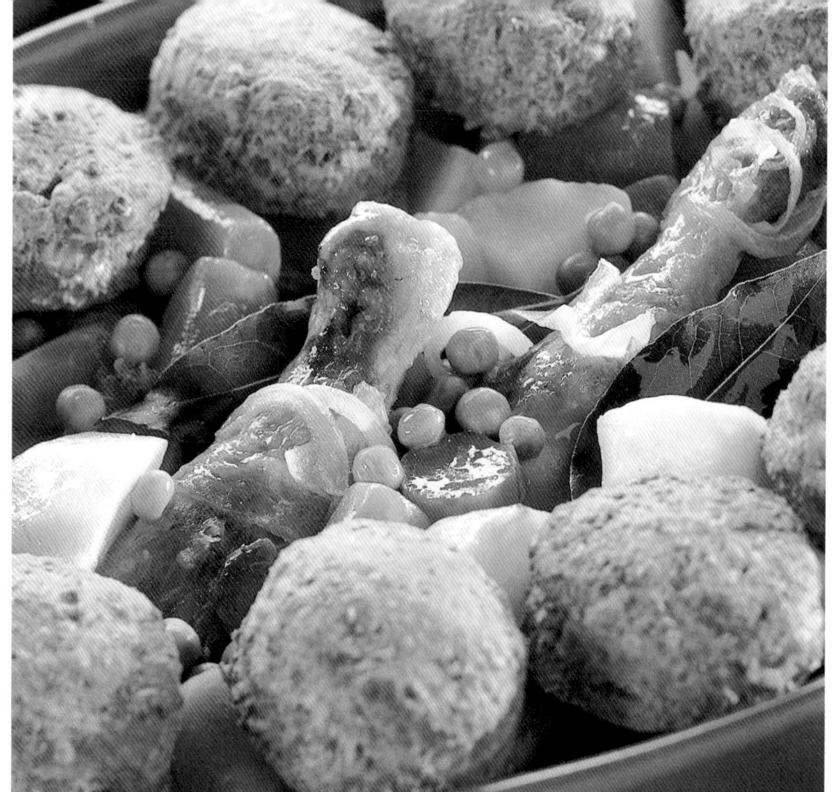

Springtime Chicken Cobbler

SERVES 4

1 tbsp vegetable oil
8 skinless chicken drumsticks
1 small onion, sliced
350 g/12 oz baby carrots
2 baby turnips
125 g/4½ oz broad beans or peas
1 tsp cornflour
300ml/½ pint chicken stock
2 bay leaves
salt and pepper

cobbler topping

250 g/9 oz plain wholemeal flour
2 tsp baking powder
2 tbsp soft sunflower margarine
2 tsp dry wholegrain mustard
55 g/2 oz low-fat mature Cheddar cheese, grated
skimmed milk, to mix, plus extra for brushing
sesame seeds, for sprinkling

1 Heat the oil in a large, heavy-based pan and fry the chicken, turning occasionally, until golden brown. Drain well and place in a casserole. Add the onion to the pan and cook, stirring, for 2–3 minutes until softened.

2 Cut the carrots and turnips into equal-size pieces. Add to the casserole with the onions and beans or peas.

3 Blend the cornflour with a little of the stock, then stir in the rest and heat gently, stirring until boiling. Pour into the casserole and add the bay leaves. Season to taste with salt and pepper.

4 Cover tightly and bake in a preheated oven, 200°C/ 400°F/Gas Mark 6, for 50–60 minutes or until the chicken juices run clear when pierced.

5 For the topping, sift the flour and baking powder. Mix in the margarine with a fork. Stir in the mustard, cheese and enough milk to make a soft dough.

6 Roll out and cut 16 rounds with a 4-cm/1½-inch cutter. Uncover the casserole, arrange the scone rounds on top of the chicken, then brush with milk and sprinkle with sesame seeds. Return to the oven and bake for 20 minutes or until the topping is golden and firm.

NUTRITION

Calories *560*; Sugars *10 g*; Protein *389 g*; Carbohydrate *64 g*; Fat *18 g*; Saturates *4 g*

moderate
15 mins
1 hr 30 mins

Sweet peppers are typical of dishes from the Basque region in France. In this recipe, Bayonne ham, from the Pyrenees, adds a delicious flavour.

Chicken Basquaise

1 Pat the chicken pieces dry with kitchen paper. Put 2 tablespoons flour in a plastic bag, season with salt and pepper and add the chicken pieces. Seal the bag and shake to coat the chicken.

2 Heat 2 tablespoons of the oil in a large flameproof casserole over a medium-high heat. Add the chicken and cook, turning frequently, for about 15 minutes until well browned all over. Transfer to a plate.

3 Heat the remaining oil in the casserole and add the onion and red peppers. Reduce the heat to medium and stir-fry until beginning to colour and soften. Add the garlic, chorizo and tomato purée and cook, stirring constantly, for about 3 minutes. Add the rice and cook, stirring to coat, for about 2 minutes until the rice is translucent.

4 Add the stock, crushed chillies and thyme, season to taste with salt and pepper and stir well. Bring to the boil. Return the chicken to the casserole, pressing it gently into the rice. Cover and cook over a very low heat for about 45 minutes until the chicken is cooked through and the rice is tender.

5 Gently stir the ham, black olives and half the parsley into the rice mixture. Re-cover and heat through for a further 5 minutes. Sprinkle with the remaining parsley and serve immediately.

SERVES 4–5

1 chicken weighing 1.35 kg/3 lb, cut into 8 pieces
flour, for dusting
3 tbsp olive oil
1 Spanish onion, sliced thickly
2 red or yellow peppers, deseeded and cut lengthways into thick strips
2 garlic cloves
150 g/5 oz spicy chorizo sausage, peeled and cut into 1-cm/½-inch pieces
1 tbsp tomato purée
200 g/7 oz long-grain rice
450 ml/16 fl oz chicken stock
1 tsp chilli flakes
½ tsp dried thyme
120 g/4 oz Bayonne or other air-dried ham, diced
12 dry-cured black olives
2 tbsp chopped fresh flat-leaved parsley
salt and pepper

NUTRITION

Calories *559*; Sugars *8 g*; Protein *50 g*; Carbohydrate *44 g*; Fat *21 g*; Saturates *6 g*

moderate

 15 mins

 1 hr 30 mins

This variation of the traditional beef dish has layers of pasta and chicken or turkey baked in red wine, tomatoes and a delicious cheese sauce.

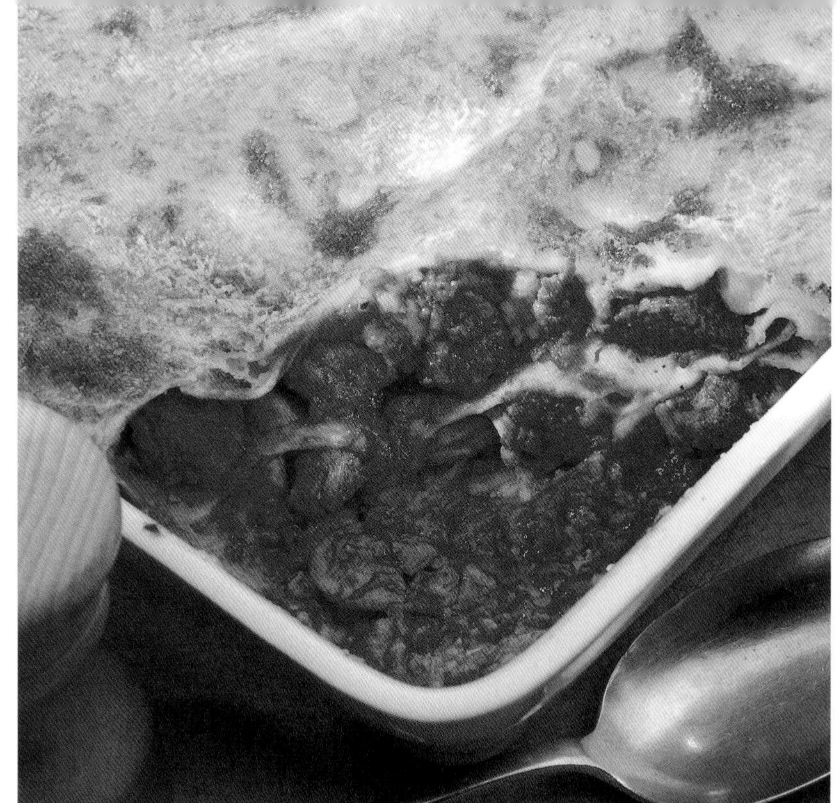

Chicken Lasagne

SERVES 4

9 sheets fresh or dried lasagne
butter, for greasing
1 tbsp olive oil
1 red onion, chopped finely
1 garlic clove, crushed
100 g/3½ oz mushrooms, wiped and sliced
350 g/12 oz chicken or turkey breast, cut into chunks
150 ml/5 fl oz red wine, diluted with 100 ml/3½ fl oz water
250 g/9 oz passata
1 tsp sugar

béchamel sauce

5 tbsp butter
5 tbsp plain flour
600 ml/1 pint milk
1 egg, beaten
75 g/2¾ oz Parmesan cheese, freshly grated
salt and pepper

NUTRITION

Calories *550*; Sugars *11 g*; Protein *35 g*; Carbohydrate *34 g*; Fat *29 g*; Saturates *12 g*

moderate
20 mins
1 hr 15 mins

1 Bring a large pan of lightly salted water to the boil. Add the sheets of lasagne and cook according to the instructions on the packet. Lightly grease a deep ovenproof dish.

2 Heat the oil in a pan. Add the onion and garlic and cook for 3–4 minutes. Add the mushrooms and chicken to the pan and stir-fry for 4 minutes or until the meat is golden-brown.

3 Add the wine, bring to the boil, then lower the heat and simmer for 5 minutes. Stir in the passata and sugar and cook for 3–5 minutes until the meat is tender and cooked through. The sauce should have thickened, but still be quite runny.

4 To make the béchamel sauce, melt the butter in a pan, stir in the flour and cook for 2 minutes. Remove the pan from the heat and gradually add the milk, mixing to form a smooth sauce. Return the pan to the heat and bring to the boil, stirring until thickened. Leave to cool slightly, then beat in the egg and half of the cheese. Season to taste.

5 Place 3 sheets of lasagne in the base of the prepared dish and spread with half of the chicken mixture. Repeat the layers. Top with the last 3 sheets of lasagne, pour over the béchamel sauce and sprinkle with the grated Parmesan cheese. Bake in a preheated oven, 190°C/375°F/Gas Mark 5, for 30 minutes until golden and the pasta is cooked.

This recipe is a type of cottage pie and is just as versatile. Add vegetables and herbs of your choice, depending on what you have at hand.

Quick Chicken Bake

1 Dry-fry the chicken, onion and carrots in a non-stick saucepan over a low heat, stirring, for about 5 minutes until the chicken has lost its pink colour.

2 Sprinkle the chicken with the flour and cook, stirring, for 2 minutes.

3 Gradually blend in the tomato purée and stock, then simmer for about 15 minutes. Season to taste with salt and pepper and add the thyme.

4 Transfer the chicken and vegetable mixture to a casserole and cool.

5 Spoon the creamed potato over the chicken mixture and sprinkle with the cheese. Bake in a preheated oven, 200°C/400°F/Gas Mark 6, for about 20 minutes, or until the cheese is bubbling and golden, then serve with peas.

SERVES 4

500 g/1lb 2 oz minced chicken
1 large onion, chopped finely
2 carrots, diced finely
25 g/1 oz plain flour
1 tbsp tomato purée
300 ml/10 fl oz chicken stock
pinch of fresh thyme
900 g/2 lb boiled potatoes, creamed with butter and milk and highly seasoned
85 g/3 oz grated Lancashire cheese
salt and pepper
peas, to serve

NUTRITION

Calories *496*; Sugars *10 g*; Protein *38 g*; Carbohydrate *52 g*; Fat *17 g*; Saturates *9 g*

moderate

25 mins

45 mins

COOK'S TIP

Instead of Lancashire cheese, you could sprinkle Cotswold cheese over the top. This is a tasty blend of Double Gloucester, onion and chives, and is ideal for melting as a topping. Alternatively, you could use a mixture of cheeses, depending on what you have available.

Low in fat and high in fibre, this colourful casserole makes a healthy and hearty meal for a cold winter's day.

Rustic Chicken *and* Orange Pot

SERVES 4

8 chicken drumsticks, skinned
1 tbsp wholemeal flour
1 tbsp olive oil
2 medium red onions
1 garlic clove, crushed
1 tsp fennel seeds
1 bay leaf
finely grated rind and juice of 1 small orange
400 g/14 oz canned chopped tomatoes
400 g/14 oz canned cannellini or flageolet beans, drained
salt and pepper

topping

3 thick slices wholemeal bread, crusts removed
2 tsp olive oil

1 Toss the chicken drumsticks in the flour to coat evenly. Heat the oil in a non-stick or heavy saucepan and fry the chicken over a fairly high heat, turning frequently, until golden brown. Transfer to a large ovenproof casserole and keep warm until required.

2 Slice the red onions into thin wedges. Add to the pan and cook for a few minutes until lightly browned. Stir in the garlic.

3 Add the fennel seeds, bay leaf, orange rind and juice, tomatoes and beans. Season with salt and pepper.

4 Cover tightly and cook in a preheated oven, 190°C/375°F/Gas Mark 5, for 30–35 minutes until the chicken juices are clear and not pink when pierced through the thickest part with a metal skewer.

5 For the topping, cut the bread into small dice and toss in the oil. Remove the lid from the casserole and top with the bread cubes. Bake for a further 15–20 minutes until the bread is golden and crisp. Serve hot.

NUTRITION

Calories *345*; Sugars *6 g*; Protein *29 g*; Carbohydrate *39 g*; Fat *10 g*; Saturates *2 g*

 moderate

 5 mins

1 hr

COOK'S TIP

Choose beans which are canned in water with no added sugar or salt. Drain and rinse well before use.

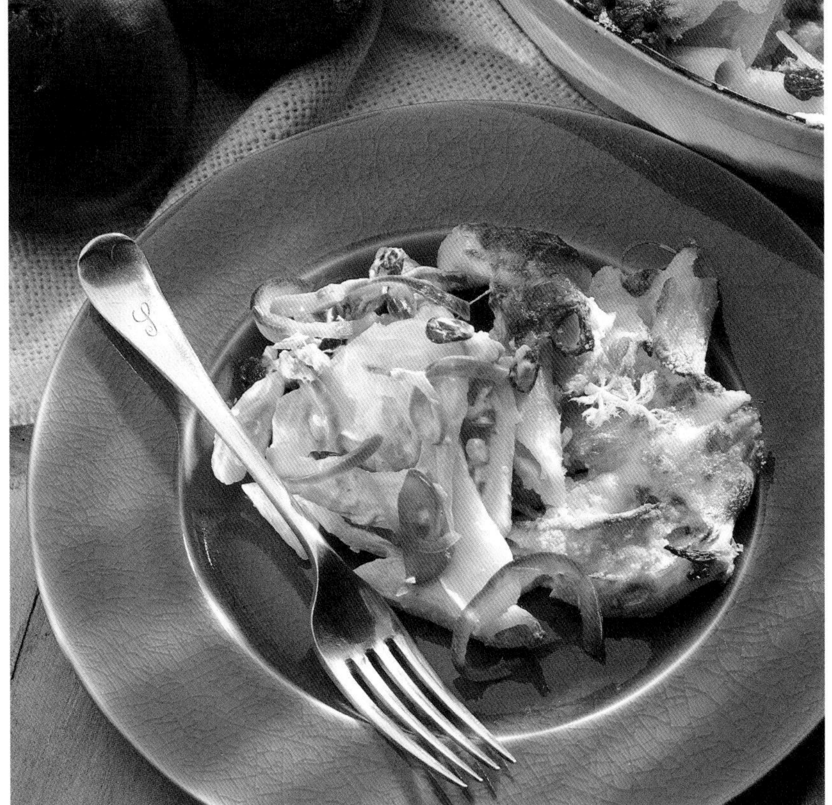

Tender lean chicken is baked with pasta in a creamy low-fat sauce which contrasts well with the fennel and the sweetness of the raisins.

Chicken Pasta Bake

1 Trim the fennel, reserving the green fronds, and slice the bulbs thinly.

2 Generously coat the onions in the lemon juice. Quarter the mushrooms.

3 Heat the oil in a large frying pan and fry the fennel, onion and mushrooms for 4–5 minutes, stirring, until just softened. Season well, transfer the mixture to a large bowl and set aside.

4 Bring a pan of lightly salted water to the boil and cook the penne according to the instructions on the packet until just cooked. Drain and mix the pasta with the vegetables.

5 Stir the raisins and chicken into the pasta mixture. Soften the soft cheese by beating it, then mix into the pasta and chicken – the heat from the pasta should make the cheese melt slightly.

6 Put the mixture into an ovenproof dish and place on a baking tray. Arrange slices of mozzarella over the top and sprinkle with the grated Parmesan.

7 Cook the Chicken Pasta Bake in a preheated oven, 200°C/400°F/Gas Mark 6, for 20–25 minutes until golden-brown.

8 Garnish with chopped fennel fronds and serve hot.

SERVES 4

2 fennel bulbs
2 red onions, sliced very thinly
1 tbsp lemon juice
125 g/4½ oz button mushrooms
1 tbsp olive oil
225 g/8 oz dried penne
55 g/2oz raisins
225 g/8 oz lean, boneless cooked chicken, skinned and shredded
375 g/13 oz low-fat soft cheese with garlic and herbs
125 g/4½ oz low-fat mozzarella cheese, sliced thinly
35 g/1¼ oz freshly grated Parmesan cheese
salt and pepper
chopped fennel fronds, to garnish

NUTRITION

Calories *643*; Sugars *20 g*; Protein *44 g*; Carbohydrate *64 g*; Fat *25 g*; Saturates *12 g*

easy

15 mins

40 mins

This aromatic chicken dish has a spicy Mexican kick. Chicken thighs have a wonderful flavour when cooked in this way.

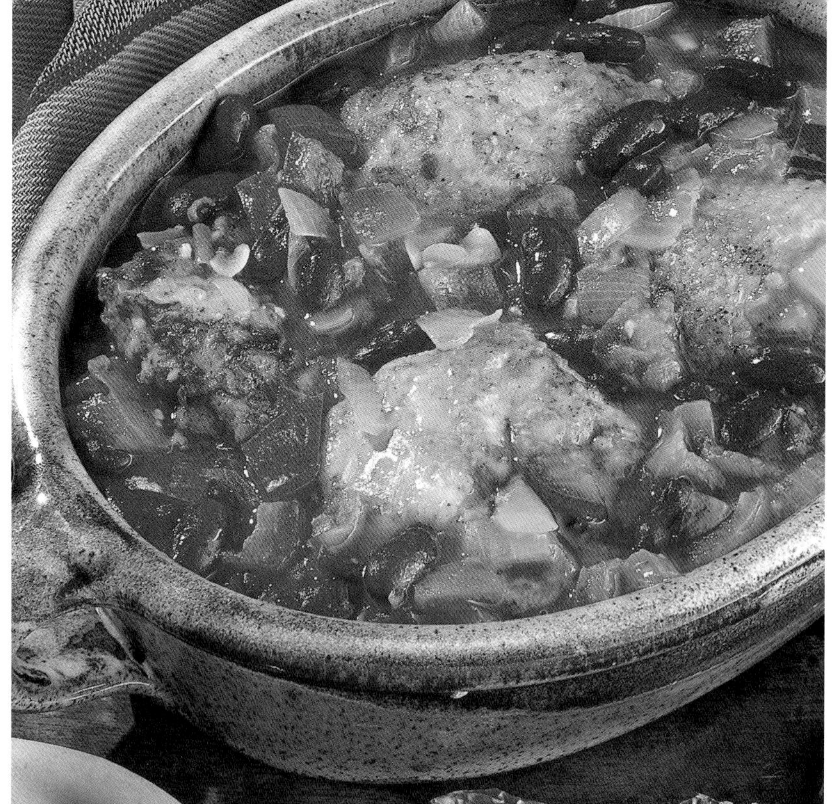

Chicken *and* Chilli Bean Pot

SERVES 4

2 tbsp plain flour
1 tsp chilli powder
8 chicken thighs or 4 chicken legs
3 tbsp vegetable oil
2 garlic cloves, crushed
1 large onion, chopped
1 green or red pepper, deseeded and chopped
300 ml/10 fl oz chicken stock
350 g/12 oz tomatoes, chopped
400 g/14 oz canned red kidney beans, rinsed and drained
2 tbsp tomato purée
salt and pepper

1 Combine the flour and chilli powder in a shallow dish and add salt and pepper to taste. Rinse the chicken, but do not dry. Dip the chicken into the seasoned flour, turning to coat it on all sides.

2 Heat the oil in a large, deep frying pan or flameproof casserole and add the chicken. Cook over a high heat, turning the pieces frequently, for 3–4 minutes until browned all over.

3 Lift the chicken out of the pan or casserole with a slotted spoon and drain thoroughly on kitchen paper.

4 Add the garlic, onion and pepper to the pan and cook over a medium heat, stirring occasionally, for 2–3 minutes until softened.

5 Add the stock, tomatoes, kidney beans and tomato purée, stirring well. Bring to the boil, then return the chicken to the pan. Reduce the heat, cover and simmer for about 30 minutes until the chicken is tender. Taste and adjust the seasoning, if necessary, and serve.

NUTRITION

Calories *333*; Sugars *10 g*; Protein *25 g*; Carbohydrate *32 g*; Fat *13 g*; Saturates *2 g*

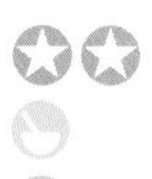

easy
10 mins
40 mins

COOK'S TIP

For extra flavour, use sun-dried tomato paste instead of tomato purée.

This unusual dish, with its mixture of chicken and shellfish, is typically Spanish. The basis of this recipe is *sofrito*, a slow-cooked mixture of onion and tomato in olive oil, with garlic and peppers.

Spanish Chicken *with* Prawns

1 Remove the skin from the chicken quarters. Heat the oil in a wide, heavy pan and fry the chicken, turning occasionally until golden-brown.

2 Using a sharp knife, deseed and slice the pepper and peel and slice the onion. Add the pepper and onion to the pan and fry gently to soften.

3 Add the garlic with the tomatoes, wine and oregano. Season well with salt and pepper, then bring to the boil, cover and simmer gently for 45 minutes or until the chicken is tender and the juices run clear when the thickest part of the chicken is pierced with a skewer.

4 Thinly slice the chorizo and add to the pan together with the prawns, then simmer for a further 5 minutes. Adjust the seasoning and serve with rice.

SERVES 4

4 chicken quarters
1 tbsp olive oil
1 red pepper
1 medium onion
2 garlic cloves, crushed
400 g/14 oz canned chopped tomatoes
200 ml/7 fl oz dry white wine
4 tbsp chopped fresh oregano
salt and pepper
125 g/4½ oz chorizo sausage
125 g/4½ oz peeled prawns
rice, to serve

NUTRITION

Calories *488*; Sugars *9 g*; Protein *69 g*; Carbohydrate *10 g*; Fat *16 g*; Saturates *5 g*

easy
20 mins
1 hr 10 mins

COOK'S TIP

Chorizo is a spicy Spanish sausage made with pork and a hot pepper such as cayenne or pimento. It is available from large supermarkets and specialist butchers.

s famous dish is known roughout the world, and it is perhaps the best known of all Italian risottos. This variation adds chicken.

Chicken Risotto *à la* Milanese

SERVES 4

125 g/4½ oz butter
900 g/2 lb chicken meat, sliced thinly
1 large onion, chopped
500 g/1 lb 2 oz arborio rice
600 ml/1 pint chicken stock
150 ml/½ pint white wine
1 tsp crumbled saffron
salt and pepper
60 g/2 oz grated Parmesan cheese, to serve

1 Heat 60 g/2 oz of the butter in a deep frying pan, and fry the chicken and onion until golden-brown.

2 Add the rice, stir well, and cook for 15 minutes on low heat.

3 Heat the stock until boiling and gradually add to the rice. Add the white wine, saffron, salt and pepper to taste and mix well. Simmer gently for 20 minutes, stirring occasionally. Add more stock if the risotto becomes too dry.

4 Leave to stand for a few minutes and just before serving add a little more stock and simmer for a further 10 minutes. Serve the risotto sprinkled with the grated Parmesan cheese and the remaining butter.

NUTRITION

Calories *857*; Sugars *1 g*; Protein *57 g*; Carbohydrate *72 g*; Fat *38 g*; Saturates *21 g*

 easy

5 mins

1 hr 5 mins

COOK'S TIP

A risotto should have moist but separate grains. Stock should be added a little at a time and only when the last addition has been completely absorbed.

If you prefer, ordinary long-grain rice can be used instead of arborio rice, but it won't give you the traditional, deliciously creamy texture that is typical of Italian risottos.

Italian Risotto

1 Heat the oil and butter or margarine in a large saucepan. Fry the leek and pepper for 1 minute then stir in the chicken and cook the mixture, stirring until golden-brown.

2 Stir in the rice and cook for 2–3 minutes.

3 Stir in the saffron strands, and salt and pepper to taste. Add the stock, a little at a time, cover and cook over a low heat, stirring occasionally, for about 20 minutes, until the rice is tender and most of the liquid is absorbed. Do not let the risotto dry out – add more stock if necessary.

4 Stir in the sweetcorn, peanuts and Parmesan cheese, then adjust the seasoning to taste. Serve hot.

SERVES 4

2 tbsp sunflower oil
15 g/½ oz butter or margarine
1 medium leek, sliced thinly
1 large yellow pepper, diced
3 skinless, boneless chicken breasts, diced
350 g/12 oz arborio rice
few strands of saffron
1.5 litres/2¾ pints chicken stock
200 g/7 oz canned sweetcorn
60 g/2 oz toasted unsalted peanuts
60 g/2 oz grated Parmesan cheese
salt and pepper

NUTRITION

Calories *701*; Sugars *7 g*; Protein *35 g*; Carbohydrate *88 g*; Fat *26 g*; Saturates *8 g*

easy

 10 mins

 30 mins

COOK'S TIP

Risottos can be frozen, before adding the Parmesan cheese, for up to 1 month, but remember to reheat this risotto thoroughly as it contains chicken.

This colourful, simple dish will tempt the appetites of all the family – it is ideal for children, who enjoy the fun shapes of the multi-coloured peppers.

Harlequin Chicken

SERVES 4

10 skinless, boneless chicken thighs
1 medium onion
1 each medium red, green and yellow peppers
1 tbsp sunflower oil
400 g/14 oz canned chopped tomatoes
2 tbsp chopped fresh parsley
pepper
wholemeal bread and a green salad, to serve

1. Using a sharp knife, cut the chicken thighs into bite-sized pieces.
2. Peel and thinly slice the onion. Halve and deseed the peppers and cut them into small diamond shapes.
3. Heat the oil in a shallow frying pan. Add the chicken thighs and onion and fry quickly until golden.
4. Add the peppers, cook for 2–3 minutes, then stir in the tomatoes and parsley and season with pepper.
5. Cover tightly and simmer for about 15 minutes, until the chicken and vegetables are tender. Serve hot with wholemeal bread and a green salad.

NUTRITION

Calories *183*; Sugars *8 g*; Protein *24 g*; Carbohydrate *8 g*; Fat *6 g*; Saturates *1 g*

 very easy

10 mins

25 mins

COOK'S TIP

If you are making this dish for small children, the chicken can be finely chopped or minced first.

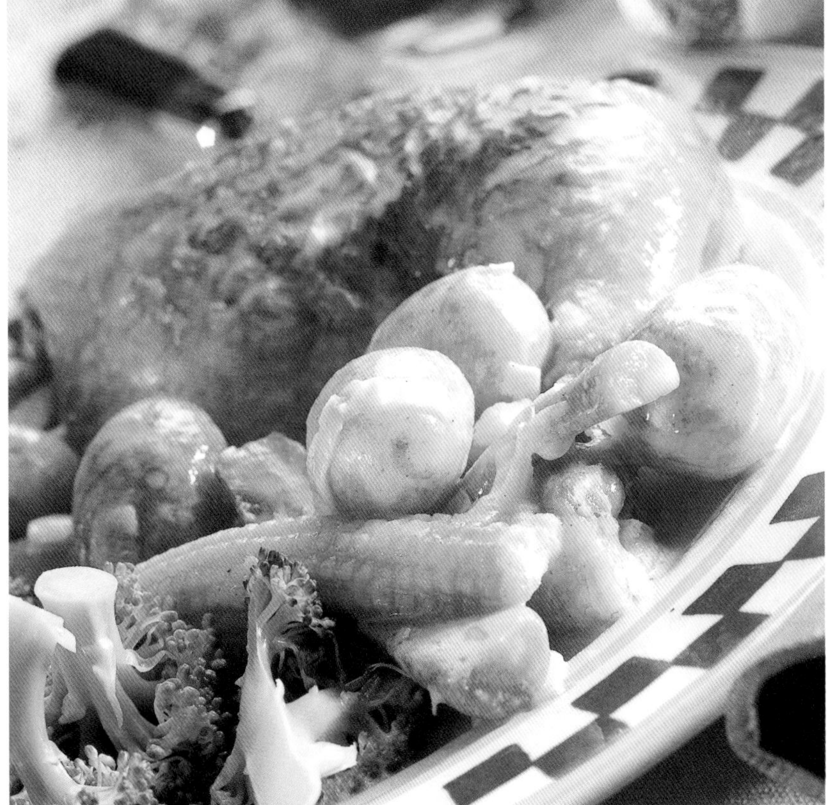

Small new potatoes are ideal for this recipe because they can be cooked whole. Cut larger potatoes in half or into chunks before using them.

Chicken *and* Potato Casserole

SERVES 4

2 tbsp vegetable oil
4 chicken portions (about 225 g/8 oz each)
2 leeks, sliced
1 garlic clove, crushed
4 tbsp plain flour
850 ml/1½ pints chicken stock
300 ml/10 fl oz dry white wine
125 g/4¼ oz baby carrots, halved lengthways
125 g/4¼ oz baby corn cobs, halved lengthways
450 g/1 lb small new potatoes
1 Fresh or Dried Bouquet Garni (see page 15)
150 ml/5 fl oz double cream
salt and pepper
rice, to serve

1 Heat the oil in a large frying pan. Cook the chicken for 10 minutes, turning until browned. Transfer to a casserole dish using a slotted spoon.

2 Add the leek and garlic and cook for 2–3 minutes, stirring. Stir in the flour, cook for another minute and remove from the heat. Stir in stock and wine, and season to taste.

3 Return the pan to the heat and bring to the boil. Stir in the carrots, baby corn, potatoes and bouquet garni. Transfer the mixture to the casserole dish.

4 Cover and cook in a preheated oven, 180°C/350°F/Gas Mark 4, for 1 hour.

5 Remove the casserole to stir in the cream, return to the oven uncovered, and cook for 15 minutes. Remove the bouquet garni, season, and serve with rice.

COOK'S TIP

Use turkey fillets instead of the chicken, if preferred, and vary the vegetables according to those you have to hand.

NUTRITION

Calories *856*; Sugars *7 g*; Protein *35 g*; Carbohydrate *40 g*; Fat *58 g*; Saturates *26 g*

 moderate

 15 mins

1 hr 35 mins

Thai curries are traditionally very hot and designed to make a little go a long way – the thin, highly spiced juices are eaten with lots of rice.

Green Chicken Curry

SERVES 4

6 skinless, boneless chicken thighs
400 ml/14 fl oz coconut milk
2 garlic cloves, crushed
2 tbsp Thai fish sauce
2 tbsp Thai green curry paste
12 baby aubergines
3 fresh green chillies, chopped finely
3 kaffir lime leaves, shredded
4 tbsp fresh coriander, chopped
salt and pepper
boiled rice, to serve

1 Cut the chicken into bite-sized pieces. Pour the coconut milk into a large pan or wok and bring to the boil over a high heat.

2 Add the chicken, garlic and fish sauce to the pan or wok and bring back to the boil. Lower the heat and simmer gently for about 30 minutes or until the chicken is just tender.

3 Remove the chicken from the mixture. Set aside and keep warm.

4 Stir the green curry paste into the pan until fully incorporated, then add the aubergines, chillies and lime leaves and simmer for 5 minutes.

5 Return the chicken to the pan or wok and bring to the boil. Season with salt and pepper to taste, then stir in the chopped coriander. Serve the curry immediately with boiled rice.

NUTRITION

Calories *193*; Sugars *9 g*; Protein *22 g*; Carbohydrate *9 g*; Fat *8 g*; Saturates *1 g*

easy
10 mins
50 mins

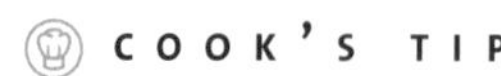

COOK'S TIP

Baby aubergines are traditionally used in this curry, but they are not always easily available. If you can't find them in an Oriental food shop, use chopped ordinary aubergine or substitute a few green peas.

This tasty chicken dish combines warm spices and almonds and is spiked with anise.

Fruity Garlic Curried Chicken

1 Heat the butter and 1 tablespoon of oil in a frying pan, add the chicken pieces and cook for 5 minutes until golden. Transfer the chicken pieces to a plate and keep warm until required.

2 Combine the onion, ginger, garlic, almonds, red pepper, cumin, coriander, turmeric, cayenne pepper and salt in a food processor or liquidizer. Blend to form a smooth paste.

3 Heat the remaining oil in a large saucepan or deep frying pan. Add the paste and fry for 10–12 minutes.

4 Add the chicken pieces, the water, star anise, lemon juice and pepper. Cover, reduce the heat and simmer gently for 25 minutes or until the chicken is tender, stirring a few times during cooking.

5 Transfer the chicken to a serving dish, sprinkle with the flaked almonds and serve with individual rice moulds.

SERVES 4

25 g/1 oz butter
7 tbsp vegetable oil
4 skinless, boneless chicken breasts, cut into 4 x 2-cm/2 x 1-inch pieces
1 medium onion, chopped roughly
2-cm/1-inch piece of fresh root ginger
3 garlic cloves, peeled
25 g/1 oz blanched almonds
1 large red pepper, chopped roughly
1 tbsp ground cumin
2 tsp ground coriander
1 tsp ground turmeric
pinch cayenne pepper
½ tsp salt
150 ml/¼ pint water
3 star anise
2 tbsp lemon juice
pepper
flaked almonds, to garnish
rice, to serve

NUTRITION

Calories *421*; Sugars *5 g*; Protein *33 g*; Carbohydrate *7 g*; Fat *30 g*; Saturates *6 g*

easy

 15 mins

 45 mins

This is a simple version of a creamy textured and mildly spiced Indian pilau. Although there are lots of ingredients, there's very little preparation needed for this dish.

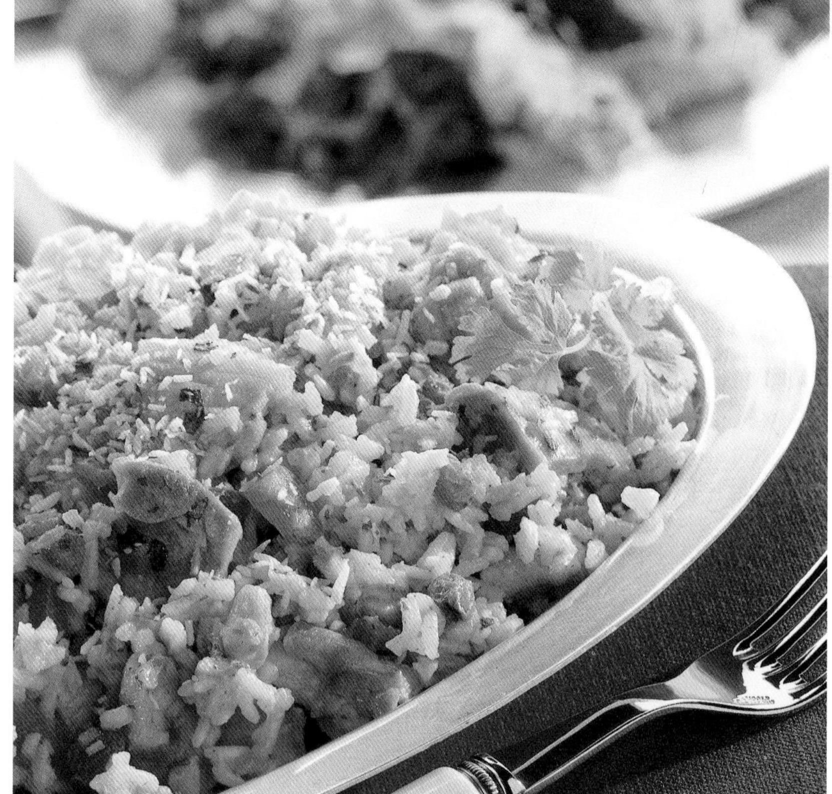

Indian Chicken *and* Sultana Pilau

SERVES 4

60 g/2 oz butter
8 skinless, boneless chicken thighs, cut into large pieces
1 medium onion, sliced
1 tsp ground turmeric
1 tsp ground cinnamon
250 g/9 oz long-grain rice
425 ml/¾ pint natural yogurt
60 g/2 oz sultanas
200 ml/7 fl oz chicken stock
1 medium tomato, chopped
2 tbsp chopped fresh coriander or parsley
2 tbsp toasted coconut
salt and pepper
fresh coriander, to garnish

1 Heat the butter in a heavy or non-stick pan and fry the chicken with the onion for about 3 minutes.

2 Stir the turmeric, cinnamon, rice and seasoning into the pan and fry gently for 3 minutes.

3 Add the yogurt, sultanas and chicken stock and mix. Cover and simmer for 10 minutes, stirring occasionally, until the rice is tender and all the stock has been absorbed. Add more stock if the mixture becomes too dry.

4 Stir in the chopped tomato and fresh coriander or parsley.

5 Sprinkle the pilau with the toasted coconut and garnish with fresh coriander.

NUTRITION

Calories *581*; Sugars *22 g*; Protein *31 g*; Carbohydrate *73 g*; Fat *19 g*; Saturates *12 g*

 easy
10 mins
20 mins

COOK'S TIP

Long-grain rice is the most widely available rice. Basmati, with its slender grains and aromatic flavour, should be used on special occasions. Rice should be washed thoroughly under cold running water before use.

Cooking in a single pot means that all of the flavours are retained. This is a substantial meal that needs only a salad and some crusty bread to accompany it.

Sage Chicken *and* Rice

1 Place the onion, garlic, celery, carrots and sprigs of fresh sage in a large saucepan and pour in the chicken stock. Bring to the boil, cover the pan and simmer for 5 minutes.

2 Cut the chicken into 2.5-cm/1-inch cubes and stir into the pan with the vegetables. Cover the pan and cook for a further 5 minutes.

3 Stir in the rice and chopped tomatoes. Add a dash of Tabasco sauce and season well. Bring to the boil, cover and simmer for 25 minutes.

4 Stir in the sliced courgettes and diced ham and continue to cook, uncovered, for a further 10 minutes, stirring occasionally, until the rice is just tender.

5 Remove and discard the sage sprigs. Garnish with a few sage leaves and serve with a fresh salad and crusty bread.

SERVES 4

1 large onion, chopped
1 garlic clove, crushed
2 sticks celery, sliced
2 carrots, diced
2 sprigs of fresh sage
300 ml/½ pint chicken stock
350 g/12 oz boneless, skinless chicken breasts
225 g/8 oz mixed brown and wild rice
400 g/14 oz canned chopped tomatoes
dash of Tabasco sauce
salt and pepper
2 medium courgettes, trimmed and sliced thinly
100 g/3½ oz lean ham, diced
fresh sage, to garnish
salad leaves and crusty bread, to serve

COOK'S TIP

If you do not have fresh sage, use 1 tsp of dried sage at Step 1.

NUTRITION

Calories *247*; Sugars *5 g*; Protein *26 g*; Carbohydrate *25 g*; Fat *5 g*; Saturates *2 g*

easy

15 mins

45 mins

Full of the flavours of autumn, this combination of lean chicken, shallots, garlic and fresh, juicy plums is a very fruity blend. Serve with bread to mop up the gravy.

Sherried Chicken, Bacon *and* Plums

SERVES 4

- 2 lean back bacon rashers, rinds removed, trimmed and chopped
- 1 tbsp sunflower oil
- 450 g/1 lb skinless, boneless chicken thighs, cut into 4 equal strips
- 1 garlic clove, crushed
- 175 g/6 oz shallots, halved
- 225 g/8 oz plums, halved or quartered (if large) and stoned
- 1 tbsp light muscovado sugar
- 150 ml/5 fl oz dry sherry
- 2 tbsp plum sauce
- 450 ml/16 fl oz Fresh Chicken Stock (see page 14)
- 2 tsp cornflour mixed with 4 tsp cold water
- 2 tbsp chopped fresh parsley, to garnish
- crusty bread, to serve

1. In a large, non-stick frying pan, dry-fry the bacon for 2–3 minutes until the juices run out. Remove the bacon from the pan with a slotted spoon, set aside and keep warm.
2. In the same frying pan, heat the oil and fry the chicken with the garlic and shallots for 4–5 minutes, stirring occasionally, until well browned all over.
3. Return the bacon to the pan and stir in the plums, sugar, sherry, plum sauce and stock. Bring to the boil and simmer for 20 minutes until the plums have softened and the chicken is cooked through.
4. Add the cornflour mixture to the pan and cook, stirring, for a further 2–3 minutes until thickened.
5. Spoon the casserole on to warm serving plates and garnish with chopped parsley. Serve with chunks of crusty bread to mop up the fruity gravy.

NUTRITION

Calories *325*; Sugars *11 g*; Protein *28 g*; Carbohydrate *16 g*; Fat *12 g*; Saturates *3 g*

easy

15 mins

35 mins

COOK'S TIP

Chunks of lean turkey or pork would also go well with this combination of flavours. The cooking time will remain the same.

This subtly spiced chicken is spiked with cayenne and paprika and finished off with a fruity sauce.

Creamy Paprika Chicken

1 Mix the flour, cayenne pepper and paprika and use to coat the chicken.

2 Shake off any excess flour. Melt the butter in a saucepan and gently fry the chicken with the onion for 4 minutes.

3 Stir in the flour and spice mixture. Add the milk slowly and cook, stirring, until the sauce thickens.

4 Simmer until the sauce is smooth.

5 Add the apple purée and grapes and simmer gently for 20 minutes.

6 Transfer the chicken and devilled sauce to a serving dish and top with soured cream and a sprinkle of paprika.

SERVES 2–3

25 g/1 oz plain flour
1 tbsp cayenne pepper
1 tsp paprika
350 g/12 oz skinless, boneless chicken, diced
25 g/1 oz butter
1 onion, chopped finely
450 ml/16 fl oz milk, warmed
4 tbsp apple purée
125 g/4½ oz green grapes
150 ml/¼ pint soured cream
paprika, to garnish

COOK'S TIP

Add more paprika if desired – as it is quite a mild spice, you can add plenty without it being too overpowering.

NUTRITION

Calories *455*; Sugars *19 g*; Protein *37 g*; Carbohydrate *29 g*; Fat *23 g*; Saturates *14 g*

very easy

10 mins

35 mins

This tasty Thai-style dish has a classic sauce of lime, peanut, coconut and chilli. You'll find coconut cream in most supermarkets or delicatessens.

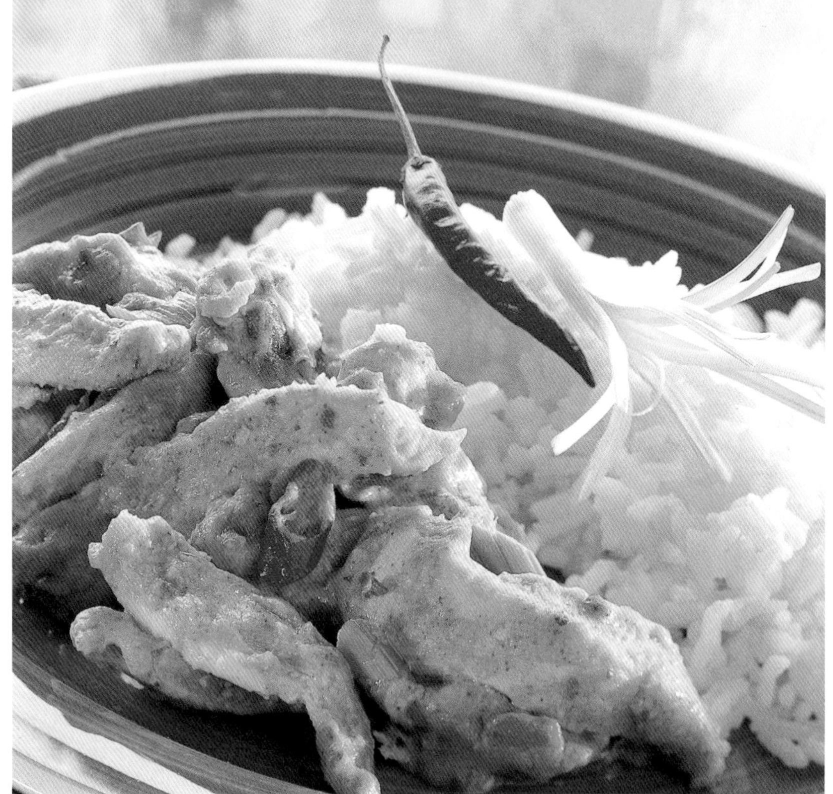

Coconut Chicken *with* Lime

SERVES 4

- 150 ml/¼ pint hot chicken stock
- 30 g/1 oz coconut cream
- 1 tbsp sunflower oil
- 8 skinless, boneless chicken thighs, cut into long, thin strips
- 1 small red chilli, sliced thinly
- 4 spring onions, sliced thinly
- 4 tbsp smooth or crunchy peanut butter
- finely grated rind and juice of 1 lime
- boiled rice, to serve
- spring onion 'flower' and red chilli, to garnish

1. Place the chicken stock in a measuring jug and crumble the creamed coconut into the stock, stirring to dissolve.
2. Heat the oil in a wok or large heavy-based frying pan and cook the chicken strips, stirring, until golden.
3. Add the sliced red chilli and the spring onions to the pan and cook gently for a few minutes, stirring to mix all the ingredients.
4. Add the peanut butter, coconut cream, lime rind and juice and simmer uncovered, stirring, for about 5 minutes.
5. Serve with boiled rice, garnished with a spring onion 'flower' and a red chilli.

NUTRITION

Calories *348*; Sugars *2 g*; Protein *36 g*; Carbohydrate *3 g*; Fat *21 g*; Saturates *8 g*

 moderate

5 mins

15 mins

COOK'S TIP

Limes are used frequently in Thai cookery. They are used in preference to lemons because they have a more acidic flavour which lends freshness and tartness to many dishes. If limes are unavailable, you can use lemons instead.

There are many versions of hot using fresh, lo ingredients. Now, there are an endless variety of ingredients available all year, perfect for traditional one-pot cooking.

Country Chicken Hot-pot

1 Remove the skin from the chicken quarters, if preferred.

2 Arrange a layer of potato slices in the bottom of a wide casserole. Season with salt and pepper, then add the thyme, rosemary and bay leaves.

3 Top with the chicken quarters, then sprinkle with the diced bacon, onion and carrots. Season well and arrange the remaining potato slices neatly on top, overlapping slightly.

4 Pour over the stout, brush the potatoes with the melted butter and cover the casserole with a lid.

5 Bake in a preheated oven, 150°C/300°F/Gas Mark 2, for about 2 hours, uncovering for the last 30 minutes to allow the potatoes to brown.

SERVES 4

- 4 chicken quarters
- 6 medium potatoes, cut into 5-mm/¼-inch slices
- salt and pepper
- 2 sprigs fresh thyme
- 2 sprigs fresh rosemary
- 2 bay leaves
- 200 g/7 oz rindless, smoked streaky bacon, diced
- 1 large onion, chopped finely
- 200 g/7 oz sliced carrots
- 150 ml/¼ pint stout
- 25 g/1 oz butter, melted

COOK'S TIP

This dish is also delicious with stewing lamb, cut into chunks. You can add different vegetables depending on what is in season – try leeks and swedes for a slightly sweeter flavour.

NUTRITION

Calories *499*; Sugars *6 g*; Protein *43 g*; Carbohydrate *44 g*; Fat *17 g*; Saturates *8 g*

easy

10 mins

2 hrs

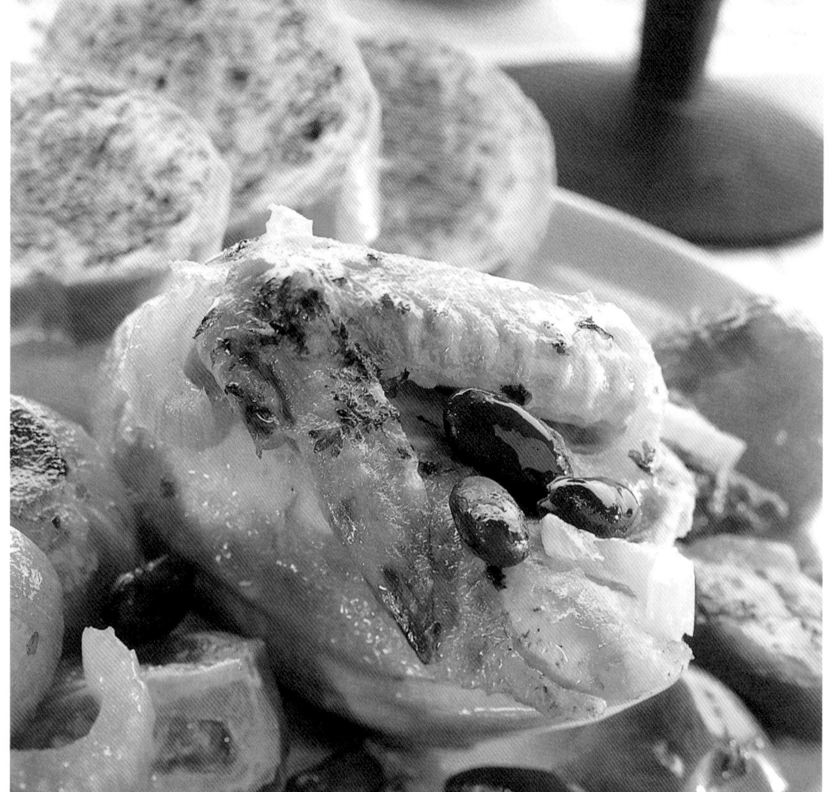

This economical bake is a complete meal – its crusty, herb-flavoured French bread topping mops up the tasty juices, and means there's no need to serve potatoes or rice separately.

Chicken, Bean *and* Celery Bake

SERVES 4

- 2 tbsp sunflower oil
- 4 chicken quarters
- 16 small whole onions, peeled
- 3 sticks celery, sliced
- 400 g/14 oz canned red kidney beans
- 4 medium tomatoes, quartered
- 200 ml/7 fl oz dry cider or stock
- 4 tbsp chopped fresh parsley
- salt and pepper
- 1 tsp paprika
- 60 g/2 oz butter
- 12 slices French bread

1. Heat the oil in a flameproof casserole and fry the chicken quarters two at a time until golden. Using a slotted spoon, remove the chicken from the pan and set aside until required.
2. Add the onions and fry until golden-brown. Add the celery and fry for 2–3 minutes. Return the chicken to the pan, then stir in the beans, tomatoes, cider, half the parsley, salt and pepper. Sprinkle with the paprika.
3. Cover and cook in a preheated oven, 200°C/400°F/Gas Mark 6, for 20–25 minutes, until the chicken juices run clear when pierced with a skewer.
4. Mix the remaining parsley with the butter and spread over the bread.
5. Uncover the casserole, arrange the bread slices overlapping on top and bake for a further 10–12 minutes, until golden and crisp.

NUTRITION

Calories *736*; Sugars *11 g*; Protein *50 g*; Carbohydrate *55 g*; Fat *35 g*; Saturates *13 g*

easy

10 mins

55 mins

COOK'S TIP

For a more unusual Italian-tasting dish, replace the garlic and parsley French bread topping with pesto.

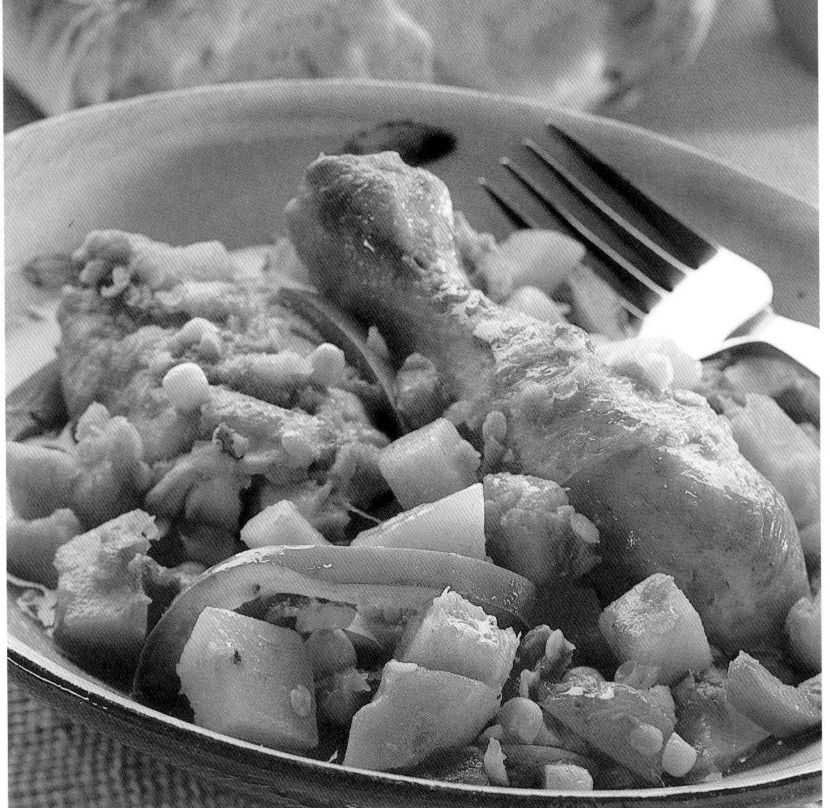

A tasty way to make chicken joints go a long way, this hearty casserole, spiced with the warm, subtle flavour of ginger, is a good choice for a Halloween party.

Caribbean Chicken Hot-pot

1 Heat the oil in a large flameproof casserole and fry the chicken joints until golden, turning frequently.

2 Using a sharp knife, peel and slice the onion, peel and dice the pumpkin or squash and deseed and slice the pepper.

3 Drain any excess fat from the pan and add the prepared onion, pumpkin and pepper. Gently fry for a few minutes until lightly browned. Add the chopped ginger, tomatoes, chicken stock and lentils. Season lightly with garlic salt and cayenne pepper.

4 Cover the casserole and place in a preheated oven, 190°C/375°F/Gas Mark 5, for about 1 hour, until the vegetables are tender and the chicken juices run clear when pierced with a skewer.

5 Add the drained sweetcorn and cook for a further 5 minutes. Season to taste and serve with crusty bread.

SERVES 4

2 tsp sunflower oil
4 chicken drumsticks
4 chicken thighs
1 medium onion
750-g/1 lb 10-oz piece of squash or pumpkin, diced
1 green pepper, sliced
2.5-cm/1-inch fresh root ginger, chopped finely
400 g/14 oz canned chopped tomatoes
300 ml/½ pint chicken stock
60 g/2 oz split lentils, washed
garlic salt
cayenne pepper
350 g/12 oz canned sweetcorn
crusty bread, to serve

COOK'S TIP

If squash or pumpkin is not available, swede makes a good substitute.

NUTRITION

Calories 277; Sugars 6 *g*; Protein 33 *g*; Carbohydrate 22 *g*; Fat 7 *g*; Saturates 1 *g*

 easy

 5 mins

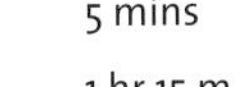 1 hr 15 mins

A colourful casserole packed with sunshine flavours from the Mediterranean. Sun-dried tomatoes add a wonderful richness and you need very few to make this really special dish.

Rich Chicken Casserole

SERVES 4

8 chicken thighs
2 tbsp olive oil
1 medium red onion, sliced
2 garlic cloves, crushed
1 large red pepper, sliced thickly
thinly pared rind and juice of 1 small orange
125 ml/4 fl oz chicken stock
400 g/14 oz canned chopped tomatoes
25 g/1 oz sun-dried tomatoes, sliced thinly
1 tbsp chopped fresh thyme
50 g/1¾ oz stoned black olives
salt and pepper
thyme sprigs and orange rind, to garnish
crusty fresh bread, to serve

1 In a heavy-based or non-stick large frying pan, dry-fry the chicken over a fairly high heat, turning occasionally, until golden brown. Drain off any excess fat from the chicken and transfer to a flameproof casserole.

2 Fry the onion, garlic and pepper in the pan over a moderate heat for 3–4 minutes. Transfer to the casserole.

3 Add the orange rind and juice, chicken stock, canned tomatoes and sun-dried tomatoes and stir to combine.

4 Bring to the boil then cover the casserole with a lid and simmer very gently over a low heat for about 1 hour, stirring occasionally. Add the chopped fresh thyme and black olives, then season with salt and pepper.

5 Scatter orange rind and thyme over the casserole and serve with crusty bread.

NUTRITION

Calories *260*; Sugars *8 g*; Protein *32 g*; Carbohydrate *8 g*; Fat *11 g*; Saturates *2 g*

moderate
5 mins
1 hr 15 mins

COOK'S TIP

Sun-dried tomatoes have a dense texture and concentrated taste, and add intense flavour to slow-cooking casseroles.

This is a good way to use up left-over rice. Use fresh or canned sweet pink grapefruit for an interesting alternative to the orange.

Orange Turkey *with* Rice

1 Heat the oil in a large frying pan and fry the onion and turkey, stirring, for 4–5 minutes until lightly browned.

2 Pour in the orange juice and add the bay leaf and seasoning. Bring to the boil and simmer for 10 minutes.

3 Meanwhile, bring a large saucepan of water to the boil and cook the broccoli florets, covered, for 2 minutes. Add the diced courgette, bring back to the boil, cover and cook for 3 minutes (do not overcook). Drain and set aside.

4 Using a sharp knife, peel off the skin and white pith from the orange.

5 Thinly slice down the orange to make round slices, then halve each slice.

6 Stir the broccoli, courgette, rice and orange slices into the turkey mixture. Gently mix together and season, then heat through for a further 3–4 minutes until piping hot.

7 Transfer the turkey rice to warm serving plates and garnish with black olives and shredded basil leaves. Serve with a tomato and onion salad.

SERVES 4

1 tbsp olive oil
1 medium onion, chopped
450 g/1 lb skinless lean turkey (such as fillet), cut into thin strips
300 ml/½ pint unsweetened orange juice
1 bay leaf
225 g/8 oz small broccoli florets
1 large courgette, diced
1 large orange
350 g/12 oz cooked brown rice
salt and pepper
tomato and onion salad, to serve

to garnish

25 g/1 oz stoned black olives in brine, drained and quartered
shredded basil leaves

NUTRITION

Calories *337*; Sugars *12 g*; Protein *32 g*; Carbohydrate *40 g*; Fat *7 g*; Saturates *1 g*

 challenging

30 mins

40 mins

Vegetables

Nutritionists tell us that we should eat more vegetables, but it isn't always easy to persuade the family to eat up their greens, especially if they are sitting in an unappetizing heap on the side of the plate. This chapter provides the answer with a spectacular collection of mouthwatering vegetable dishes – soups, bakes, risottos, casseroles and curries. Beans, peas, lentils, broccoli, cauliflower, mushrooms, peppers, onions, courgettes, tomatoes, even the humble potato, take a starring role and are combined with each other for a colourful, melt-in-the-mouth medley or with other ingredients, such as pasta, to satisfy even the hungriest appetite. A vegetarian main course is an easy way to ring the changes in the weekly menu and, as vegetables tend to cook quite quickly, it will give the family cook a welcome break. From Mushroom and Cheese Risotto to Coconut Vegetable Curry, vegetables have never looked – or tasted – so good.

A slightly hot and spicy Indian flavour is given to this soup with the use of garam masala, chilli, cumin and coriander.

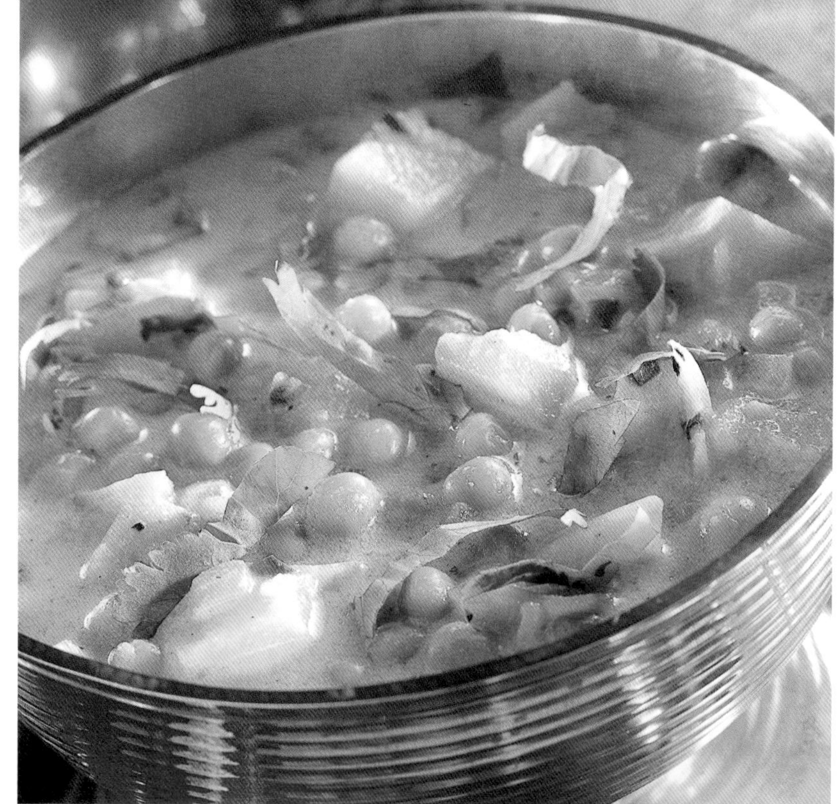

Indian Potato *and* Pea Soup

SERVES 4

2 tbsp vegetable oil
225 g/8 oz floury potatoes, diced
1 large onion, chopped
2 garlic cloves, crushed
1 tsp garam masala
1 tsp ground coriander
1 tsp ground cumin
850 ml/1½ pints vegetable stock
1 fresh red chilli, chopped
100 g/3½ oz frozen peas
4 tbsp natural yogurt
salt and pepper
chopped coriander, to garnish
warm bread, to serve

1 Heat the vegetable oil in a large, heavy-based saucepan. Add the potatoes, onion and garlic and sauté over a low heat, stirring, for about 5 minutes.

2 Add the garam masala, ground coriander and ground cumin and cook, stirring constantly, for 1 minute.

3 Stir in the vegetable stock and red chilli and bring the mixture to the boil. Reduce the heat, cover the pan and simmer for 20 minutes, until the potatoes begin to break down.

4 Add the peas and cook for a further 5 minutes. Stir in the yogurt and season with salt and pepper to taste.

5 Pour the hot soup into warm soup bowls, garnish with fresh coriander and serve with warm bread.

NUTRITION

Calories *153*; Sugars *8 g*; Protein *6 g*; Carbohydrate *18 g*; Fat *6 g*; Saturates *1 g*

very easy

15 mins

30 mins

COOK'S TIP

For slightly less heat, deseed the chilli before adding it to the soup. Always wash your hands after handling chillies because they contain volatile oils that can irritate the skin and make your eyes burn if you touch your face.

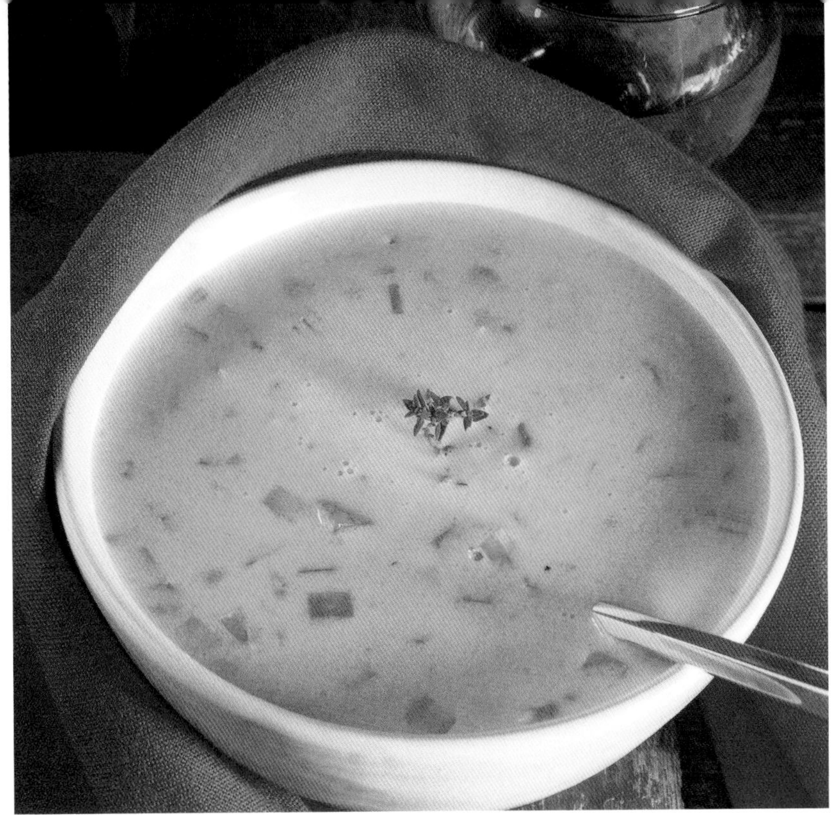

This hearty soup is wonderful made in the middle of winter with fresh seasonal vegetables. Use a really well-flavoured mature Cheddar cheese.

Cheese *and* Vegetable Chowder

1 Melt the butter in a large heavy-based saucepan over a medium-low heat. Add the onion, leek and garlic. Cover and cook for about 5 minutes, stirring frequently, until the vegetables are starting to soften.

2 Stir the flour into the vegetables and cook for 2 minutes. Add a little of the stock and stir, scraping the bottom of the pan to mix in the flour. Bring to the boil, stirring frequently, and slowly stir in the rest of the stock.

3 Add the carrots, celery, turnip, potato, thyme and bay leaf. Reduce the heat, cover the pan and cook the soup gently for about 35 minutes, stirring occasionally, until the vegetables are tender. Remove the bay leaf and the thyme sprigs and discard.

4 Stir in the cream and simmer over a very low heat for 5 minutes.

5 Add the cheese a handful at a time, stirring constantly for 1 minute after each addition to make sure it is completely melted. Taste the soup and adjust the seasoning, adding salt if needed, and pepper to taste.

6 Ladle the soup into warm bowls, sprinkle with parsley and serve.

SERVES 4

25 g/1 oz butter
1 large onion, chopped finely
1 large leek, split lengthways and sliced thinly
1–2 garlic cloves, crushed
55 g/2 oz plain flour
1.2 litres/2 pints vegetable stock
3 carrots, diced finely
2 celery sticks, diced finely
1 turnip, diced finely
1 large potato, diced finely
3–4 sprigs of fresh thyme or ⅛ tsp dried thyme
1 bay leaf
350 ml/12 fl oz single cream
300 g/10½ oz mature Cheddar cheese, grated
salt and pepper
chopped fresh parsley, to garnish

NUTRITION

Calories *669*; Sugars *13 g*; Protein *26 g*; Carbohydrate *33 g*; Fat *49 g*; Saturates *30 g*

moderate

 15 mins

 50 mins

Mediterranean vegetables, roasted in olive oil and flavoured with thyme, are the basis for this soup.

Roasted Vegetable Soup

SERVES 6

2–3 tbsp olive oil
700 g/1 lb 9 oz ripe tomatoes, skinned, cored and halved
3 large yellow peppers, halved, cored and deseeded
3 courgettes, halved lengthways
1 small aubergine, halved lengthways
4 garlic cloves, halved
2 onions, cut into eighths
pinch of dried thyme
1 litre/1¾ pints vegetable stock
125 ml/4 fl oz single cream
salt and pepper
shredded fresh basil leaves, to garnish

NUTRITION

Calories *163*; Sugars *13 g*; Protein *5 g*; Carbohydrate *15 g*; Fat *10 g*; Saturates *3 g*

moderate
15 mins
1 hr 10 mins

1 Brush a large shallow baking dish with olive oil. Laying them cut-side down, arrange the tomatoes, peppers, courgettes and aubergine in one layer (use two dishes, if necessary). Tuck the garlic cloves and onion pieces into the gaps and drizzle the vegetables with olive oil. Season lightly with salt and pepper and sprinkle with the thyme.

2 Place the vegetables in a preheated oven at 190°C/375°F/Gas Mark 5 and bake, uncovered, for 30–35 minutes, or until soft and browned around the edges. Leave to cool, then scrape out the aubergine flesh and remove the skin from the peppers.

3 Working in batches, put the aubergine and pepper flesh, together with the courgettes, into a food processor and chop to the consistency of salsa or pickle; do not purée. Alternatively, place in a bowl and chop with a knife.

4 Combine the stock with the chopped vegetable mixture in a saucepan and simmer over a medium heat for 20–30 minutes until all the vegetables are tender and the flavours have completely blended.

5 Stir in the cream and simmer the soup over a low heat for about 5 minutes, stirring occasionally, until hot. Taste and adjust the seasoning, if necessary. Ladle the soup into warm bowls, garnish with basil and serve.

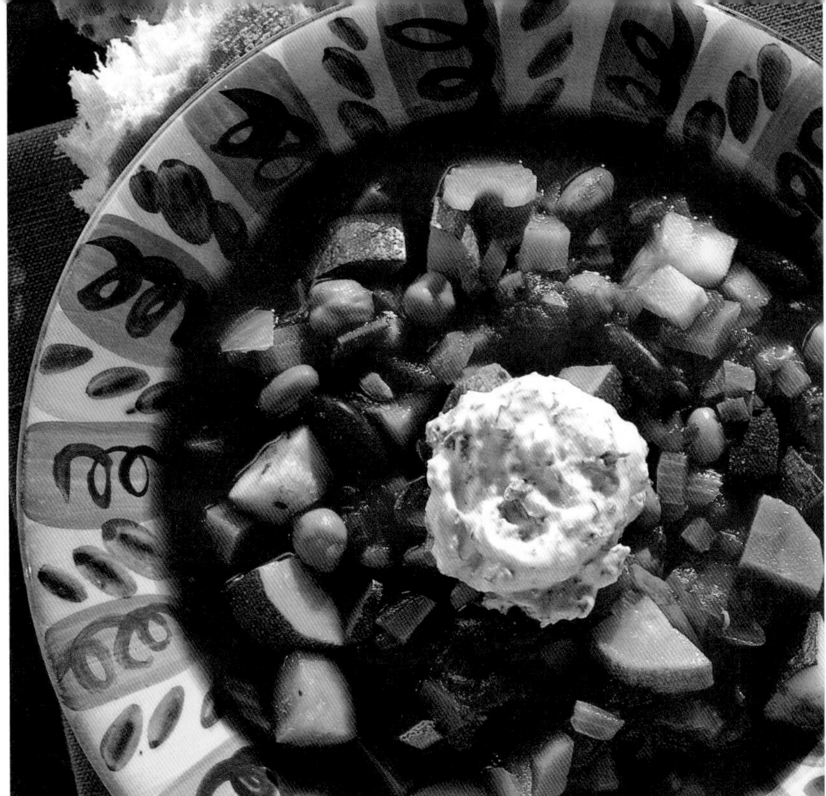

This thick, satisfying blend of beans and vegetables in a rich red wine and tomato stock, based on an Italian favourite, would make a tasty supper dish.

Mixed Bean Soup

1 Place the prepared onion, garlic, celery and carrot in a large saucepan. Stir in the tomatoes, red wine, vegetable stock and oregano.

2 Bring the vegetable mixture to the boil, cover and leave to simmer for 15 minutes. Stir the mixed beans and pulses into the mixture with the courgettes, and continue to cook, uncovered, for a further 5 minutes.

3 Add the tomato purée to the mixture and season well with salt and pepper to taste. Then heat through, stirring occasionally, for a further 2–3 minutes, but be careful not to allow the mixture to boil again.

4 Ladle the soup into warm bowls and serve with a spoonful of pesto on each portion and accompanied with chunks of crusty bread.

SERVES 4

1 medium onion, chopped
1 garlic clove, chopped finely
2 celery sticks, sliced
1 large carrot, diced
400 g/14 oz canned chopped tomatoes
150 ml/5 fl oz Italian dry red wine
1.2 litres/2 pints fresh vegetable stock
1 tsp dried oregano
425 g/15 oz canned mixed beans and pulses
2 medium courgettes, diced
1 tbsp tomato purée
salt and pepper

to serve

pesto (see page 99)
crusty bread

NUTRITION

Calories *192*; Sugars *10 g*; Protein *10 g*; Carbohydrate *23 g*; Fat *5 g*; Saturates *1 g*

COOK'S TIP

Use a jar of good-quality pesto from the supermarket as the garnish if you are too busy to make your own.

moderate

15 mins

35 mins

This soup is best made with white onions, which have a milder flavour than the more usual brown variety. If you cannot get hold of them, try using large Spanish onions instead.

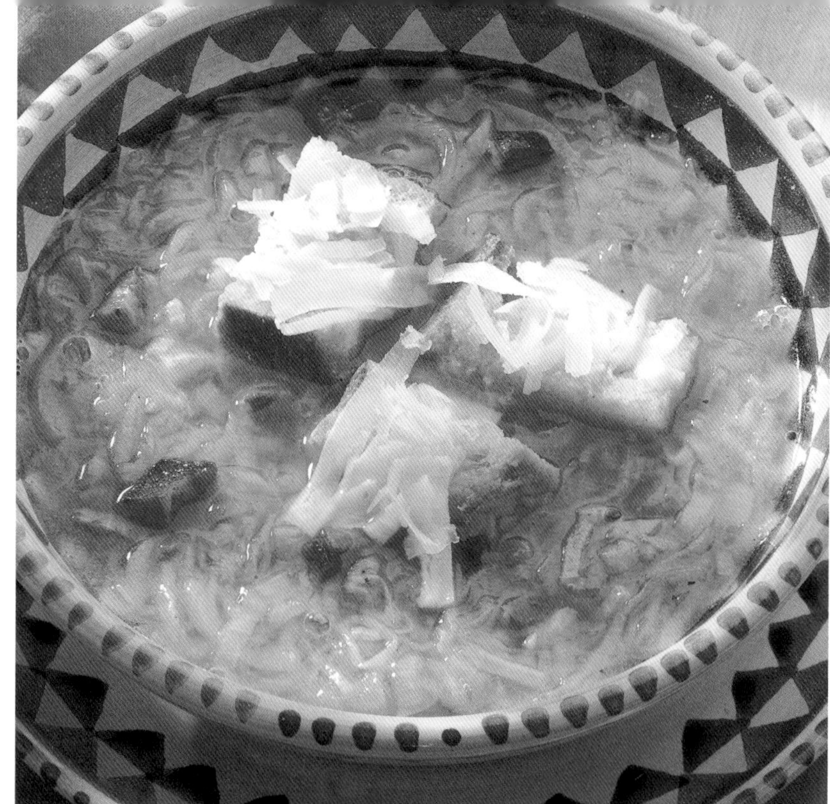

Tuscan Onion Soup

SERVES 4

- 50 g/1¾ oz pancetta, diced
- 1 tbsp olive oil
- 4 large white onions, sliced thinly in rings
- 3 garlic cloves, chopped
- 850 ml/1½ pints hot chicken or ham stock
- 4 slices ciabatta or other Italian bread
- 50 g/1¾ oz butter
- 75 g/2¾ oz Gruyère or Cheddar, grated coarsely
- salt and pepper

1. Dry-fry the pancetta in a large saucepan for 3–4 minutes, or until it begins to brown. Remove the pancetta from the pan and set aside until required.
2. Add the oil to the pan and cook the onions and garlic over a high heat for 4 minutes. Reduce the heat, cover and cook for 15 minutes, or until the onions and garlic are lightly caramelised.
3. Add the stock to the saucepan and bring to the boil. Reduce the heat and leave the mixture to simmer, covered, for about 10 minutes.
4. Toast the slices of ciabatta on both sides, under a preheated grill, for 2–3 minutes, or until golden. Spread the ciabatta with butter and top with the Gruyère or Cheddar cheese. Cut the bread into bite-sized pieces.
5. Add the reserved pancetta to the soup and season to taste with salt and pepper. Pour into 4 soup bowls and top with the toasted bread.

NUTRITION

Calories *390*; Sugars *0g*; Protein *9g*; Carbohydrate *15 g*; Fat *33 g*; Saturates *14 g*

very easy

5–10 mins

40–45 mins

COOK'S TIP

Pancetta is similar to bacon, but it is air- and salt-cured for about 6 months. It is available from most delicatessens and some large supermarkets. If you cannot obtain pancetta, use unsmoked bacon instead.

A *minestra* is a soup cooked with pasta; in this case farfalline, a small bow-shaped variety, is used. Served with lentils, this hearty soup is a whole meal in itself.

Brown Lentil Soup *with* Pasta

SERVES 4

- 4 streaky bacon rashers, cut into small squares
- 1 onion, chopped
- 2 garlic cloves, crushed
- 2 celery sticks, chopped
- 50 g/1¾ oz farfalline or spaghetti, broken into small pieces
- 420 g/14½ oz canned brown lentils, drained
- 1.2 litres/2 pints hot ham or vegetable stock
- 2 tbsp chopped fresh mint

1 Place the bacon in a large frying pan together with the onions, garlic and celery. Dry-fry for 4–5 minutes, stirring, until the onion is tender and the bacon is just beginning to brown.

2 Add the farfalline or spaghetti pieces to the pan and cook, stirring, for about 1 minute to coat the pasta in the oil.

3 Add the lentils and the stock and bring to the boil. Reduce the heat and leave to simmer for 12–15 minutes, or until the pasta is tender.

4 Remove the pan from the heat and stir in the chopped fresh mint.

5 Transfer the soup to warm soup bowls and serve immediately.

COOK'S TIP

If you prefer to use dried lentils, add the stock before the pasta and cook for 1–1¼ hours, or until the lentils are tender. Add the pasta and cook for a further 12–15 minutes.

NUTRITION

Calories 225; Sugars *1 g*; Protein *13 g*; Carbohydrate 27 *g*; Fat *8 g*; Saturates *3 g*

easy

5 mins

25 mins

ith the flavour of
is soup makes a
ıpper dish when
served with crusty bread
and a crisp salad.

Lentil *and* Pasta Soup

SERVES 4

1 tbsp olive oil
1 medium onion, chopped
4 garlic cloves, chopped finely
350 g/12 oz carrot, sliced
1 stick celery, sliced
225 g/8 oz split red lentils, washed
600 ml/1 pint vegetable stock
700 ml/1¼ pints boiling water
150 g/5½ oz pasta
150 ml/5 fl oz natural low-fat fromage frais, plus extra to serve
salt and pepper
2 tbsp chopped fresh parsley, to garnish

1 Heat the olive oil in a large saucepan and gently fry the prepared onion, garlic, carrot and celery, stirring gently, for about 5 minutes or until the vegetables begin to soften.

2 Add the lentils, stock and boiling water. Season well, stir and bring back to the boil. Simmer, uncovered, for 15 minutes until the lentils are completely tender. Allow to cool for 10 minutes.

3 Meanwhile, bring another saucepan of water to the boil and cook the pasta according to the instructions on the packet. Drain well and set aside.

4 Place the soup in a blender and process until smooth. Return to a saucepan and add the pasta. Bring back to a simmer and heat for 2–3 minutes until piping hot. Remove from the heat and stir in the fromage frais. Taste and adjust the seasoning if necessary.

5 Serve sprinkled with freshly ground black pepper and chopped parsley and with extra fromage frais if wished.

NUTRITION

Calories *390*; Sugars *12 g*; Protein *20 g*; Carbohydrate *71 g*; Fat *5 g*; Saturates *1 g*

 easy
15 mins
55 mins

COOK'S TIP

Avoid boiling the soup once the fromage frais has been added or it will separate and become watery, spoiling the appearance of the soup.

This soup takes advantage of summer vegetables bursting with flavour. If you find fresh flageolets or other fresh beans, be sure to include them.

Green Vegetable Soup

1 Heat the oil in a large pan. Cook the onion and leek over a low heat, stirring occasionally, for 5 minutes. Add the celery, carrot and garlic, cover and cook for a further 5 minutes.

2 Add the water, potato, parsnip, kohlrabi or turnip and French beans. Bring to the boil, reduce the heat, cover and simmer for 5 minutes.

3 Add the peas, courgettes and flageolet beans and season to taste. Cover and simmer for about 25 minutes until all the vegetables are tender.

4 Meanwhile, make the pesto. Put all the ingredients in a food processor and process until smooth, scraping down the sides as necessary. Alternatively, pound together using a pestle and mortar.

5 Add the spinach to the soup and simmer for 5 minutes. Stir in a spoonful of the pesto. Ladle into bowls and pass the remaining pesto separately.

SERVES 6

1 tbsp olive oil
1 onion, chopped finely
1 large leek, split and sliced thinly
1 celery stick, sliced thinly
1 carrot, quartered and sliced thinly
1 garlic clove, chopped finely
1.4 litres/2½ pints water
1 potato, diced
1 parsnip, diced finely
1 small kohlrabi or turnip, diced
150 g/5½ oz French beans, cut in small pieces
150 g/5½ oz fresh or frozen peas
2 small courgettes, quartered and sliced
400 g/14 oz canned flageolet beans, drained and rinsed
100 g/3½ oz spinach leaves, shredded finely
salt and pepper

pesto

1 large garlic clove, chopped very finely
15 g/½ oz basil leaves
4 tbsp extra virgin olive oil
85 g/3 oz grated Parmesan cheese

NUTRITION

Calories *260*; Sugars *7 g*; Protein *12 g*; Carbohydrate *21 g*; Fat *15 g*; Saturates *4 g*

easy
20 mins
50 mins

This simple recipe includes sweet potato with its distinctive flavour and colour, combined with a hint of orange and fresh coriander.

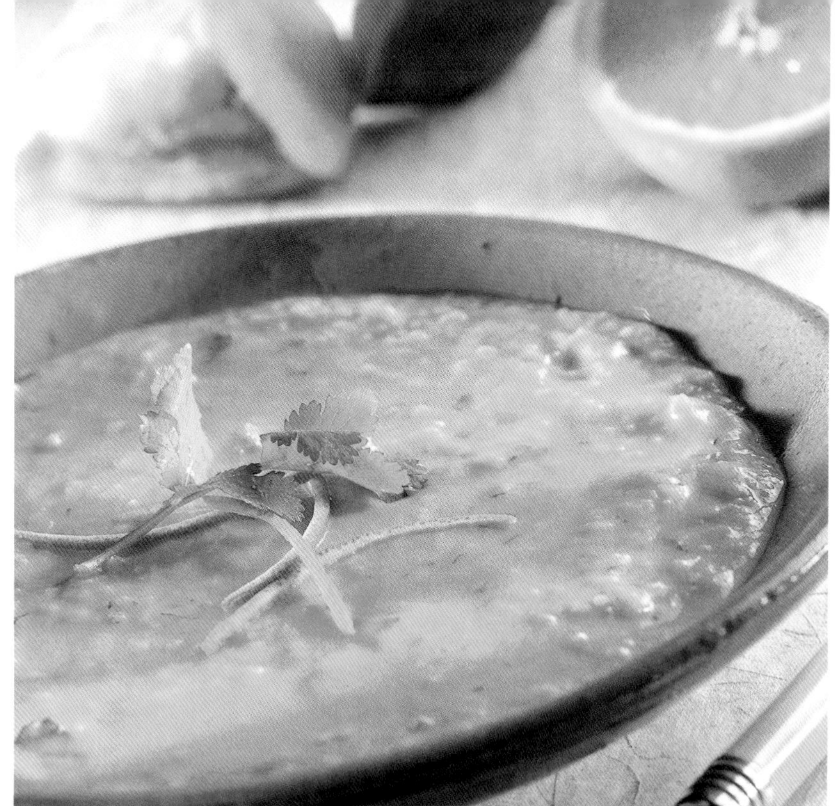

Sweet Potato *and* Onion Soup

SERVES 4

2 tbsp vegetable oil
900 g/2 lb sweet potatoes, diced
1 carrot, diced
2 onions, sliced
2 garlic cloves, crushed
600 ml/1 pint vegetable stock
300 ml/10 fl oz unsweetened orange juice
225 ml/8 fl oz low-fat natural yogurt
2 tbsp chopped fresh coriander
salt and pepper

to garnish
sprigs of fresh coriander
strips of orange rind

1 Heat the vegetable oil in a large, heavy-based saucepan and add the sweet potatoes, carrot, onions and garlic. Sauté the vegetables over a low heat, stirring constantly, for 5 minutes, until softened.

2 Pour in the vegetable stock and orange juice and bring to the boil.

3 Reduce the heat, cover and simmer for 20 minutes, or until the sweet potatoes and carrot are tender.

4 Transfer the mixture to a food processor or blender in batches and process for 1 minute, until puréed. Return the purée to the rinsed-out saucepan.

5 Stir in the yogurt and coriander and season with salt and pepper to taste.

6 Serve in warm soup bowls and garnish with coriander and orange rind.

NUTRITION
Calories *320*; Sugars *26 g*; Protein *7 g*; Carbohydrate *62 g*; Fat *7 g*; Saturates *1 g*

very easy

15 mins

30 mins

COOK'S TIP

This soup can be chilled before serving, if preferred. If chilling, stir the yogurt into the dish just before serving. Serve in chilled bowls.

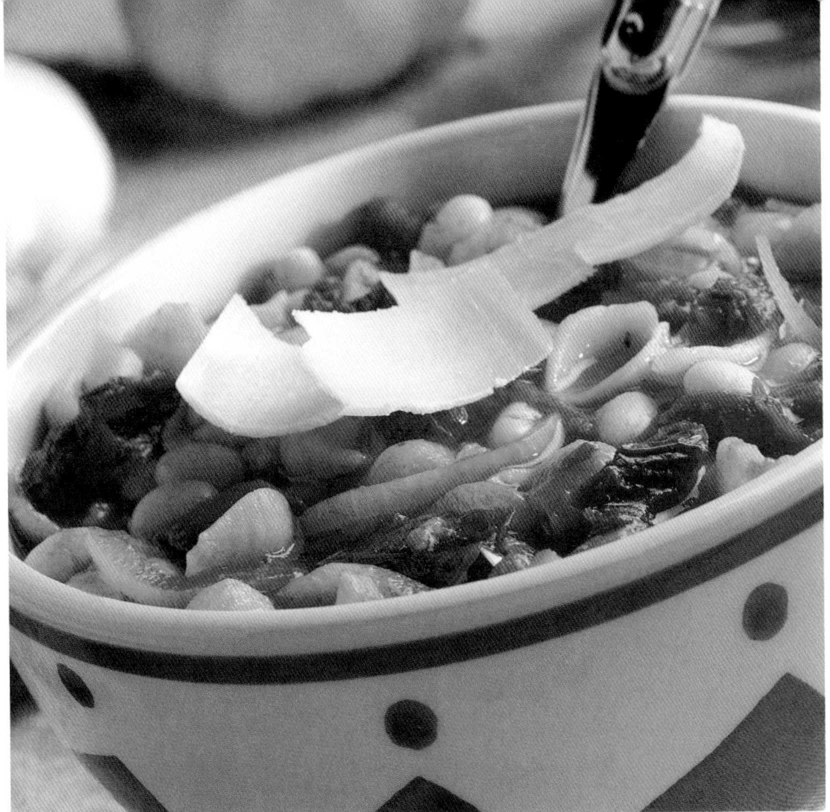

This soup makes an excellent winter lunch served with warm crusty bread and a slice of cheese.

Haricot Bean *and* Pasta Soup

1 Put the haricot beans in a large saucepan, add sufficient cold water to cover and bring to the boil. Boil vigorously over a high heat for 15 minutes. Drain the beans and keep warm.

2 Heat the oil in a pan over a medium heat and fry the onions for 2–3 minutes or until they are just beginning to change colour. Stir in the garlic and cook for 1 minute. Stir in the tomatoes, oregano and tomato purée.

3 Add the water and the beans to the pan. Bring to the boil, cover, then lower the heat and simmer for about 45 minutes, or until the beans are tender.

4 Add the pasta to the pan and season to taste with salt and pepper. Stir in the sun-dried tomatoes, bring back to the boil, partly cover and simmer for 10 minutes, or until the pasta is tender, but still firm to the bite.

5 Stir the coriander or parsley into the soup. Ladle the soup into a warm tureen, sprinkle over the Parmesan cheese and serve immediately.

SERVES 4

250 g/9 oz haricot beans, soaked for 3 hours in cold water and drained
4 tbsp olive oil
2 large onions, sliced
3 garlic cloves, chopped
425 g/14 oz canned chopped tomatoes
1 tsp dried oregano
1 tsp tomato purée
850 ml/1½ pints water
90 g/3½ oz dried fusilli or conchigliette
115 g/4 oz sun-dried tomatoes, drained and sliced thinly
1 tbsp chopped fresh coriander or flat-leaved parsley
salt and pepper
2 tbsp Parmesan cheese shavings, to serve

NUTRITION

Calories *519*; Sugars *13 g*; Protein *20 g*; Carbohydrate *67 g*; Fat *21 g*; Saturates *3 g*

easy

 3 hrs 10 mins

 1 hr 15 mins

COOK'S TIP

If preferred, place the beans in a pan of cold water and bring to the boil. Remove from the heat and leave the beans to cool in the water. Drain and rinse the beans before using.

This soup is a delicious and filling treat on cold winter evenings.

Noodle Soup

SERVES 4

- 3 rashers smoked, rindless bacon, diced
- 1 large onion, chopped
- 15 g/½ oz butter
- 450 g/1 lb dried peas, soaked in cold water for 2 hours and drained
- 2.3 litres/4 pints chicken stock
- 225 g/8 oz dried egg noodles
- 150 ml/5 fl oz double cream
- salt and pepper
- chopped fresh parsley, to garnish
- Parmesan cheese croûtons (see Cook's Tip), to serve

1 Put the bacon, onion and butter into a large saucepan and cook over a low heat for about 6 minutes.

2 Add the peas and the chicken stock to the pan and bring to the boil. Season lightly with salt and pepper, cover and simmer for 1½ hours.

3 Add the egg noodles to the pan and simmer for a further 15 minutes.

4 Pour in the cream and blend thoroughly. Transfer to a warm tureen, garnish with parsley, top with Parmesan cheese croûtons and serve.

NUTRITION

Calories *835*; Sugars *8 g*; Protein *37 g*; Carbohydrate *105 g*; Fat *33 g*; Saturates *16 g*

 easy

2 hrs 10 mins

2 hrs 10 mins

COOK'S TIP

To make Parmesan cheese croûtons, cut a French stick into slices. Coat lightly with olive oil and sprinkle with Parmesan. Grill for about 30 seconds.

Adding soft cheese to this soup just before serving makes it very special, while the rice and croûtons provide an excellent contrast of textures.

Broccoli Soup

1 Divide the broccoli into small florets and cut off the stems. Peel the large stems and then chop all the stems into small pieces.

2 Heat the butter and oil in a large saucepan over a medium heat and add the onion, leek and carrot. Cook the vegetables for 3–4 minutes, stirring frequently, until the onion is soft.

3 Add the broccoli stems, rice, water, bay leaf and a pinch of salt. Bring just to the boil and reduce the heat to low. Cover the pan and simmer the soup for 15 minutes. Add the broccoli florets and continue cooking, covered, for 15–20 minutes until the rice and vegetables are tender. Remove the bay leaf.

4 Season the soup with nutmeg, pepper and, if needed, more salt. Stir in the cream and soft cheese. Simmer over a low heat for a few minutes until heated through, stirring occasionally. Adjust the seasoning if necessary. Ladle into warm bowls and serve sprinkled with the croûtons.

SERVES 4

400 g/14 oz broccoli (from 1 large head)
2 tsp butter
1 tsp oil
1 onion, chopped finely
1 leek, sliced thinly
1 small carrot, chopped finely
3 tbsp white rice
850 ml/1½ pints water
1 bay leaf
freshly grated nutmeg
4 tbsp double cream
100 g/3½ oz soft cheese
salt and pepper
croûtons, to serve (see Cook's Tip)

NUTRITION

Calories *384*; Sugars *7 g*; Protein *8 g*; Carbohydrate *21 g*; Fat *30 g*; Saturates *18 g*

moderate

15 mins

50 mins

COOK'S TIP

To make croûtons, remove the crusts from thick slices of bread, then cut the bread into dice. Fry in vegetable oil, stirring constantly, until evenly browned, then drain on kitchen paper.

Mild red chilli powder and pan-browned garlic give flavour to this simple, homely soup. Quick to make, it's an ideal choice for a light lunch.

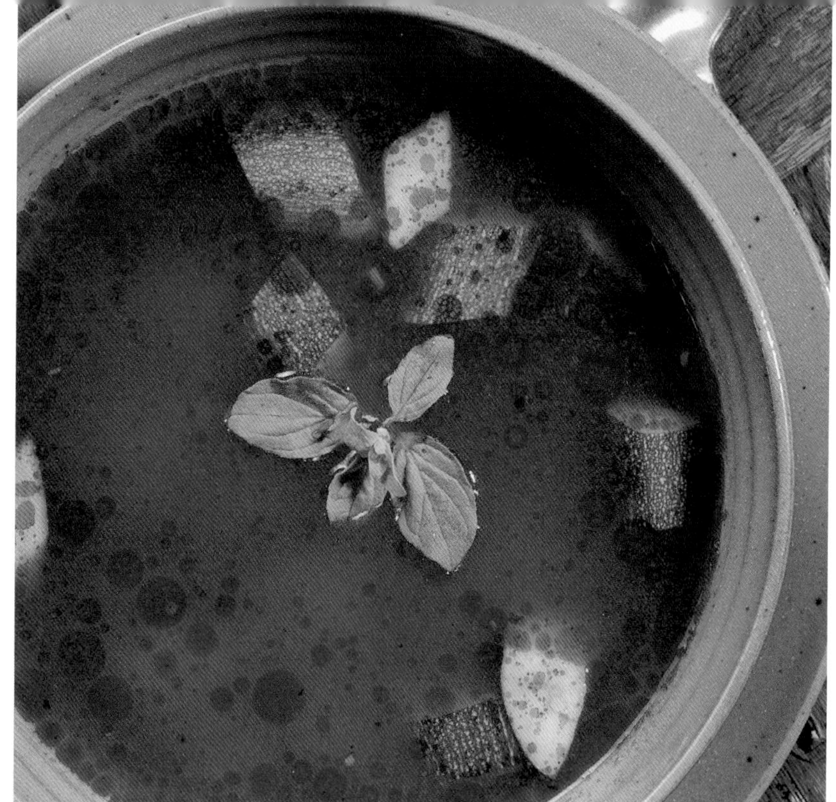

Spicy Courgette Soup

SERVES 4

- 2 tbsp vegetable oil
- 4 garlic cloves, sliced thinly
- 1–2 tbsp mild red chilli powder
- ¼–½ tsp ground cumin
- 1.5 litres/2¾ pints chicken, vegetable or beef stock
- 2 courgettes, cut into bite-sized chunks
- 4 tbsp long-grain rice
- salt and pepper
- fresh oregano sprigs, to garnish
- lime wedges, to serve (optional)

1. Heat the oil in a heavy-based pan, add the garlic and cook, stirring frequently, for about 2 minutes until softened and just beginning to change colour. Stir in the chilli powder and cumin and cook over a medium-low heat, stirring constantly, for a minute.
2. Stir in the stock, courgettes and rice, then cook over a medium-high heat for about 10 minutes until the courgettes are just tender and the rice is cooked through. Season the soup to taste with salt and pepper.
3. Ladle into warmed bowls, garnish with oregano and serve with lime wedges.

NUTRITION

Calories *98*; Sugars *1 g*; Protein *2 g*; Carbohydrate *8 g*; Fat *7 g*; Saturates *1 g*

very easy

5 mins

15 mins

COOK'S TIP

Instead of rice, use tiny pasta, such as orzo or very thin pasta known as fideo. Use yellow summer squash instead of the courgettes and add cooked pinto beans in place of the rice. Diced tomatoes also make a tasty addition.

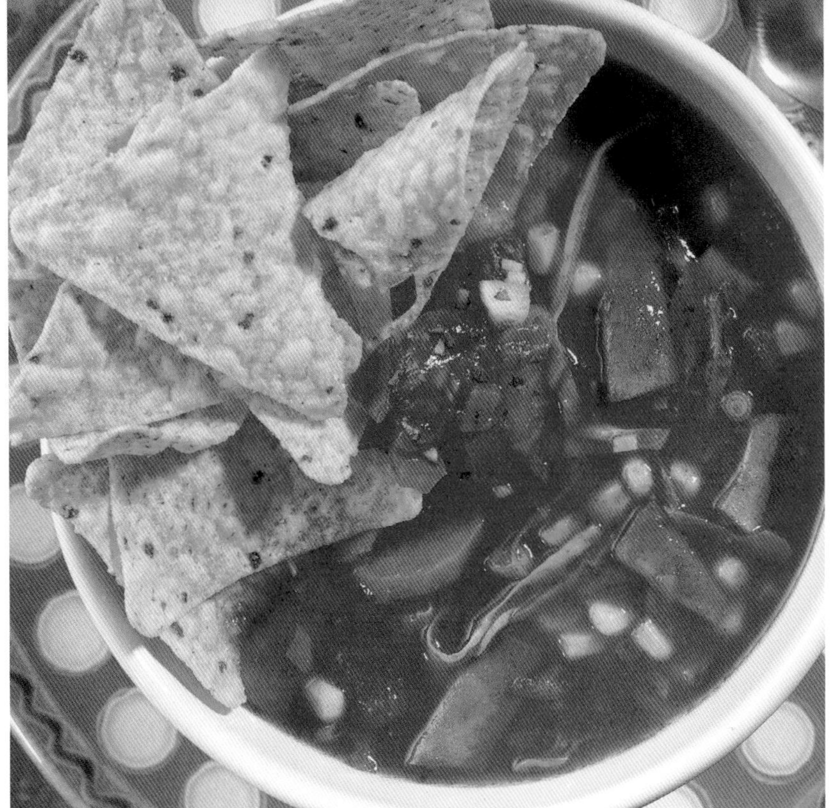

Crisp tortilla chips act as croûtons in this hearty vegetable soup which is found throughout Mexico. Add cheese to melt into the soup, if you wish.

Mexican Vegetable Soup

1 Heat the oil in a heavy-based pan. Add the onion and garlic and cook for a few minutes until softened, then sprinkle in the cumin and chilli powder. Stir in the carrot, potato, tomatoes, courgette and cabbage and cook, stirring occasionally, for 2 minutes.

2 Pour in the stock. Cover and cook over a medium heat for about 20 minutes until the vegetables are tender.

3 Add extra water if necessary, then stir in the sweetcorn and French beans and cook for a further 5–10 minutes or until the beans are tender. Season with salt and pepper to taste, bearing in mind that the tortilla chips may be salty.

4 Ladle the soup into soup bowls and sprinkle each portion with fresh coriander. Top with a spoon of salsa, then add a handful of tortilla chips.

SERVES 4

2 tbsp vegetable or extra virgin olive oil
1 onion, chopped finely
4 garlic cloves, chopped finely
¼–½ tsp ground cumin
2–3 tsp mild chilli powder
1 carrot, sliced
1 waxy potato, diced
350 g/12 oz diced fresh or canned tomatoes
1 courgette, diced
¼ small cabbage, shredded
1 litre/1¾ pints vegetable or chicken stock or water
1 corn cob, the kernels cut off the cob or canned sweetcorn
about 10 French beans, cut into bite-sized lengths
salt and pepper

to serve

4–6 tbsp chopped fresh coriander
salsa of your choice or chopped fresh chilli, to taste
tortilla chips

NUTRITION

Calories *201*; Sugars *9 g*; Protein *6 g*; Carbohydrate *27 g*; Fat *9 g*; Saturates *1 g*

easy

 10 mins

 40 mins

This is a well-known method of cooking vegetables and is perfect with shallots or onions, served with a crisp salad.

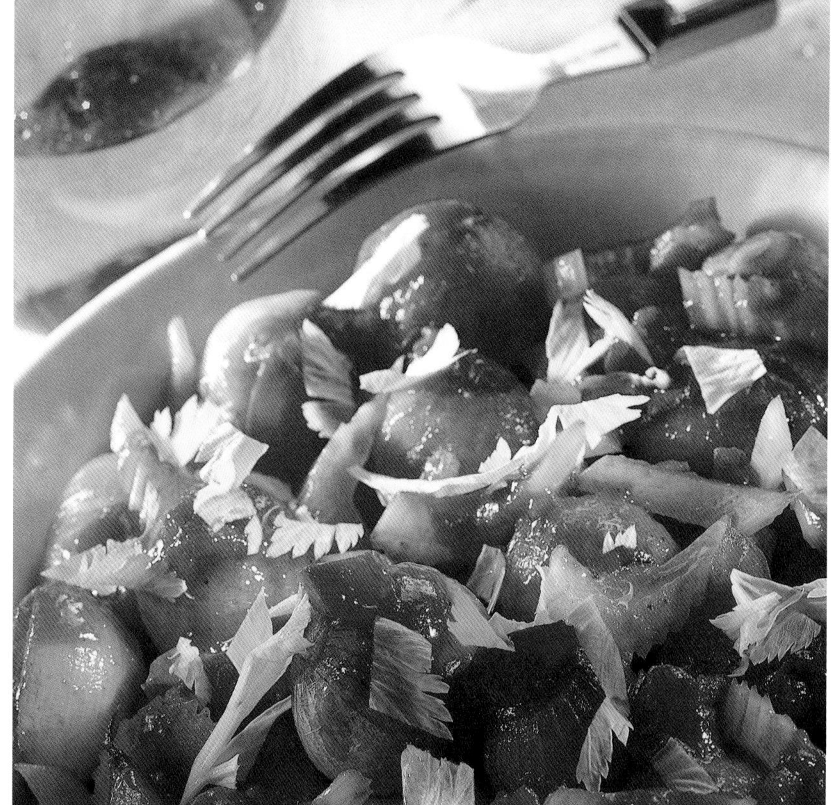

Onions *à la* Grecque

SERVES 4

450 g/1 lb shallots
3 tbsp olive oil
3 tbsp clear honey
2 tbsp garlic wine vinegar
3 tbsp dry white wine
1 tbsp tomato purée
2 celery sticks, sliced
2 tomatoes, deseeded and chopped
salt and pepper
chopped celery leaves, to garnish

1 Peel the shallots. Heat the oil in a large saucepan, add the shallots and cook, stirring, for 3–5 minutes, or until they begin to brown.

2 Add the honey and cook over a high heat for a further 30 seconds, then add the garlic wine vinegar and dry white wine, stirring well.

3 Stir in the tomato purée, the celery and the tomatoes, and bring the mixture to the boil. Cook over a high heat for 5–6 minutes. Season to taste and leave to cool slightly.

4 Garnish with chopped celery leaves and serve warm. Alternatively chill in the refrigerator before serving.

NUTRITION

Calories *200*; Sugars *26 g*; Protein *2 g*; Carbohydrate *28 g*; Fat *9 g*; Saturates *1 g*

 very easy
10 mins
15 mins

Poppy seeds add texture and flavour to this recipe and counteract the sweet flavour of the carrots.

Carrot *and* Orange Bake

1 Cook the carrots and leek in boiling lightly salted water for 5–6 minutes. Drain well and transfer to a shallow ovenproof dish until required.

2 Mix together the orange juice, honey, garlic, mixed spice and thyme and pour the mixture over the vegetables. Season with salt and pepper to taste.

3 Cover the dish and cook in a preheated oven, 180°C/350°F/Gas Mark 4, for 30 minutes, or until the vegetables are tender.

4 Remove the lid and sprinkle with poppy seeds. Transfer the bake to a warmed serving dish, garnish with the fresh thyme sprigs and orange rind and serve immediately.

SERVES 4

675 g/1½ lb carrots, cut into thin strips
1 leek, sliced
300 ml/½ pint fresh orange juice
2 tbsp clear honey
1 garlic clove, crushed
1 tsp mixed spice
2 tsp chopped thyme
1 tbsp poppy seeds
salt and pepper

to garnish
sprigs of fresh thyme
strips of orange rind

NUTRITION

Calories *138*; Sugars *31 g*; Protein *2 g*; Carbohydrate *32 g*; Fat *1 g*; Saturates *0.2 g*

easy

 20 mins

 40 mins

COOK'S TIP

Lemon or lime juice could be used instead of the orange juice, if you prefer. Garnish with lemon or lime rind.

This quick one-pan dish is ideal for a snack. Packed with colour and flavour, it is very versatile because you can add other vegetables.

Pepper *and* Mushroom Hash

SERVES 4

675 g/1½ lb potatoes, cubed
1 tbsp olive oil
2 garlic cloves, crushed
1 green pepper, deseeded and cubed
1 yellow pepper, deseeded and cubed
3 tomatoes, diced
75 g/2¾ oz button mushrooms, halved
1 tbsp Worcestershire sauce
2 tbsp chopped fresh basil
salt and pepper
sprigs of fresh basil, to garnish
warm crusty bread, to serve

1 Cook the potatoes in a saucepan of boiling salted water for 7–8 minutes. Drain well and reserve.

2 Heat the olive oil in a large, heavy-based frying pan. Add the potatoes and cook, stirring constantly, for 8–10 minutes, until browned.

3 Add the garlic and peppers and cook, stirring frequently, for 2–3 minutes.

4 Stir in the tomatoes and mushrooms and cook, stirring frequently, for 5–6 minutes.

5 Stir in the Worcestershire sauce and basil and season to taste with salt and pepper. Transfer to a warm serving dish, garnish with basil sprigs and serve with warm crusty bread.

NUTRITION
Calories *182*; Sugars *6 g*; Protein *5 g*; Carbohydrate *34 g*; Fat *4 g*; Saturates *0.5 g*

easy
 5 mins
 30 mins

COOK'S TIP

Most brands of Worcestershire sauce contain anchovies, so if you are a vegetarian check the label to make sure you choose a vegetarian variety.

This dish contains many Greek flavours such as lemon, garlic, oregano and olives, for a really flavoursome recipe.

Greek Beans

1 Put the haricot beans in a flameproof casserole dish.

2 Add the olive oil and crushed garlic and cook over a gentle heat, stirring occasionally, for 4–5 minutes.

3 Add the stock, bay leaf, oregano, tomato purée, lemon juice and red onion. Cover and simmer for about 1 hour or until the sauce has thickened.

4 Stir in the black olives, then season the beans with salt and pepper to taste. The beans are delicious served either warm or cold.

SERVES 4

400 g/14 oz canned haricot beans, drained
1 tbsp olive oil
3 garlic cloves, crushed
425 ml/¾ pint vegetable stock
1 bay leaf
2 sprigs oregano
1 tbsp tomato purée
juice of 1 lemon
1 small red onion, chopped
25 g/1 oz stoned black olives, halved
salt and pepper

NUTRITION

Calories *115*; Sugars *4 g*; Protein *6 g*; Carbohydrate *15 g*; Fat *4 g*; Saturates *0.6 g*

very easy
 5 mins
 1 hr

COOK'S TIP

You can substitute other canned beans for the haricot beans – try cannellini or black-eyed beans or chickpeas instead. Drain and rinse them before use as canned beans often have sugar or salt added.

The tomatoes in this recipe give the rice its distinctive pinkish colour. The texture of the rice will be slightly 'wet'.

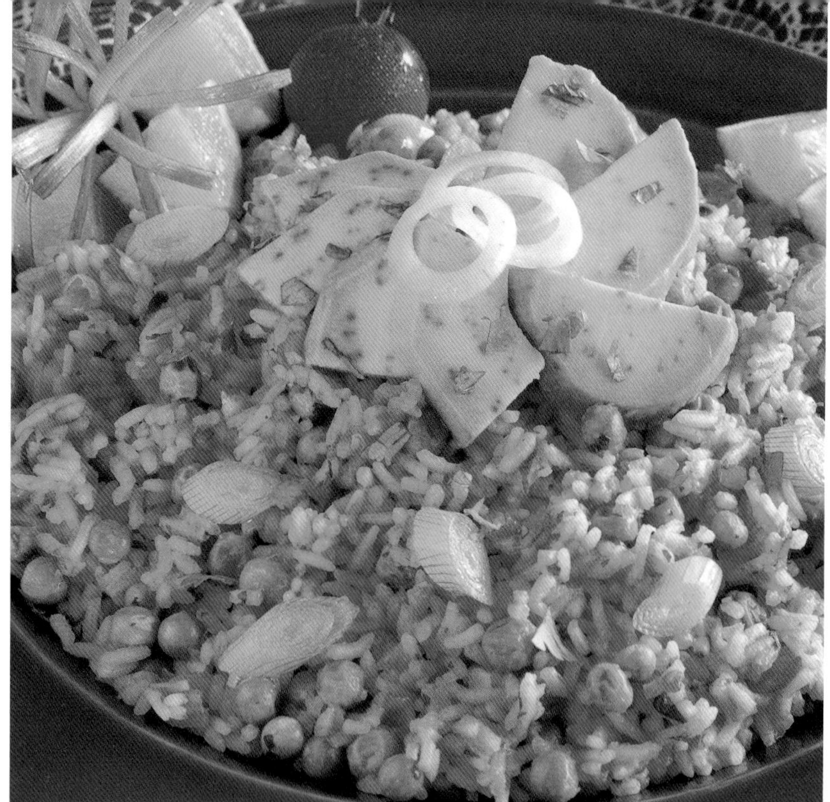

Mexican Tomato Rice

SERVES 6 – 8

400 g/14 oz long-grain rice
1 large onion, chopped
2–3 garlic cloves, crushed
350 g/12 oz canned Italian plum tomatoes
3–4 tbsp olive oil
1 litre/1¾ pints chicken stock
1 tbsp tomato purée
1 habañero or other hot chilli
175 g/6 oz frozen peas, thawed
4 tbsp chopped fresh coriander
salt and pepper

to serve

1 large avocado, peeled, stoned, sliced and sprinkled with lime juice
lime wedges
4 spring onions, chopped
1 tbsp chopped fresh coriander

1 Cover the rice with hot water and set aside to stand for 15 minutes. Drain, then rinse under cold running water.

2 Place the onion and garlic in a food processor and process until a smooth purée forms. Scrape the purée into a small bowl and set aside. Put the tomatoes in the food processor and process until smooth, then strain into another bowl, pushing through any solids with the back of a wooden spoon.

3 Heat the oil in a flameproof casserole over a medium heat. Add the rice and cook, stirring frequently, for 4 minutes until golden and translucent. Add the onion purée and cook, stirring frequently, for a further 2 minutes. Add the stock, processed canned tomatoes and tomato purée and bring to the boil.

4 Using a pin or long needle, carefully pierce the chilli in 2–3 places. Add to the rice, season to taste with salt and pepper and reduce the heat to low. Cover and simmer for about 25 minutes until the rice is tender and the liquid just absorbed. Discard the chilli, stir in the peas and coriander and cook for about 5 minutes to heat through.

5 To serve, gently fork the rice mixture into a warmed large, shallow serving bowl. Arrange the avocado slices and lime wedges on top. Sprinkle over the chopped spring onions and chopped coriander and serve immediately.

NUTRITION

Calories *311*; Sugars *4 g*; Protein *7 g*; Carbohydrate *50 g*; Fat *11 g*; Saturates *2 g*

 easy

30 mins

40 mins

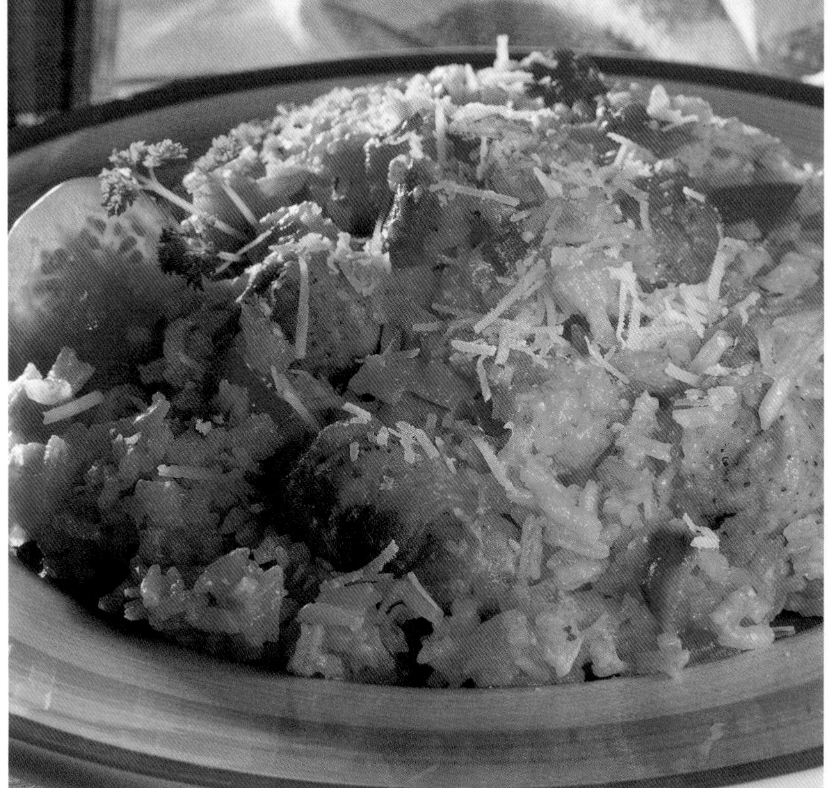

A great quick supper for the family, this dish is incredibly simple to put together, yet is truly scrumptious!

Baked Tomato Rice

1 Heat the vegetable oil in a large flameproof casserole over a medium heat. Add the onion and red pepper and cook, stirring frequently, for about 5 minutes until soft and lightly coloured. Stir in the garlic and thyme and cook for 1 further minute.

2 Add the rice and cook, stirring frequently, for about 2 minutes until the rice is well coated and translucent. Stir in the stock, tomatoes and bay leaf. Bring to the boil and simmer vigorously for 5 minutes until the stock is almost completely absorbed.

3 Stir in the basil, Cheddar cheese, chives and pork sausages and bake, covered, in a preheated oven, 180°C/350°F/Gas Mark 4, for about 25 minutes.

4 Sprinkle with the Parmesan cheese and return to the oven, uncovered, for 5 minutes until the top is golden. Serve hot, straight from the casserole.

SERVES 4

2 tbsp vegetable oil
1 onion, chopped coarsely
1 red pepper, deseeded and chopped
2 garlic cloves, chopped finely
½ tsp dried thyme
300 g/10½ oz long-grain rice
1 litre/1¾ pints chicken or vegetable stock
225 g/8 oz canned chopped tomatoes
1 bay leaf
2 tbsp shredded fresh basil
175 g/6 oz mature Cheddar cheese, grated
2 tbsp chopped fresh chives
4 herbed pork sausages, cooked and cut into 1-cm/½-inch pieces
2–3 tbsp freshly grated Parmesan cheese

NUTRITION

Calories *708*; Sugars *7 g*; Protein *27 g*; Carbohydrate *76 g*; Fat *35 g*; Saturates *16 g*

easy

5 mins

45 mins

COOK'S TIP

For a vegetarian version, replace the pork sausages with 400 g/14 oz canned drained butter beans, kidney beans or sweetcorn. Alternatively, try a mixture of sautéed mushrooms and courgettes.

This tasty risotto gets its vibrant green colour from the spinach and mint. Serve with Italian-style rustic bread and salad for an informal supper.

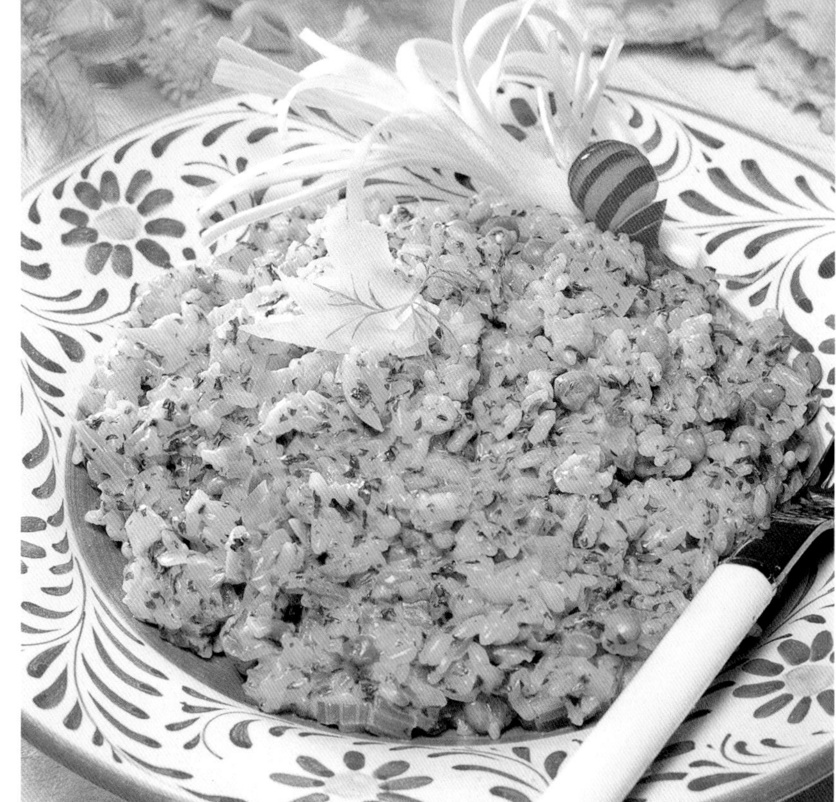

Minted Green Risotto

SERVES 6

- 2 tbsp unsalted butter
- 450 g/1 lb fresh shelled peas or thawed frozen peas
- 1 kg/2 lb 4 oz young spinach leaves, washed and drained
- 1 bunch of fresh mint, leaves stripped from stalks
- 2 tbsp chopped fresh basil
- 2 tbsp chopped fresh oregano
- pinch of freshly grated nutmeg
- 4 tbsp mascarpone cheese or double cream
- 2 tbsp vegetable oil
- 1 onion, chopped finely
- 4 celery sticks, including leaves, chopped finely
- 2 garlic cloves, chopped finely
- ½ tsp dried thyme
- 300 g/10½ oz arborio or carnaroli rice
- 50 ml/2 fl oz dry white vermouth
- 1 litre/1¾ pints chicken or vegetable stock, simmering
- 85 g/3 oz freshly grated Parmesan cheese

NUTRITION

Calories *512*; Sugars *7 g*; Protein *20 g*; Carbohydrate *51 g*; Fat *24 g*; Saturates *12 g*

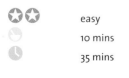

 easy

10 mins

35 mins

1 Heat half the butter in a deep frying pan over a medium-high heat until sizzling. Add the peas, spinach, mint leaves, basil and oregano and season with the nutmeg. Cook, stirring frequently, for about 3 minutes until the spinach and mint leaves are wilted. Cool slightly.

2 Pour the spinach mixture into a food processor and process for 15 seconds. Add the mascarpone or cream and process again for about 1 minute. Transfer to a bowl and set aside.

3 Heat the oil and remaining butter in a large, heavy-based saucepan over a medium heat. Add the onion, celery, garlic and thyme and cook for about 2 minutes until the vegetables are softened. Add the rice and cook, stirring frequently, for about 2 minutes until the rice is translucent and well coated.

4 Add the vermouth to the rice; it will bubble and steam rapidly. When it is almost absorbed, add a ladleful (about 225 ml/8 fl oz) of the simmering stock. Cook, stirring constantly, until the stock is completely absorbed.

5 Continue adding the stock, about half a ladleful at a time, allowing each addition to be absorbed before adding the next. This should take 20–25 minutes. The risotto should have a creamy consistency and the rice should be just tender. Stir in the spinach-cream mixture and the Parmesan. Serve the risotto immediately.

The beetroot and red wine give this risotto its stunning colour and also impart a rich sweet flavour, which is unusual but surprisingly delicious.

Hot Pink Risotto

1 Put the dried cherries or cranberries in a saucepan with the wine and bring to the boil. Simmer for 2–3 minutes until slightly reduced. Remove from the heat and set aside.

2 Heat the oil in a large heavy-based saucepan over a medium heat. Add the onion, celery and thyme and cook, stirring occasionally, for about 2 minutes until just beginning to soften. Add the garlic and rice and cook, stirring constantly, until the rice is well coated.

3 Add a ladleful (about 225 ml/8 fl oz) of the simmering stock; it will bubble and steam rapidly. Cook, stirring constantly, until the stock is absorbed.

4 Continue adding the stock, about half a ladleful at a time, allowing each addition to be absorbed before adding the next. This should take 20–25 minutes. The risotto should have a creamy consistency and the rice should be tender, but still firm to the bite. Half way through the cooking time, remove the cherries or cranberries from the wine with a slotted spoon and add to the risotto with the beetroot and half the wine. Continue adding the stock or remaining wine.

5 Stir in the dill and chives and season to taste with salt and pepper. Serve with the Parmesan, if wished.

SERVES 4–6

175 g/6 oz dried sour cherries or dried cranberries
225 ml/8 fl oz fruity red wine, such as Valpolicella
3 tbsp olive oil
1 large red onion, chopped finely
2 celery sticks, chopped finely
½ tsp dried thyme
1 garlic clove, chopped finely
350 g/12 oz arborio or carnaroli rice
1.2 litres/2 pints chicken or vegetable stock, simmering
4 cooked beetroot (not in vinegar), diced
2 tbsp chopped fresh dill
2 tbsp snipped fresh chives
salt and pepper
55 g/2 oz freshly grated Parmesan cheese, to serve (optional)

NUTRITION

Calories *397*; Sugars *9 g*; Protein *11 g*; Carbohydrate *61 g*; Fat *11 g*; Saturates *3 g*

 easy

 10 mins

40 mins

Although this is the easiest, most basic risotto, it is one of the most delicious. Because there are few ingredients, use the best of each.

Easy Cheese Risotto

SERVES 4–6

- 4–6 tbsp unsalted butter
- 1 onion, chopped finely
- 300 g/10½ oz arborio or carnaroli rice
- 125 ml/4 fl oz dry white vermouth or white wine
- 1.2 litres/2 pints chicken or vegetable stock, simmering
- 85 g/3 oz freshly grated Parmesan cheese, plus extra for sprinkling
- salt and pepper

1 Heat about 2 tablespoons of the butter in a large heavy-based saucepan over a medium heat. Add the onion and cook for about 2 minutes until just beginning to soften. Add the rice and cook, stirring frequently, for about 2 minutes until translucent and well coated with the butter.

2 Pour in the vermouth: it will bubble and steam rapidly and evaporate almost immediately. Add a ladleful (about 225 ml/8 fl oz) of the simmering stock and cook, stirring constantly, until the stock is completely absorbed.

3 Continue adding the stock, about half a ladleful at a time, allowing each addition to be absorbed before adding the next – never allow the rice to cook 'dry'. This should take 20–25 minutes. The risotto should have a creamy consistency and the rice grains should be tender, but still firm to the bite.

4 Switch off the heat and stir in the remaining butter and Parmesan. Season with salt and pepper to taste. Cover, leave to stand for about 1 minute, then serve with extra Parmesan for sprinkling.

NUTRITION

Calories *353*; Sugars *2 g*; Protein *10 g*; Carbohydrate *40 g*; Fat *15 g*; Saturates *9 g*

 easy

5 mins

30 mins

COOK'S TIP

If you prefer not to use butter, soften the onion in 2 tablespoons olive oil and stir in about 2 tablespoons extra virgin olive oil with the Parmesan at the end.

It's worth searching around for wild rocket as its robust peppery flavour makes all the difference to this dish.

Rocket *and* Tomato Risotto

1 Heat the oil and half the butter in a large frying pan. Add the onion and cook for about 2 minutes until just beginning to soften. Stir in the garlic and rice and cook, stirring frequently, until the rice is translucent and well coated.

2 Pour in the vermouth; it will evaporate almost immediately. Add a ladleful (about 225 ml/8 fl oz) of the stock and cook, stirring, until it is absorbed.

3 Continue adding the stock, about half a ladleful at a time, allowing each addition to be absorbed before adding the next. Just before the rice is tender, stir in the chopped tomatoes and rocket. Shred the basil leaves and immediately stir into the risotto. Continue to cook, adding more stock, until the risotto is creamy and the rice is tender, but still firm to the bite.

4 Remove from the heat and stir in the remaining butter, the grated Parmesan and mozzarella. Season to taste with salt and pepper. Remove the pan from the heat, cover and leave to stand for about 1 minute. Serve immediately, before the mozzarella melts completely.

SERVES 4 – 6

2 tbsp olive oil
2 tbsp unsalted butter
1 large onion, chopped finely
2 garlic cloves, chopped finely
350 g/12 oz arborio rice
125 ml/4 fl oz dry white vermouth
1.5 litres/2¾ pints chicken or vegetable stock, simmering
6 vine-ripened or Italian plum tomatoes, deseeded and chopped
125 g/4½ oz wild rocket
handful of fresh basil leaves
115 g/4 oz freshly grated Parmesan cheese
225 g/8 oz fresh Italian buffalo mozzarella, grated coarsely or diced
salt and pepper

NUTRITION

Calories *546*; Sugars *6 g*; Protein *23 g*; Carbohydrate *57 g*; Fat *24 g*; Saturates *12 g*

easy

10 mins

30 mins

Make this creamy risotto with Italian arborio rice and freshly grated Parmesan cheese for the best results.

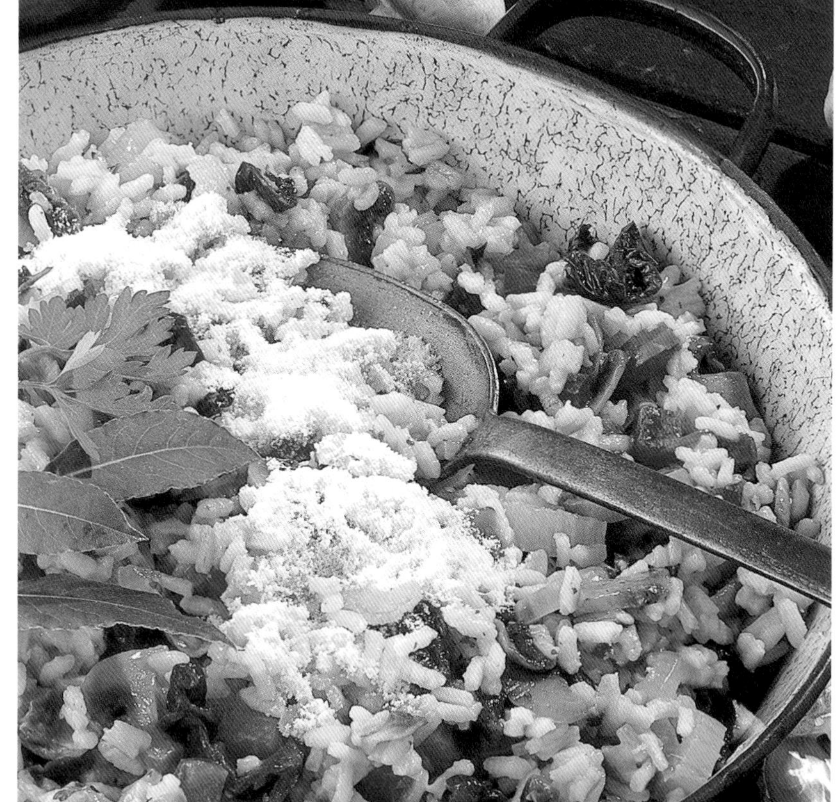

Mushroom *and* Cheese Risotto

SERVES 4

2 tbsp olive or vegetable oil
225 g/8 oz arborio rice
2 garlic cloves, crushed
1 onion, chopped
2 celery sticks, chopped
1 red or green pepper, deseeded and chopped
225 g/8 oz mushrooms, sliced
1 tbsp chopped fresh oregano or 1 tsp dried oregano
1 litre/1¾ pints vegetable stock
55 g /2 oz sun-dried tomatoes in olive oil, drained and chopped (optional)
55 g/2 oz finely grated Parmesan cheese
salt and pepper

to garnish
fresh flat-leaved parsley sprigs
fresh bay leaves

1 Heat the oil in a wok or large frying pan. Add the rice and cook, stirring constantly, for 5 minutes.

2 Add the garlic, onion, celery and pepper and cook, stirring constantly, for 5 minutes. Add the mushrooms and cook for 3–4 minutes.

3 Stir in the oregano and stock. Heat until just boiling, then reduce the heat, cover and simmer for 20 minutes or until the rice is tender and creamy.

4 Add the sun-dried tomatoes, if using, and season to taste with salt and pepper. Stir in half of the grated Parmesan cheese. Top with the remaining cheese, garnish with flat-leaved parsley and bay leaves and serve.

NUTRITION
Calories *358*; Sugars *3 g*; Protein *11 g*; Carbohydrate *50 g*; Fat *14 g*; Saturates *5 g*

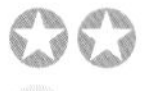 easy
20 mins
40 mins

This fragrant risotto makes a delicate first course for a special meal. Serve with a sprinkling of grated Parmesan, if wished.

Orange-scented Risotto

1 Toast the pine kernels in a frying pan over a medium heat for about 3 minutes, stirring and shaking frequently, until golden-brown. Set aside.

2 Heat half the butter in a large heavy-based pan over a medium heat. Add the shallots and leek and cook for about 2 minutes until they begin to soften. Add the rice and cook, stirring frequently, for about 2 minutes until the rice is translucent and well coated.

3 Pour in the liqueur or vermouth; it will evaporate almost immediately. Add a ladleful (about 225 ml/8 fl oz) of the stock and cook, stirring, until absorbed. Continue adding the stock, about half a ladleful at a time, allowing each addition to be absorbed before adding the next – take care never to allow the rice to cook 'dry'.

4 After about 15 minutes, add the orange rind and juice and continue to cook, adding more stock, until the rice is tender, but still firm to the bite. The risotto should have a creamy consistency.

5 Remove from the heat and stir in the remaining butter and 2 tablespoons of the chives. Season to taste with salt and pepper. Spoon into serving dishes and sprinkle with the toasted pine kernels and the remaining chives.

SERVES 4

2 tbsp pine kernels
4 tbsp unsalted butter
2 shallots, chopped finely
1 leek, shredded finely
400 g/14 oz arborio or carnaroli rice
2 tbsp orange-flavoured liqueur or dry white vermouth
1.5 litres/2¾ pints chicken or vegetable stock, simmering
grated rind of 1 orange
juice of 2 oranges, strained
3 tbsp snipped fresh chives
salt and pepper

NUTRITION

Calories *599*; Sugars *9 g*; Protein *10 g*; Carbohydrate *95 g*; Fat *22 g*; Saturates *9 g*

moderate

10 mins

35 mins

This vegetarian version of paella is packed with vegetables and nuts for a truly delicious and simple dish.

Cashew Nut Paella

SERVES 4

2 tbsp olive oil
1 tbsp butter
1 red onion, chopped
150 g/5½ oz arborio rice
1 tsp ground turmeric
1 tsp ground cumin
½ tsp chilli powder
3 garlic cloves, crushed
1 fresh green chilli, deseeded and sliced
1 green pepper, deseeded and diced
1 red pepper, deseeded and diced
85 g/3 oz baby corn cobs
2 tbsp stoned black olives
1 large tomato, deseeded and diced
450 ml/16 fl oz vegetable stock
85 g/3 oz unsalted cashew nuts
55 g/2 oz frozen peas
2 tbsp chopped fresh parsley
pinch of cayenne pepper
salt and pepper
fresh herbs, to garnish

NUTRITION

Calories *406*; Sugars *8 g*; Protein *10 g*; Carbohydrate *44 g*; Fat *22 g*; Saturates *6 g*

 easy
 15 mins
35 mins

1 Heat the olive oil and butter in a large frying pan or paella pan until the butter has melted.

2 Add the onion and cook over a medium heat, stirring constantly, for 2–3 minutes until softened.

3 Stir in the rice, turmeric, cumin, chilli powder, garlic, sliced chilli, green and red peppers, corn cobs, olives and tomato and cook over a medium heat, stirring occasionally, for 1–2 minutes.

4 Pour in the stock and bring the mixture to the boil. Reduce the heat and cook gently, stirring constantly, for a further 20 minutes.

5 Add the cashew nuts and peas and continue to cook, stirring occasionally, for a further 5 minutes. Season to taste with salt and pepper and sprinkle with chopped fresh parsley and a pinch of cayenne pepper. Transfer the paella to warm serving plates, garnish with fresh herbs and serve immediately.

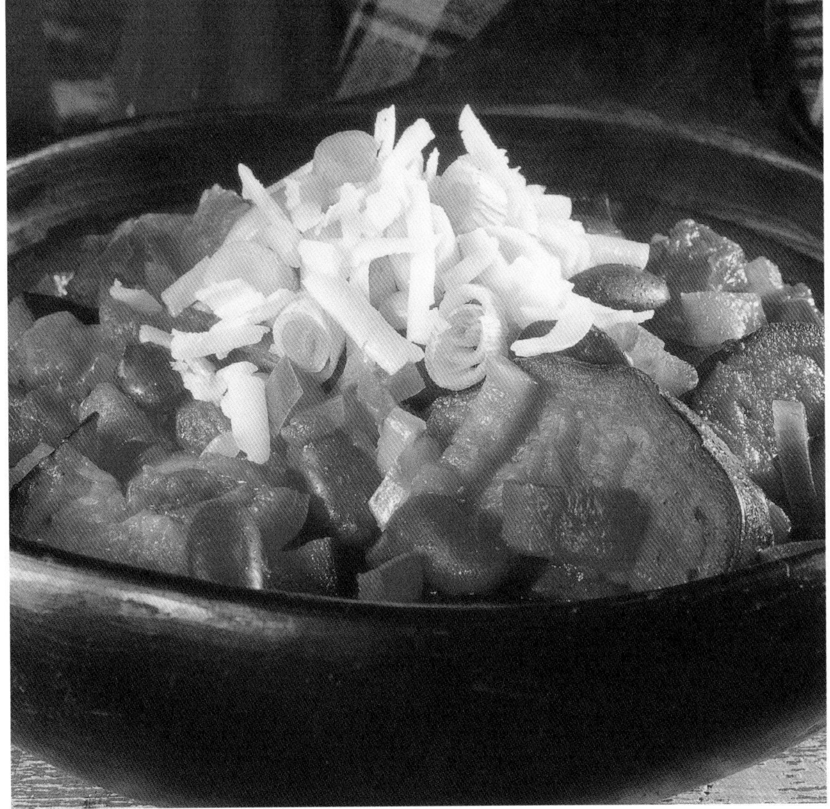

This is a hearty and flavoursome soup that is good on its own or spooned over cooked rice or baked potatoes for a more substantial meal.

Vegetable Chilli

1 Brush the aubergine slices on 1 side with olive oil. Heat half the oil in a large, heavy-based frying pan over a medium-high heat. Add the aubergine slices, oiled-side up, and cook for 5–6 minutes until browned on one side. Turn the slices over, cook on the other side until browned and transfer to a plate. Cut into bite-sized pieces.

2 Heat the remaining oil in a large saucepan over a medium heat. Add the onion and peppers and cook, stirring occasionally, for 3–4 minutes until the onion is just softened, but not browned. Add the garlic and continue cooking for 2–3 minutes or until the onion is just beginning to colour.

3 Add the tomatoes, chilli powder, cumin and oregano. Season to taste with salt and pepper. Bring just to the boil, reduce the heat, cover and simmer gently for 15 minutes.

4 Add the sliced courgettes, aubergine pieces and kidney beans. Stir in the water and the tomato purée. Bring back to the boil, then cover the pan and continue simmering for about 45 minutes or until the vegetables are tender. Taste and then adjust the seasoning if necessary. If you prefer a hotter dish, stir in a little more chilli powder.

5 Ladle into warmed bowls and top with spring onions and cheese.

SERVES 4

- 1 medium aubergine, peeled if wished, cut into 2.5-cm/1-inch slices
- 1 tbsp olive oil, plus extra for brushing
- 1 large red or yellow onion, chopped finely
- 2 red or yellow peppers, deseeded and chopped finely
- 3–4 garlic cloves, finely chopped or crushed
- 800 g/1 lb 12 oz canned chopped tomatoes
- 1 tbsp mild chilli powder
- ½ tsp ground cumin
- ½ tsp dried oregano
- 2 small courgettes, quartered lengthways and sliced
- 400 g/14 oz canned kidney beans, drained and rinsed
- 450 ml/16 fl oz water
- 1 tbsp tomato purée
- 6 spring onions, chopped finely
- 115 g/4 oz grated Cheddar cheese
- salt and pepper

NUTRITION

Calories *213*; Sugars *11 g*; Protein *12 g*; Carbohydrate *21 g*; Fat *10 g*; Saturates *5 g*

easy

 10 mins

 1 hr 15 mins

Millet makes an interesting alternative to rice, which is the more traditional ingredient for a pilau. Serve with a crisp Oriental salad.

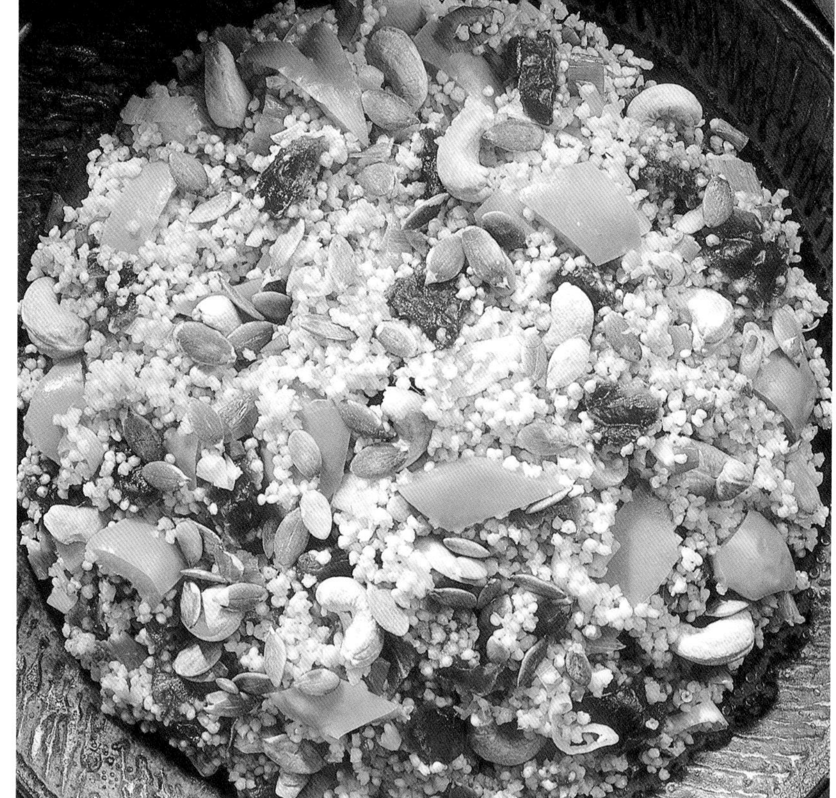

Asian-style Millet Pilau

SERVES 4

- 300 g/10½ oz millet grains
- 1 tbsp vegetable oil
- 1 bunch spring onions, white and green parts, chopped
- 1 garlic clove, crushed
- 1 tsp grated fresh root ginger
- 1 orange pepper, seeded and diced
- 600 ml/1 pint water
- 1 orange
- 115 g/4 oz chopped stoned dates
- 2 tsp sesame oil
- 115 g/4 oz roasted cashew nuts
- 2 tbsp pumpkin seeds
- salt and pepper
- Oriental salad vegetables, to serve

1 Place the millet in a large pan and toast over a medium heat, shaking the pan occasionally, for 4–5 minutes, until the grains begin to crack and pop.

2 Heat the oil in another pan. Add the spring onions, garlic, ginger and pepper and cook over a medium heat, stirring frequently, for 2–3 minutes until just softened, but not browned. Add the millet and pour in the water.

3 Using a vegetable peeler, pare the rind from the orange and add the rind to the pan. Squeeze the juice from the orange into the pan. Season to taste with salt and pepper.

4 Bring to the boil, reduce the heat, cover and cook gently for 20 minutes until all the liquid has been absorbed. Remove the pan from the heat, stir in the dates and sesame oil and set aside to stand for 10 minutes.

5 Remove and discard the orange rind and stir in the cashew nuts. Pile into a warmed serving dish, sprinkle with pumpkin seeds and serve immediately with Oriental salad vegetables.

NUTRITION

Calories *660*; Sugars *28 g*; Protein *15 g*; Carbohydrate *94 g*; Fat *27 g*; Saturates *5 g*

easy

20 mins

30 mins

This colourful and interesting mixture of vegetables, cooked in a spicy sauce, is excellent served with rice and naan bread.

Vegetable Curry

1 Cut the turnips or swede, aubergine and potatoes into 1-cm/½-inch cubes. Divide the cauliflower into small florets. Leave the mushrooms whole or slice them thickly if preferred. Slice the onion and carrots.

2 Heat the ghee or oil in a large pan. Add the onion, turnip or swede, potato and cauliflower and cook over a low heat, stirring frequently, for 3 minutes.

3 Add the garlic, ginger, chillies, paprika, ground coriander and curry powder and cook, stirring, for 1 minute.

4 Add the stock, tomatoes, aubergine and mushrooms and season with salt. Cover and simmer, stirring occasionally, for about 30 minutes or until tender. Add the green pepper and carrots, cover and cook for a further 5 minutes.

5 Blend the cornflour with the coconut milk to a smooth paste and stir into the mixture. Add the ground almonds and simmer, stirring constantly, for 2 minutes. Taste and adjust the seasoning if necessary. Transfer to serving plates and serve hot, garnished with coriander sprigs.

SERVES 4

225 g/8 oz turnips or swede
1 aubergine
350 g/12 oz new potatoes
225 g/8 oz cauliflower
225 g/8 oz button mushrooms
1 large onion
3 carrots
6 tbsp vegetable ghee or vegetable oil
2 garlic cloves, crushed
4 tsp finely chopped fresh root ginger
1–2 fresh green chillies, deseeded and chopped
1 tbsp paprika
2 tsp ground coriander
1 tbsp mild or medium curry powder
450 ml/16 fl oz vegetable stock
400 g/14 oz canned chopped tomatoes
1 green pepper, deseeded and sliced
1 tbsp cornflour
150 ml/5 fl oz coconut milk
2–3 tbsp ground almonds
salt
sprigs fresh coriander, to garnish

NUTRITION

Calories *421*; Sugars *20 g*; Protein *12 g*; Carbohydrate *42 g*; Fat *24 g*; Saturates *3 g*

easy

 10 mins

 45 mins

This unusual vegetarian dish is best served as a side dish with other curries and with rice to soak up the wonderfully rich, spiced juices.

Spiced Cashew Nut Curry

SERVES 4

250 g/9 oz unsalted cashew nuts
1 tsp coriander seeds
1 tsp cumin seeds
2 cardamom pods, crushed
1 tbsp sunflower oil
1 onion, sliced thinly
1 garlic clove, crushed
1 small fresh green chilli, deseeded and chopped
1 cinnamon stick
½ tsp ground turmeric
4 tbsp coconut cream
300 ml/10 fl oz hot vegetable stock
3 kaffir lime leaves, shredded finely
salt and pepper
boiled jasmine rice, to serve

1 Soak the cashew nuts in cold water overnight. Drain thoroughly. Crush the coriander seeds, cumin seeds and cardamom pods with a pestle and mortar.

2 Heat the oil and stir-fry the onion and garlic for 2–3 minutes to soften, but not brown. Add the chilli, crushed spices, cinnamon stick and turmeric and stir-fry for a further minute.

3 Add the coconut cream and the hot stock to the pan. Bring to the boil, then add the cashew nuts and lime leaves.

4 Cover the pan, lower the heat and simmer for about 20 minutes. Serve hot, accompanied by jasmine rice.

NUTRITION

Calories *455*; Sugars *6 g*; Protein *13 g*; Carbohydrate *16 g*; Fat *39 g*; Saturates *11 g*

very easy
8 hrs 15 mins
25 mins

COOK'S TIP

All spices give the best flavour when freshly crushed, but if you prefer, you can use ground spices instead of crushing them yourself in a mortar with a pestle.

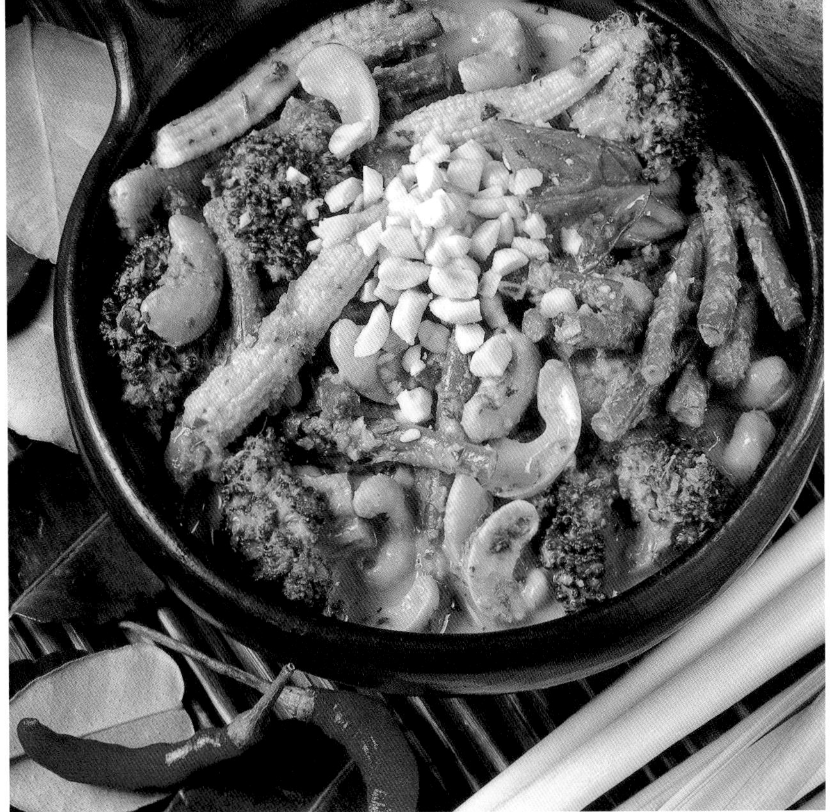

This is a wonderfully quick dish to prepare. If you don't have time to prepare the curry paste, it can be bought ready-made.

Red Curry *with* Cashews

1 To make the curry paste, grind all the ingredients in a large mortar with a pestle or in a grinder. Alternatively, process briefly in a food processor. (The quantity of red curry paste is more than is required for this recipe. Store for up to 3 weeks in a sealed jar in the refrigerator.)

2 Put a wok or large, heavy-based frying pan over a high heat, add 3 tablespoons of the red curry paste and stir until it gives off its aroma. Reduce the heat to medium.

3 Add the coconut milk, kaffir lime leaf, light soy sauce, baby corn cobs, broccoli florets, French beans and cashew nuts. Bring to the boil and simmer for about 10 minutes until the vegetables are cooked, but still firm and crunchy.

4 Remove and discard the lime leaf and stir in the basil leaves and coriander. Transfer to a warmed serving dish, garnish with peanuts and serve.

SERVES 4

250 ml/9 fl oz coconut milk
1 kaffir lime leaf
¼ tsp light soy sauce
4 baby corn cobs, halved lengthways
115 g/4 oz broccoli florets
115 g/4 oz French beans, cut into pieces
4 tbsp cashew nuts
15 fresh basil leaves
1 tbsp chopped fresh coriander
1 tbsp chopped roasted peanuts, to garnish

red curry paste

7 fresh red chillies, deseeded and blanched
2 tsp cumin seeds
2 tsp coriander seeds
2.5-cm/1-inch piece of galangal, chopped
½ lemon grass stalk, chopped
1 tsp salt
grated rind of 1 lime
4 garlic cloves, chopped
3 shallots, chopped
2 kaffir lime leaves, shredded
1 tbsp vegetable oil

NUTRITION

Calories *274*; Sugars *5 g*; Protein *10 g*; Carbohydrate *38 g*; Fat *10 g*; Saturates *3 g*

easy

 25 mins

 15 mins

A mildly spiced but richly flavoured Indian-style dish full of different textures and flavours. Serve with naan bread to soak up the tasty sauce.

Coconut Vegetable Curry

SERVES 4

1 large aubergine, cut into 2.5-cm/1-inch cubes
2 tbsp vegetable oil
2 garlic cloves, crushed
1 fresh green chilli, deseeded and chopped finely
1 tsp grated fresh root ginger
1 onion, chopped finely
2 tsp garam masala
8 cardamom pods
1 tsp ground turmeric
1 tbsp tomato purée
700 ml/1¼ pints Fresh Vegetable Stock (see page 14)
1 tbsp lemon juice
225 g/8 oz potatoes, diced
250 g/9 oz small cauliflower florets
225 g/8 oz okra, trimmed
225 g/8 oz frozen peas
150 ml/5 fl oz coconut milk
salt and pepper
flaked coconut, to garnish
naan bread, to serve

NUTRITION

Calories *159*; Sugars *8 g*; Protein *8 g*; Carbohydrate *19 g*; Fat *6 g*; Saturates *1 g*

easy

1 hr 45 mins

35 mins

1 Layer the aubergine in a bowl, sprinkling with salt as you go. Set aside for 30 minutes. Rinse well under running water. Drain and dry. Set aside.

2 Heat the oil in a large pan and gently cook the garlic, chilli, ginger, onion and spices for 4–5 minutes.

3 Stir in the tomato purée, stock, lemon juice, potatoes and cauliflower and mix well. Bring to the boil, cover and simmer for 15 minutes.

4 Stir in the aubergine, okra, peas and coconut milk and season with salt and pepper to taste. Continue to simmer, uncovered, for a further 10 minutes until tender. Discard the cardamom pods. Pile the curry on to a warmed serving platter, garnish with flaked coconut and serve with naan bread.

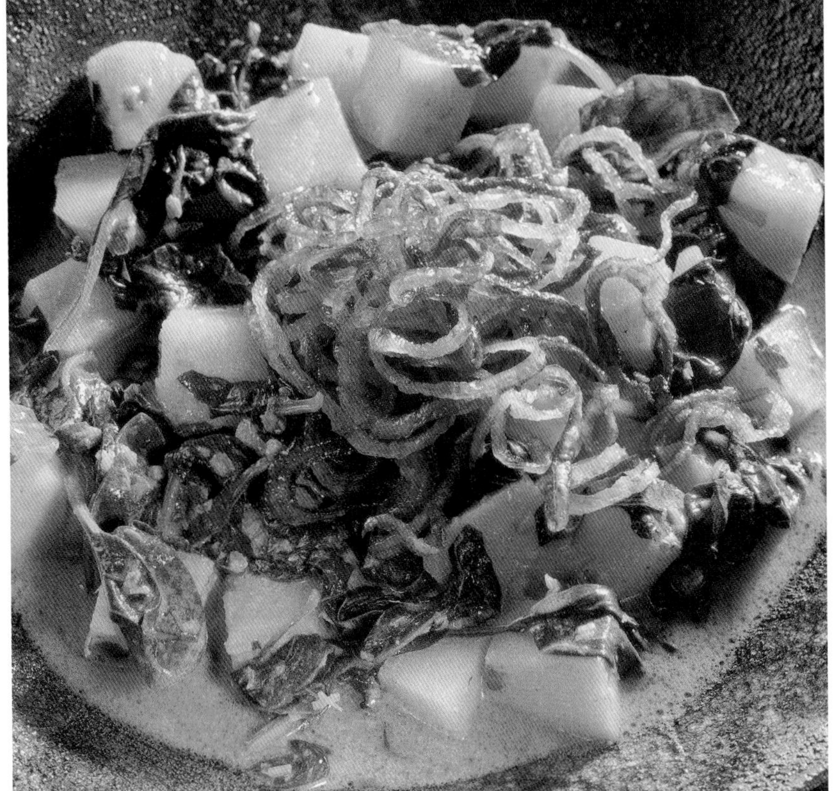

Potatoes are not highly regarded in Thai cookery because rice is the traditional staple. This dish is a tasty exception.

Yellow Curry

1 Place the garlic, galangal, lemon grass and coriander seeds in a mortar and pound continuously with a pestle until a smooth paste forms.

2 Heat 2 tablespoons of the oil in a frying pan or wok. Stir in the garlic paste and stir-fry for 30 seconds. Stir in the curry paste and turmeric, then add the coconut milk and bring the mixture to the boil.

3 Add the potatoes and stock. Return to the boil, then lower the heat and simmer, uncovered, for 10–12 minutes until the potatoes are almost tender.

4 Stir in the spinach and simmer until the leaves are wilted.

5 Fry the onion in the remaining oil until crisp and golden brown. Place on top of the curry just before serving.

SERVES 4

2 garlic cloves, chopped finely
3-cm/1¼-inch piece of galangal, chopped finely
1 lemon grass stalk, chopped finely
1 tsp coriander seeds
3 tbsp vegetable oil
2 tsp Thai red curry paste
½ tsp ground turmeric
200 ml/7 fl oz coconut milk
250 g/9 oz potatoes, cubed
100 ml/3½ fl oz vegetable stock
200 g/7 oz young spinach leaves
1 small onion, sliced thinly into rings

NUTRITION

Calories *160*; Sugars *4 g*; Protein *3 g*; Carbohydrate *15 g*; Fat *10 g*; Saturates *1 g*

easy

 5 mins

 15 mins

COOK'S TIP

Choose a firm, waxy potato for this dish, one that will keep its shape during cooking, in preference to a floury variety that will break up easily once cooked.

Seasonal fresh vegetables are casseroled with lentils, then topped with a ring of fresh cheese scones to make this tasty cobbler.

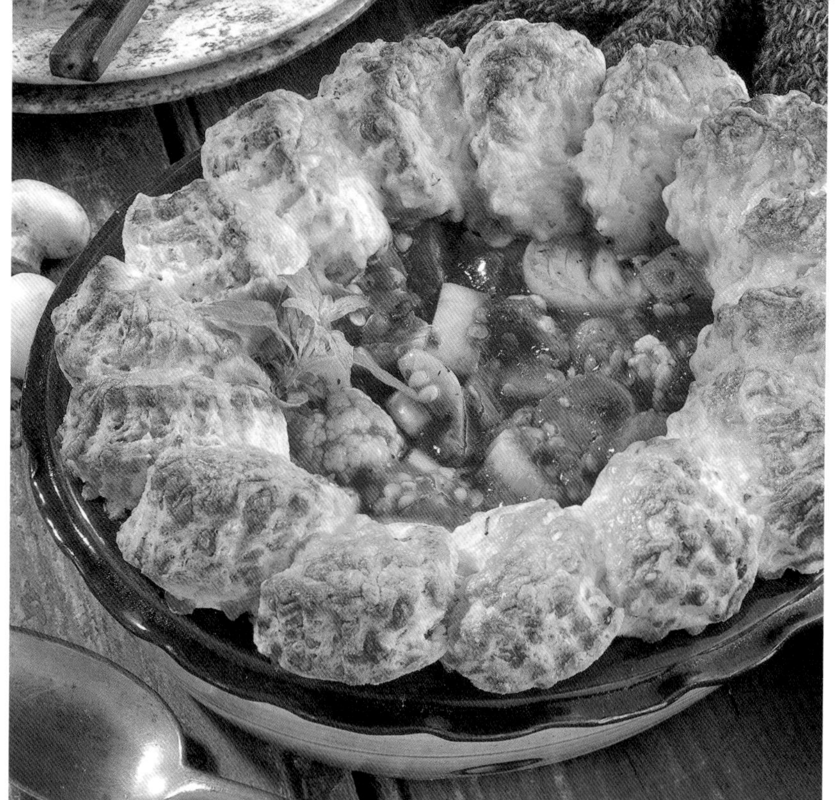

Winter Vegetable Cobbler

SERVES 4

- 1 tbsp olive oil
- 1 garlic clove, crushed
- 8 small onions, halved
- 2 celery sticks, sliced
- 225 g/8 oz swede, chopped
- 2 carrots, sliced
- ½ small cauliflower, broken into florets
- 225 g/8 oz mushrooms, sliced
- 400 g/14 oz canned chopped tomatoes
- 55 g/2 oz red lentils, washed
- 2 tbsp cornflour
- 3–4 tbsp water
- 300 ml/10 fl oz vegetable stock
- 2 tsp Tabasco sauce
- 2 tsp chopped oregano, plus sprigs to garnish

cobbler topping

- 225 g/8 oz self-raising flour
- 4 tbsp butter
- 115 g/4 oz grated mature Cheddar cheese
- 2 tsp chopped fresh oregano
- 1 egg, lightly beaten
- 150 ml/5 fl oz milk
- salt

NUTRITION

Calories *734*; Sugars *22 g*; Protein *27 g*; Carbohydrate *96 g*; Fat *30 g*; Saturates *16 g*

 moderate

20 mins

40 mins

1 Heat the oil and cook the garlic and onions for 5 minutes. Add the celery, swede, carrots and cauliflower and cook for 2–3 minutes. Add the mushrooms, tomatoes and lentils. Mix the cornflour and water and stir into the pan with the stock, Tabasco and oregano.

2 Transfer to an ovenproof dish, cover and bake in a preheated oven, 180°C/350°F/Gas Mark 4, for 20 minutes.

3 To make the topping, sift the flour with a pinch of salt into a bowl. Rub in the butter, then stir in most of the cheese and the chopped oregano. Beat the egg with the milk and add enough to the dry ingredients to make a soft dough. Knead, roll out to 1 cm/½ inch thick and cut into 5-cm/2-inch rounds.

4 Remove the dish from the oven and increase the temperature to 200°C/400°F/Gas Mark 6. Arrange the scones around the edge of the dish, brush with the remaining egg and milk and sprinkle with the reserved cheese. Cook for a further 10–12 minutes. Garnish and serve.

This is a really hearty dish, perfect for winter days when a filling hot dish is just what you need to keep the cold out.

Lentil *and* Rice Casserole

1 Place the lentils, rice and vegetable stock in a large flameproof casserole and cook over a low heat, stirring occasionally, for 20 minutes.

2 Add the leek, garlic, tomatoes and their can juice, ground cumin, chilli powder, garam masala, sliced pepper, broccoli, corn cobs and French beans to the pan. Stir.

3 Bring the mixture to the boil, reduce the heat, cover and simmer for a further 10–15 minutes or until the vegetables are tender.

4 Add the shredded basil and season with salt and pepper to taste.

5 Garnish with fresh basil sprigs and serve immediately.

SERVES 4

225 g/8 oz split red lentils, washed
55 g/2 oz long-grain rice
1.2 litres/2 pints vegetable stock
1 leek, cut into chunks
3 garlic cloves, crushed
400 g/14 oz canned chopped tomatoes
1 tsp ground cumin
1 tsp chilli powder
1 tsp garam masala
1 red pepper, deseeded and sliced
100 g/3½ oz small broccoli florets
8 baby corn cobs, halved lengthways
55 g/2 oz French beans, halved
1 tbsp shredded fresh basil
salt and pepper
fresh basil sprigs, to garnish

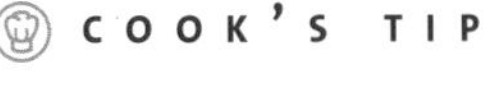

You can vary the rice in this recipe – use brown or wild rice, if you prefer.

NUTRITION

Calories *312*; Sugars *9 g*; Protein *20 g*; Carbohydrate *51 g*; Fat *2 g*; Saturates *0.4 g*

 easy

15 mins

 40 mins

The red of the tomatoes is a great contrast to the cauliflower and herbs, making this dish appealing to both the eye and the palate.

Cauliflower Bake

SERVES 4

- 500 g/1 lb 2 oz cauliflower, broken into florets
- 600 g/1 lb 5 oz potatoes, cubed
- 100 g/3½ oz cherry tomatoes

sauce

- 2 tbsp butter or margarine
- 1 leek, sliced
- 1 garlic clove, crushed
- 3 tbsp plain flour
- 300 ml/10 fl oz milk
- 85 g/3 oz mixed cheese, such as Cheddar, Parmesan and Gruyère, grated
- ½ tsp paprika
- 2 tbsp chopped fresh flat-leaved parsley
- salt and pepper
- chopped fresh parsley, to garnish

1 Cook the cauliflower in a saucepan of boiling water for 10 minutes. Drain well and reserve. Meanwhile, cook the potatoes in a pan of boiling water for 10 minutes, drain and reserve.

2 To make the sauce, melt the butter or margarine in a saucepan and sauté the leek and garlic for 1 minute. Stir in the flour and cook, stirring constantly, for 1 minute. Remove the pan from the heat and gradually stir in the milk, 55 g/2 oz of the cheese, the paprika and parsley. Return the pan to the heat and bring to the boil, stirring constantly. Season with salt and pepper to taste.

3 Spoon the cauliflower into a deep ovenproof dish. Add the cherry tomatoes and top with the potatoes. Pour the sauce over the potatoes and sprinkle on the remaining grated cheese.

4 Cook in a preheated oven, 180°C/350°F/Gas Mark 4, for 20 minutes or until the vegetables are cooked through and the cheese is golden-brown and bubbling. Garnish and serve immediately.

NUTRITION

Calories *305*; Sugars *9 g*; Protein *15 g*; Carbohydrate *31 g*; Fat *14 g*; Saturates *6 g*

easy

10 mins

40 mins

COOK'S TIP

This dish could be made with broccoli instead of cauliflower.

This is a very colourful and nutritious dish, packed full of crunchy vegetables in a tasty white wine sauce.

Potato-topped Vegetables

1 Cook the carrot, cauliflower, broccoli, fennel and beans in a large saucepan of boiling water for 10 minutes until just tender. Drain the vegetables thoroughly and set aside.

2 Melt the butter in a saucepan. Stir in the flour and cook for 1 minute. Remove from the heat and stir in the stock, wine and milk. Return to the heat and bring to the boil, stirring until thickened. Stir in the reserved vegetables, mushrooms and sage.

3 Meanwhile, make the topping. Cook the potatoes in boiling water for 10–15 minutes. Drain and mash with the butter, yogurt and half the cheese. Stir in the fennel seeds. Season to taste.

4 Spoon the vegetable mixture into a 1-litre/1¾-pint pie dish. Spoon the potato over the top and sprinkle with the remaining cheese. Cook in a preheated oven, 190°C/375°F/Gas Mark 5, for 30–35 minutes or until golden. Serve hot.

SERVES 4

- 1 carrot, diced
- 175 g/6 oz cauliflower florets
- 175 g/6 oz broccoli florets
- 1 fennel bulb, sliced
- 85 g/3 oz French beans, halved
- 2 tbsp butter
- 2½ tbsp plain flour
- 150 ml/5 fl oz vegetable stock
- 150 ml/5 fl oz dry white wine
- 150 ml/5 fl oz milk
- 175 g/6 oz chestnut mushrooms, quartered
- 2 tbsp chopped fresh sage

topping

- 900 g/2 lb floury potatoes, diced
- 2 tbsp butter
- 4 tbsp natural yogurt
- 70 g/2½ oz Parmesan cheese, freshly grated
- 1 tsp fennel seeds
- salt and pepper

NUTRITION

Calories *413* Sugars *11 g*; Protein *19 g*; Carbohydrate *41 g*; Fat *18 g*; Saturates *11 g*

easy

 20 mins

 1 hr 15 mins

This dish can be cooked in a single large dish or in four individual Yorkshire pudding tins.

Vegetable Toad-in-the-hole

SERVES 4

100 g/3½ oz plain flour
2 eggs, beaten
200 ml/7 fl oz milk
2 tbsp wholegrain mustard
2 tbsp vegetable oil

filling

25 g/1 oz butter
2 garlic cloves, crushed
1 onion, cut into eight
75 g/2¾ oz baby carrots, halved lengthways
50 g/1¾ oz French beans
50 g/1¾ oz canned sweetcorn, drained
2 tomatoes, seeded and cut into chunks
1 tsp wholegrain mustard
1 tbsp chopped mixed herbs
salt and pepper

1 To make the batter, sift the flour and a pinch of salt into a bowl. Beat in the eggs and milk to make a batter. Stir in the mustard and leave to stand.

2 Pour the oil into a shallow ovenproof dish and heat in a preheated oven, 200°C/400°F/ Gas Mark 6, for 10 minutes.

3 To make the filling, melt the butter in a frying pan and sauté the garlic and onion, stirring constantly, for 2 minutes. Cook the carrots and beans in a saucepan of boiling water for 7 minutes, or until tender. Drain well.

4 Add the sweetcorn and tomatoes to the frying pan with the mustard and chopped mixed herbs. Season well and add the carrots and beans.

5 Remove the heated dish from the oven and pour in the batter. Spoon the vegetables into the centre, return to the oven and cook for 30–35 minutes, until the batter has risen and set. Serve immediately.

NUTRITION

Calories *313*; Sugars *9 g*; Protein *9 g*; Carbohydrate *31 g*; Fat *18 g*; Saturates *7 g*

 moderate
15 mins
55 mins

This is a dish of Persian origin, not Chinese as it sounds. Aubergines are fried and mixed with tomatoes, mint, sugar and vinegar.

Sweet *and* Sour Vegetables

1 Using a sharp knife, cut the aubergines into cubes. Put them in a colander, sprinkle with plenty of salt and leave to stand for 30 minutes. Rinse thoroughly under cold running water to remove all traces of the salt and drain thoroughly. This process removes all the bitter juices from the aubergines. Pat dry with kitchen paper.

2 Heat the oil in a large, heavy-based frying pan.

3 Add the aubergine and sauté over a medium heat, stirring, for 1–2 minutes, until beginning to colour.

4 Stir in the garlic and onion wedges and cook, stirring constantly, for a further 2–3 minutes.

5 Stir in the tomatoes, mint and vegetable stock. Lower the heat, cover with a lid and simmer for about 15–20 minutes, or until the aubergine is tender.

6 Add the brown sugar, red wine vinegar and chilli flakes, then season with salt and pepper and cook for a further 2–3 minutes, stirring constantly.

7 Transfer to a warmed serving dish, garnish the aubergine with fresh mint sprigs and serve immediately.

SERVES 4

2 large aubergines
6 tbsp olive oil
4 garlic cloves, crushed
1 onion, cut into eight
4 large tomatoes, deseeded and chopped
3 tbsp chopped mint
150 ml/¼ pint vegetable stock
4 tsp brown sugar
2 tbsp red wine vinegar
1 tsp chilli flakes
salt and pepper
sprigs of fresh mint, to garnish

NUTRITION

Calories *218*; Sugars *12 g*; Protein *3 g*; Carbohydrate *14 g*; Fat *17 g*; Saturates *3 g*

easy

 45 mins

 30 mins

This colourful and tasty lasagne has layers of vegetables in tomato sauce and aubergines, all topped with a rich cheese sauce.

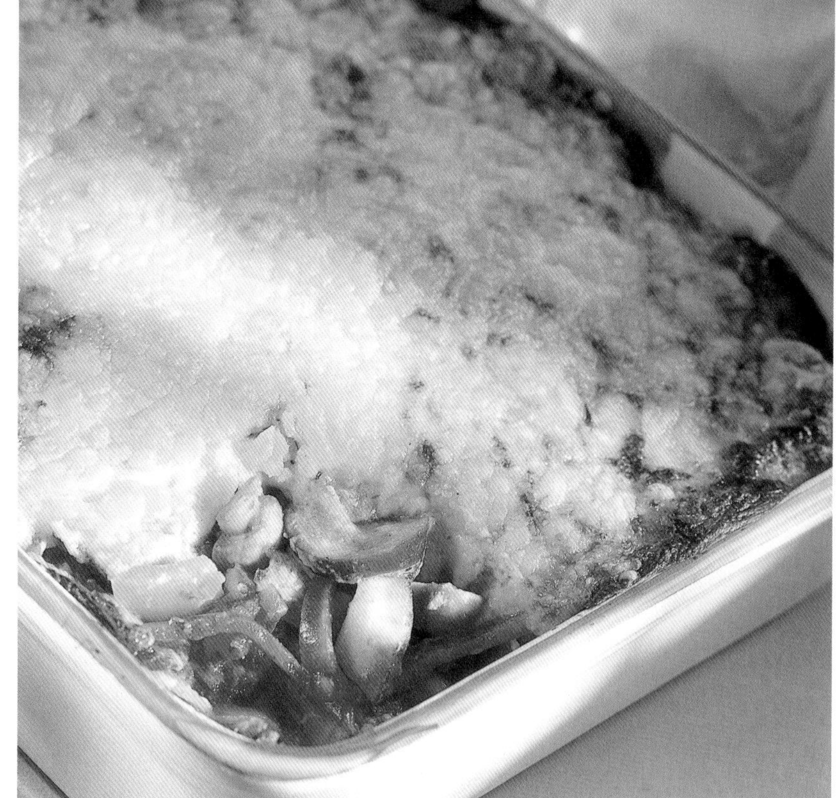

Vegetable Lasagne

SERVES 4

1 aubergine, sliced
3 tbsp olive oil
2 garlic cloves, crushed
1 red onion, halved and sliced
3 mixed peppers, deseeded and diced
225 g/8 oz mixed mushrooms, sliced
2 celery sticks, sliced
1 courgette, diced
½ tsp chilli powder
½ tsp ground cumin
2 tomatoes, chopped
300 ml/½ pint passata
2 tbsp chopped basil
8 no pre-cook lasagne verdi sheets
salt and pepper

cheese sauce

2 tbsp butter or margarine
1 tbsp flour
150ml/¼ pint vegetable stock
300 ml/½ pint milk
75 g/2¾ oz grated Cheddar cheese
1 tsp Dijon mustard
1 tbsp chopped basil
1 egg, beaten

NUTRITION

Calories *544*; Sugars *18 g*; Protein *20 g*; Carbohydrate *61 g*; Fat *26 g*; Saturates *12 g*

easy

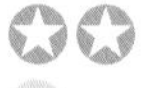

35 mins

55 mins

1 Place the aubergine slices in a colander, sprinkle them with salt and leave for 20 minutes. Rinse under cold running water, drain and reserve.

2 Heat the oil in a pan and sauté the garlic and onion for 1–2 minutes. Add the peppers, mushrooms, celery and courgette and cook, stirring constantly, for 3–4 minutes.

3 Stir in the spices and cook for 1 minute. Mix in the chopped tomatoes, passata and basil and season to taste with salt and pepper.

4 For the sauce, melt the butter in a pan, stir in the flour and cook for 1 minute. Remove from the heat, stir in the stock and milk, return to the heat and add half the cheese and the mustard. Boil, stirring, until thickened. Stir in the basil. Remove from the heat and stir in the egg.

5 Place half the lasagne sheets in an ovenproof dish. Top with half the vegetable mixture then half the aubergines. Repeat the layers and spoon the cheese sauce over the top.

6 Sprinkle the lasagne with the remaining cheese and cook in a preheated oven, 180°C/350°F/Gas Mark 4, for 40 minutes, until the top is golden brown.

This is a really simple, family dish which is inexpensive and easy to prepare and cook. Serve with a salad or fresh green vegetables.

Macaroni Cheese *and* Tomato

1 To make the tomato sauce, heat the oil in a heavy-based pan. Add the shallots and garlic and cook, stirring constantly, for 1 minute. Add the tomatoes and basil and season with salt and pepper to taste. Cook over a medium heat, stirring constantly, for 10 minutes.

2 Meanwhile, bring a large pan of lightly salted water to the boil. Add the macaroni, bring back to the boil and cook for 8 minutes or until tender, but still firm to the bite. Drain well.

3 Combine the grated Cheddar and Parmesan in a bowl. Grease a deep, ovenproof dish. Spoon one third of the tomato sauce into the base of the dish, cover with one third of the macaroni and then top with one third of the mixed cheeses. Season to taste with salt and pepper. Repeat these layers twice, ending with a layer of grated cheese.

4 Combine the breadcrumbs and basil and sprinkle evenly over the top. Dot the topping with the butter or margarine and cook in a preheated oven, 190°C/375°F/Gas Mark 5, for 25 minutes or until the the topping is golden-brown and bubbling. Serve immediately.

SERVES 4

225 g/8 oz dried elbow macaroni
175 g/6 oz grated Cheddar cheese
100 g/3½ oz grated Parmesan cheese
1 tbsp butter or margarine, plus extra for greasing
4 tbsp fresh white breadcrumbs
1 tbsp chopped fresh basil

tomato sauce

1 tbsp olive oil
1 shallot, chopped finely
2 garlic cloves, crushed
500 g/1 lb 2 oz canned chopped tomatoes
1 tbsp chopped fresh basil
salt and pepper

NUTRITION

Calories *592*; Sugars *6 g*; Protein *28 g*; Carbohydrate *57 g*; Fat *29 g*; Saturates *17 g*

 easy

 15 mins

35–40 mins

Fish *and* Seafood

The range of seafood available these days is immense, but sometimes it is difficult to know how to cook unfamiliar fish. The answer might be to put it in a pot and make a fabulous stew. Jambalaya (see page 156), Italian Fish Stew (see page 157) or Bouillabaisse (see page 159) are as different as their countries of origin, equally delicious and incredibly easy to make. Another answer might be to stir it with rice to make an elegant Crab Risotto (see page 170) or to combine it with chillies and other spices in a one-pot Goan Fish Curry (see page 155). Then, again, there are soups and chowders, bakes and pasta dishes – and not an unhealthy chip in sight. There are recipes for inexpensive family meals and dishes for sophisticated entertaining, featuring seafood of all kinds from cod to prawns and from sardines to squid – even a lobster one-pot.

This is a traditional, creamy Scottish soup. As the smoked haddock has quite a strong flavour, it has been mixed with some fresh cod.

Cullen Skink

SERVES 4

225 g/8 oz undyed smoked haddock fillet
2 tbsp butter
1 onion, chopped finely
600 ml/1 pint milk
350 g/12 oz potatoes, diced
350 g/12 oz cod, boned, skinned and cubed
150 ml/5 fl oz double cream
2 tbsp chopped fresh parsley
lemon juice, to taste
salt and pepper

to garnish
lemon slices
parsley sprigs

1 Put the haddock fillet in a large frying pan and cover with boiling water. Leave for 10 minutes. Drain, reserving 300 ml/10 fl oz of the soaking water. Flake the fish, taking care to remove all the bones.

2 Heat the butter in a large saucepan and add the onion. Cook gently for 10 minutes until softened. Add the milk and bring to a gentle simmer before adding the potatoes. Cook for 10 minutes.

3 Add the reserved haddock flakes and cod. Simmer for an additional 10 minutes until the cod is tender.

4 Remove about one third of the fish and potatoes, put in a food processor and blend until smooth. Alternatively, push through a sieve into a bowl. Return to the soup with the cream, parsley and seasoning. Taste and add a little lemon juice, if desired. Add a little of the reserved soaking water if the soup seems too thick. Reheat gently and serve the soup immediately.

NUTRITION

Calories *108*; Sugars *2.3 g*; Protein *7.4 g*; Carbohydrate *5.6 g*; Fat *6.4 g*; Saturates *4 g*

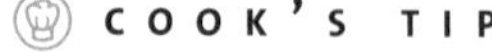

 moderate
20 mins
40 mins

COOK'S TIP

Look for Finnan haddock, if you can find it. Do not use yellow-dyed haddock fillet, which is often actually whiting and not haddock at all.

Juicy chunks of fish and sumptuous shellfish are cooked in a flavoursome stock. Serve with toasted bread rubbed with garlic.

Mediterranean Fish Soup

1 Heat the olive oil in a large, heavy-based saucepan and gently fry the onion and garlic for 2–3 minutes, until just softened.

2 Pour in the stock and wine and bring to the boil.

3 Tie the bay leaf and herbs together with string and add to the saucepan with the fish and mussels. Stir, cover and simmer for 5 minutes.

4 Stir in the tomatoes and prawns and continue to cook for a further 3–4 minutes, until piping hot and the fish is cooked through.

5 Discard the herbs and any mussels that have not opened. Season with salt and pepper to taste, then ladle into warm soup bowls.

6 Garnish with sprigs of fresh thyme and serve with lemon wedges and toasted bread rubbed with garlic.

SERVES 4

- 1 tbsp olive oil
- 1 large onion, chopped
- 2 garlic cloves, chopped finely
- 450 ml/15 fl oz Fresh Fish Stock (see page 14)
- 150 ml/5 fl oz dry white wine
- 1 bay leaf
- 1 sprig each of fresh thyme, rosemary and oregano
- 450 g/1 lb firm white fish fillets, such as cod, monkfish or halibut, skinned and cut into 2.5-cm/1-inch cubes
- 450 g/1 lb fresh mussels, prepared
- 400 g/14 oz canned chopped tomatoes
- 225 g/8 oz peeled, cooked prawns, thawed if frozen
- salt and pepper
- sprigs of fresh thyme, to garnish

to serve

- lemon wedges
- 4 slices toasted French bread, rubbed with a cut garlic clove

NUTRITION

Calories *316*; Sugars *4 g*; Protein *53 g*; Carbohydrate *5 g*; Fat *7 g*; Saturates *1 g*

moderate

1 hr

15 mins

Any mixture of fish is suitable for this recipe, from simple smoked and white fish to salmon or mussels, depending on the occasion.

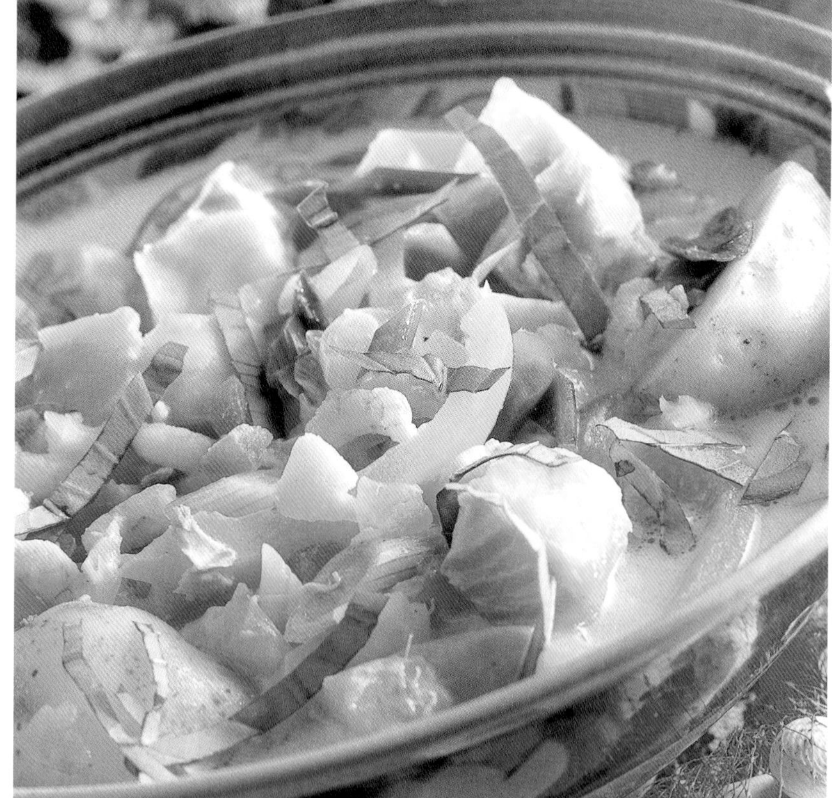

Mixed Fish Soup

SERVES 4

2 tbsp vegetable oil
450 g/1 lb small new potatoes, halved
1 bunch spring onions, sliced
1 yellow pepper, sliced
2 garlic cloves, crushed
225 ml/8 fl oz dry white wine
600 ml/1 pint fish stock
225 g/8 oz white fish fillet, skinned and cubed
225 g/8 oz smoked cod fillet, skinned and cubed
2 tomatoes, peeled, deseeded and chopped
100 g/3½ oz peeled cooked prawns
150 ml/5 fl oz double cream
2 tbsp shredded fresh basil

1 Heat the vegetable oil in a large saucepan and add the halved potatoes, spring onions, pepper and garlic. Sauté the vegetables gently for 3 minutes, stirring constantly.

2 Add the white wine and fish stock and bring to the boil. Reduce the heat and simmer for 10–15 minutes.

3 Add the fish fillet cubes and chopped tomatoes and continue to cook for 10 minutes or until the fish is cooked through completely.

4 Stir in the cooked prawns, the cream and the shredded basil and cook for 2–3 minutes. Pour the soup into warmed bowls and serve immediately.

NUTRITION

Calories *458*; Sugars *5 g*; Protein *28 g*; Carbohydrate *22 g*; Fat *25 g*; Saturates *12 g*

 easy
10 mins
35 mins

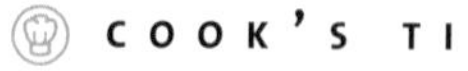

COOK'S TIP

For a soup that is slightly less rich, omit the wine and stir natural yogurt into the soup instead of the double cream.

This is also known as Tom Yam Gung. Oriental supermarkets may sell tom yam sauce ready prepared in jars, sometimes labelled 'Chillies in Oil'.

Thai Fish Soup

1 First make the tom yam sauce. Heat the oil in a small pan, cook the garlic briefly until just brown, remove with a slotted spoon and set aside. Cook the shallot in the oil until brown and crisp. Remove with a slotted spoon, add the chillies, and fry until they darken. Remove and drain on kitchen paper. Take the pan off the hob and save the oil for later use.

2 In a small food processor or spice grinder, grind the dried shrimps, if using, then add the reserved chillies, garlic and shallot. Grind to a smooth paste. Return the paste to the original pan over a low heat. Mix in the fish sauce and sugar. Remove from the heat.

3 Heat the stock and 2 tablespoons of the tom yam sauce in a large saucepan. Add the lime leaves, lemon grass, lemon juice, fish sauce, chillies and sugar. Simmer for 2 minutes.

4 Add the mushrooms and prawns and cook for a further 2–3 minutes until the prawns are cooked. Ladle the soup into warm bowls and serve immediately, garnished with spring onion.

SERVES 4

450 ml/16 fl oz light chicken stock
2 lime leaves, chopped
5-cm/2-inch piece of lemon grass, chopped
3 tbsp lemon juice
3 tbsp Thai fish sauce
2 small, hot green chillies, deseeded and chopped finely
½ tsp sugar
8 small shiitake mushrooms, halved
450 g/1 lb raw prawns, peeled if necessary and deveined
spring onions, to garnish

tom yam sauce

4 tbsp vegetable oil
5 garlic cloves, chopped finely
1 large shallot, chopped finely
2 large hot dried red chillies, chopped
1 tbsp dried shrimps (optional)
1 tbsp Thai fish sauce
2 tsp sugar

NUTRITION

Calories *230*; Sugars *4 g*; Protein *22 g*; Carbohydrate *9 g*; Fat *12 g*; Saturates *1 g*

 moderate

25 mins

5 mins

This soup is based on the classic Chinese chicken and sweetcorn soup, but the delicate flavour of the crab works very well.

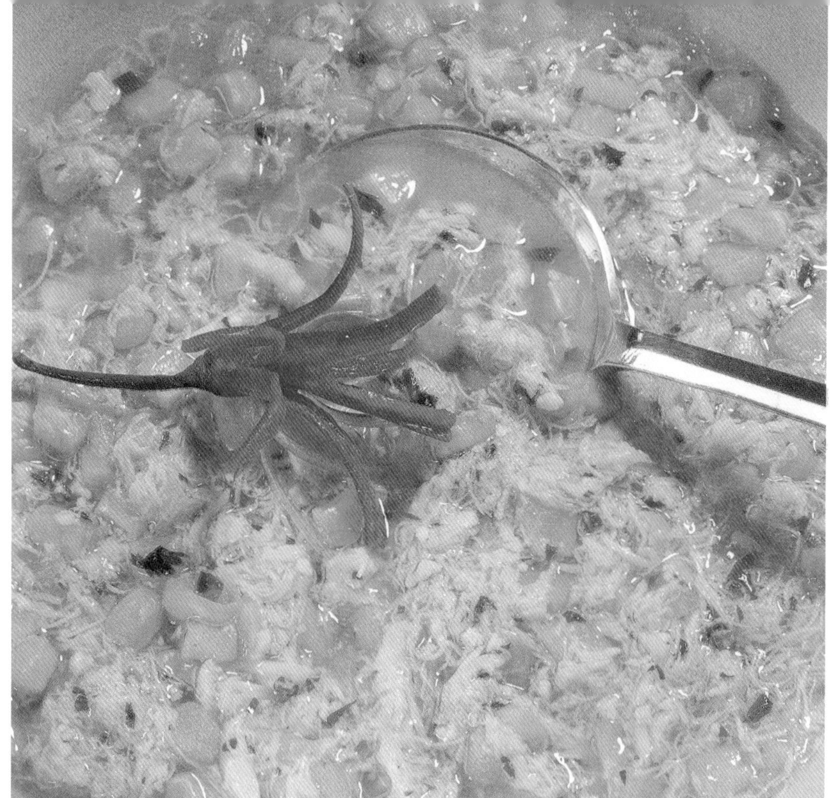

Chinese Crab *and* Sweetcorn Soup

SERVES 4

- 1 tbsp vegetable oil
- 1 small onion, chopped finely
- 1 garlic clove, chopped finely
- 1 tsp grated fresh root ginger
- 1 small red chilli, deseeded and finely chopped
- 2 tbsp dry sherry or Chinese rice wine
- 225 g/8 oz fresh white crab meat
- 326 g/11 oz can sweetcorn, drained
- 600 ml/1 pint light chicken stock
- 1 tbsp light soy sauce
- 2 tbsp chopped fresh coriander
- 2 eggs, beaten
- salt and pepper
- chilli 'flowers', to garnish

1 Heat the oil in a large saucepan and add the onion. Cook gently for 5 minutes until softened. Add the garlic, ginger and chilli and cook gently for a further minute.

2 Add the sherry or rice wine and bubble until reduced by half. Add the crab meat, sweetcorn, chicken stock and soy sauce. Bring to the boil and simmer gently for 5 minutes. Stir in the coriander. Season to taste.

3 Remove from the heat and pour in the eggs. Wait for a few seconds and then stir well, to break the eggs into ribbons. Serve the soup immediately, garnished with chilli 'flowers'.

NUTRITION

Calories *248*; Sugars *8 g*; Protein *18 g*; Carbohydrate *20 g*; Fat *10 g*; Saturates *2 g*

easy

10 mins

15 mins

COOK'S TIP

For convenience, you could use canned crab meat. Make sure it is well drained before adding it to the soup.

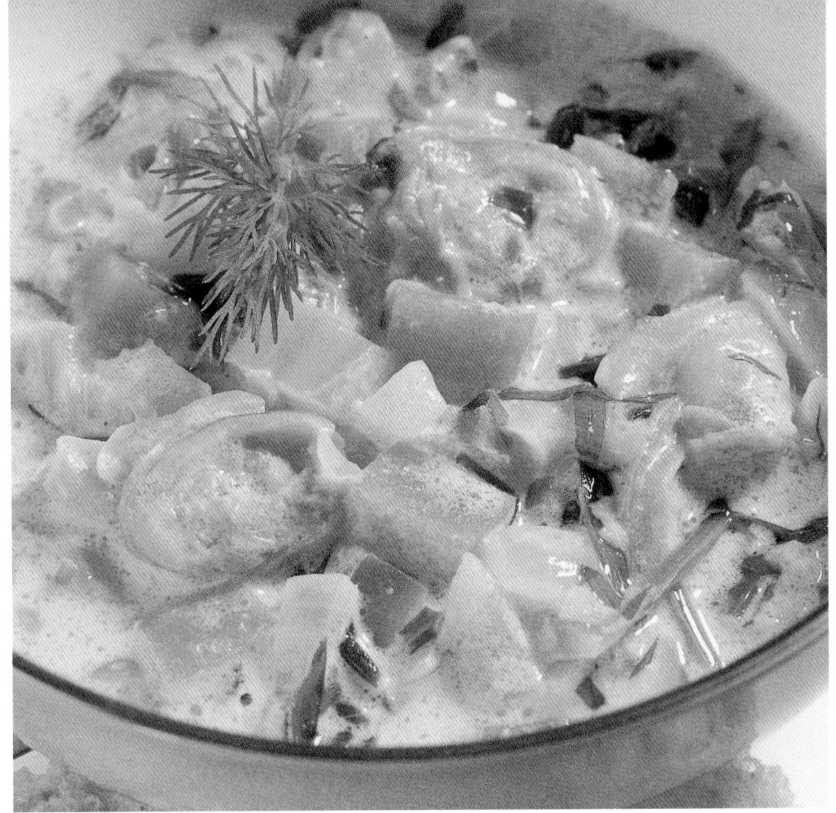

This recipe is intended to be served in small quantities. It is very rich and full of flavour.

Clam *and* Sorrel Soup

1 Put the clams in a large saucepan with the onion and wine. Cover and cook over a high heat for 3–4 minutes until the clams have opened. Strain, reserving the cooking liquid, but discarding the onion. Set aside the clams until they are cool enough to handle.

2 In a clean saucepan, melt the butter over a low heat. Add the carrot, shallots and celery and cook very gently for 10 minutes until softened but not coloured. Add the reserved cooking liquid and bay leaves and simmer for a further 10 minutes.

3 Meanwhile, roughly chop the clams, if large. Add to the soup with the cream and sorrel. Simmer for a further 2–3 minutes until the sorrel has collapsed. Season with pepper and serve immediately, garnished with dill, with plenty of crusty bread.

SERVES 4

900 g/2 lb live clams, scrubbed
1 onion, chopped finely
150 ml/5 fl oz dry white wine
50 g/1¼ oz butter
1 small carrot, diced finely
2 shallots, diced finely
1 stick celery, diced finely
2 bay leaves
150 ml/5 fl oz double cream
25 g/1 oz shredded sorrel
pepper
crusty bread, to serve
dill, to garnish

NUTRITION

Calories *348*; Sugars *5 g*; Protein *10 g*; Carbohydrate *7 g*; Fat *29 g*; Saturates *18 g*

 easy
20 mins
30 mins

COOK'S TIP

Sorrel is a large-leafed herb with a slightly sour, lemony flavour that goes very well with fish. It is increasingly easy to find in larger supermarkets, but is also incredibly easy to grow, as a plant.

Packed full of flavour, this delicious fish dish is really a meal in itself, but it is ideal accompanied by a crisp side salad.

Fish *and* Crab Chowder

SERVES 4

1 large onion, chopped finely
2 celery sticks, chopped finely
150 ml/5 fl oz dry white wine
600 ml/1 pint fish stock
600 ml/1 pint skimmed milk
1 bay leaf
225 g/8 oz smoked cod fillet, skinned and cut into 2.5-cm/1-inch cubes
225 g/8 oz smoked haddock fillets, skinned and cut into 2.5-cm/1-inch cubes
350 g/12 oz canned crab meat, drained
225 g/8 oz French beans, sliced into 2.5-cm/1-inch pieces, blanched
225 g/8 oz cooked brown rice
4 tsp cornflour mixed with 4 tbsp water
salt and pepper
mixed green salad, to serve

1 Place the onion, celery and wine in a large, heavy-based saucepan. Bring to the boil, cover and cook over a low heat for 5 minutes.

2 Uncover the pan and cook for a further 5 minutes, until almost all of the liquid has evaporated.

3 Pour in the stock and milk and add the bay leaf, then bring to the boil. Reduce the heat, then stir in the cod and haddock. Simmer over a low heat, uncovered, for 5 minutes.

4 Add the crab meat, beans and cooked brown rice and simmer gently for 2–3 minutes, until just heated through. Remove the bay leaf with a slotted spoon and discard.

5 Stir in the cornflour mixture until the soup has thickened slightly. Season with salt and pepper to taste and ladle into warm soup bowls. Serve with a mixed green salad.

NUTRITION

Calories *440*; Sugars *10 g*; Protein *49 g*; Carbohydrate *43 g*; Fat *7 g*; Saturates *1 g*

 easy

40 mins

25 mins

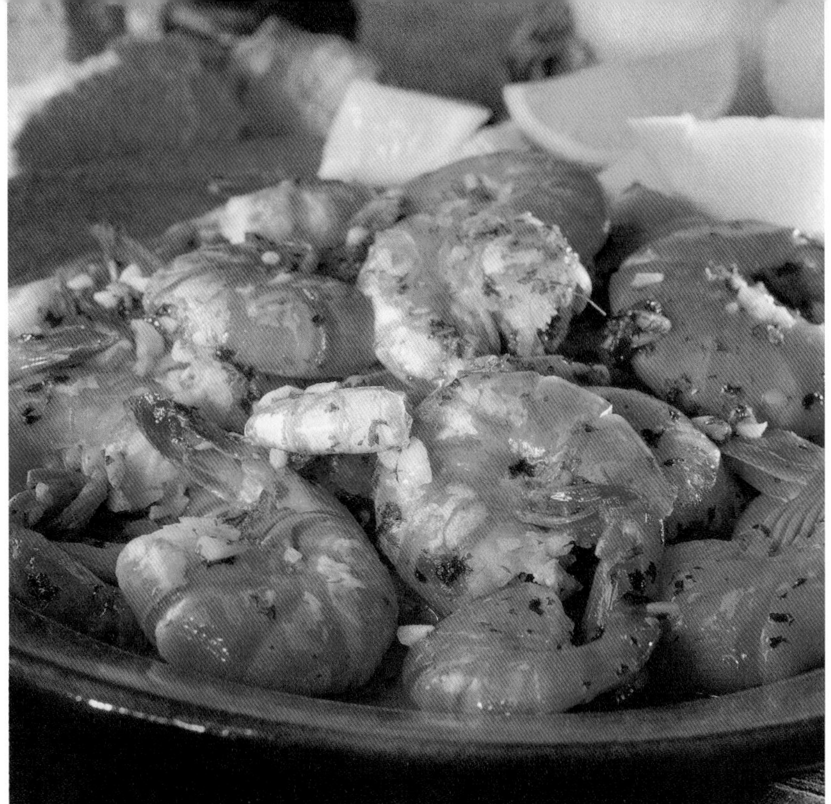

In Spain, giant garlic prawns are cooked in small half-glazed earthenware dishes called *cazuelas*. The prawns arrive at your table sizzling.

Giant Garlic Prawns

1 Heat the olive oil in a large, heavy-based frying pan over a low heat. Add the garlic and chillies and cook, stirring occasionally, for 1–2 minutes until softened but not coloured.

2 Add the prawns and stir-fry for 2–3 minutes until heated through and coated in the oil and garlic mixture.

3 Turn off the heat and add the chopped parsley, stirring well to mix. Season to taste with salt and pepper.

4 Divide the prawns and garlic-flavoured oil between warmed serving dishes and serve with lots of crusty bread. Garnish with lemon wedges.

SERVES 4

125 ml/4 fl oz olive oil
4 garlic cloves, chopped finely
2 hot fresh red chillies, deseeded and finely chopped
450 g/1 lb cooked king prawns
2 tbsp chopped fresh flat-leaved parsley
salt and pepper
lemon wedges, to garnish
crusty bread, to serve

COOK'S TIP

If you can get hold of raw prawns, cook them as above but increase the cooking time to 5–6 minutes until the prawns are cooked through and turn bright pink. If you are using frozen prawns, make sure they are thoroughly thawed before cooking.

NUTRITION

Calories *385*; Sugars *0 g*; Protein *26 g*; Carbohydrate *1 g*; Fat *31 g*; Saturates *5 g*

very easy

5 mins

5–8 mins

This soup-like main course rice dish is packed with a tempting array of fresh seafood and is typically Thai in flavour.

Rice *with* Seafood

SERVES 4

12 live mussels, scrubbed and bearded
2 litres/3½ pints fish stock
2 tbsp vegetable oil
1 garlic clove, crushed
1 tsp grated fresh root ginger
1 fresh red bird's-eye chilli, chopped
2 spring onions, chopped
225 g/8 oz long-grain rice
2 small squid, cleaned and sliced
100 g/3½ oz firm white fish fillet, such as halibut or monkfish, cut into chunks
100 g/3½ oz raw prawns, peeled
2 tbsp Thai fish sauce
3 tbsp chopped fresh coriander

1 Discard any mussels with damaged shells or open ones that do not close when firmly tapped with a knife. Pour 4 tablespoons of the stock into a large pan. Add the mussels, cover and cook over a medium heat, shaking the pan until the mussels open. Remove from the heat and discard any which have failed to open.

2 Heat the oil in a large frying pan or wok and fry the garlic, ginger, chilli and spring onions for 30 seconds. Add the remaining stock and bring to the boil.

3 Stir in the rice, then add the squid, fish chunks and prawns. Lower the heat and simmer gently for 15 minutes or until the rice is cooked. Add the fish sauce and mussels.

4 Ladle into wide bowls and sprinkle with chopped coriander before serving.

NUTRITION

Calories *370*; Sugars *0 g*; Protein *27 g*; Carbohydrate *52 g*; Fat *8 g*; Saturates *1 g*

moderate

5–10 mins

20 mins

COOK'S TIP

You could use leftover cooked rice for this dish. Just simmer the seafood gently until cooked, then stir in the rice at the end.

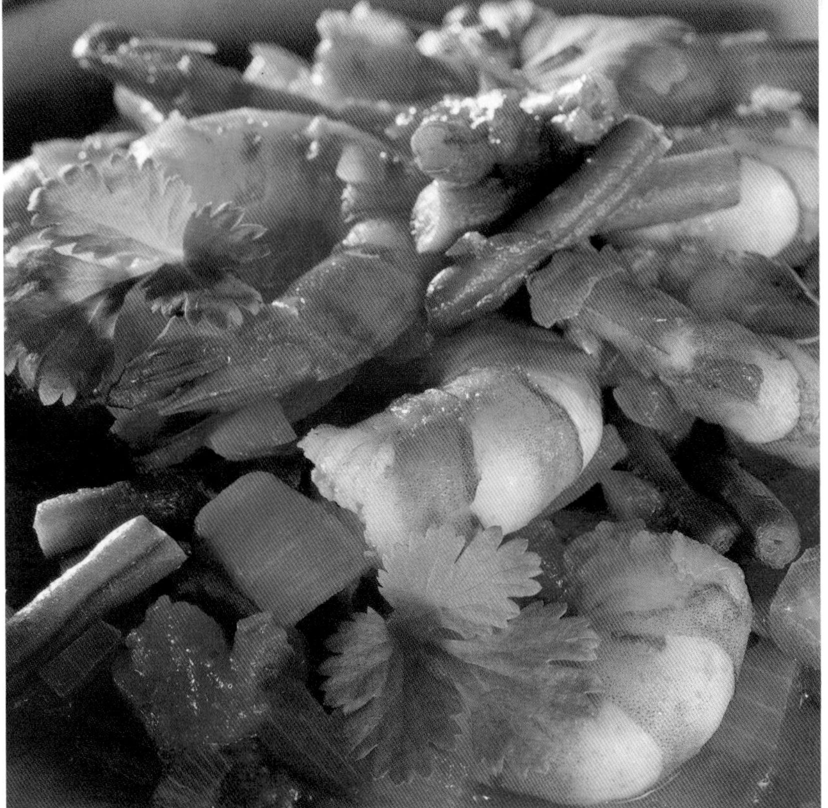

The sweet briny flesh of prawns is wonderful paired with the smoky scent of chipotle chillies.

Prawns *in* Green Sauce

1 Heat the oil in a large pan. Add the onions and garlic and cook over a low heat, stirring occasionally, for about 5–10 minutes until softened. Add the tomatoes and cook for 2 minutes.

2 Add the French beans, cumin, allspice, cinnamon, chipotle chilli and marinade and fish stock. Bring to the boil, then reduce the heat and simmer for a few minutes to combine the flavours.

3 Add the prawns and cook, stirring gently, for 1–2 minutes only, then remove the pan from the heat and set the prawns aside to steep in the hot liquid to finish cooking. They are cooked when they have turned a bright pink colour.

4 Serve the prawns immediately, garnished with the fresh coriander and accompanied by the lime wedges.

SERVES 4

2 tbsp vegetable oil
3 onions, chopped
5 garlic cloves, chopped
5–7 ripe tomatoes, diced
175–225 g/6–8 oz French beans, cut into 5-cm/2-inch pieces and blanched for 1 minute
¼ tsp ground cumin
pinch of ground allspice
pinch of ground cinnamon
½–1 canned chipotle chilli in adobo marinade, with some of the marinade
450 ml/16 fl oz fish stock or water mixed with a fish stock cube
450 g/1 lb raw prawns, peeled
sprigs of fresh coriander
1 lime, cut into wedges

NUTRITION

Calories *225*; Sugars *13 g*; Protein *24 g*; Carbohydrate *17 g*; Fat *8 g*; Saturates *1 g*

 easy

  10 mins

 15–20 mins

COOK'S TIP

If you can find them, use bottled nopales (edible cacti), cut into strips, to add an exotic touch to the dish.

A Thai-influenced dish of rice, cooked in coconut milk, with spicy monkfish and fresh peas – what could be better?

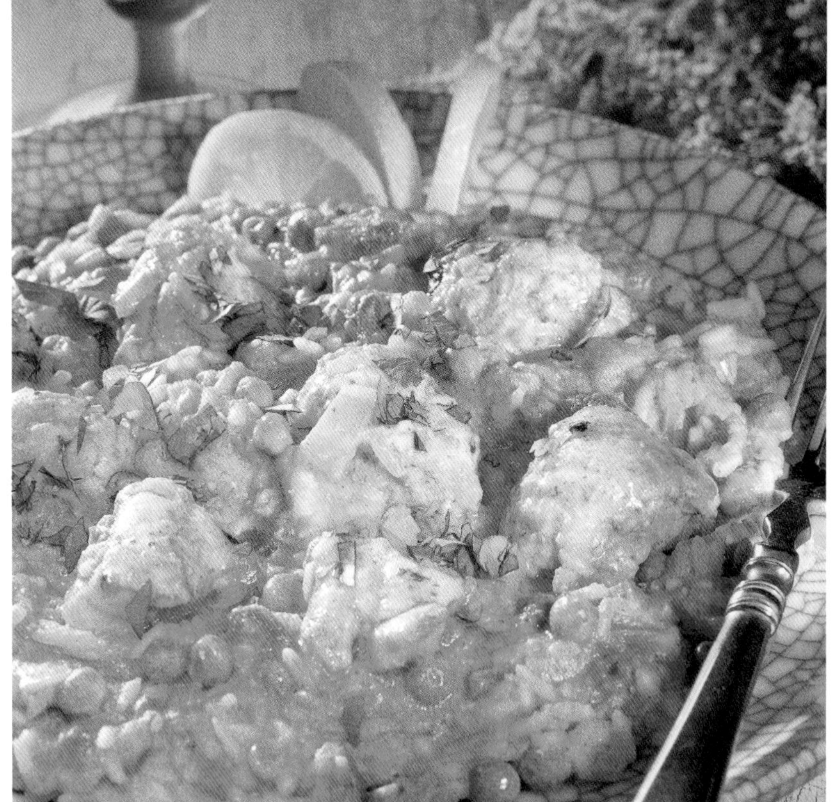

Spicy Monkfish Rice

SERVES 4

1 fresh hot red chilli, deseeded and chopped
1 tsp chilli flakes
2 garlic cloves, chopped
pinch of saffron
3 tbsp roughly chopped fresh mint leaves
4 tbsp olive oil
2 tbsp lemon juice
375 g/12 oz monkfish fillet, cut into bite-sized pieces
1 onion, chopped finely
225 g/8 oz long-grain rice
400g/14 oz canned chopped tomatoes
200 ml/7 fl oz coconut milk
115 g/4 oz peas
salt and pepper
2 tbsp chopped fresh coriander, to garnish

1 Process the chilli, chill flakes, garlic, saffron, mint, olive oil and lemon juice in a food processor or blender until combined, but not smooth.

2 Put the monkfish into a non-metallic dish and pour over the spice paste, turning to coat. Cover and set aside for 20 minutes to marinate.

3 Heat a large pan until very hot. Using a slotted spoon, lift the monkfish from the marinade and add, in batches, to the hot pan. Cook for 3–4 minutes until browned and firm. Remove with a draining spoon and set aside.

4 Add the onion and remaining marinade to the pan and cook for 5 minutes until softened and lightly browned. Add the rice and stir until well coated. Add the tomatoes and coconut milk. Bring to the boil, cover and simmer very gently for 15 minutes. Stir in the peas, season and arrange the fish over the top. Cover with foil and continue to cook over a very low heat for 5 minutes. Serve garnished with the chopped coriander.

NUTRITION

Calories *440*; Sugars *8 g*; Protein *22 g*; Carbohydrate *60 g*; Fat *14 g*; Saturates *2 g*

easy

 30 mins

 30 mins

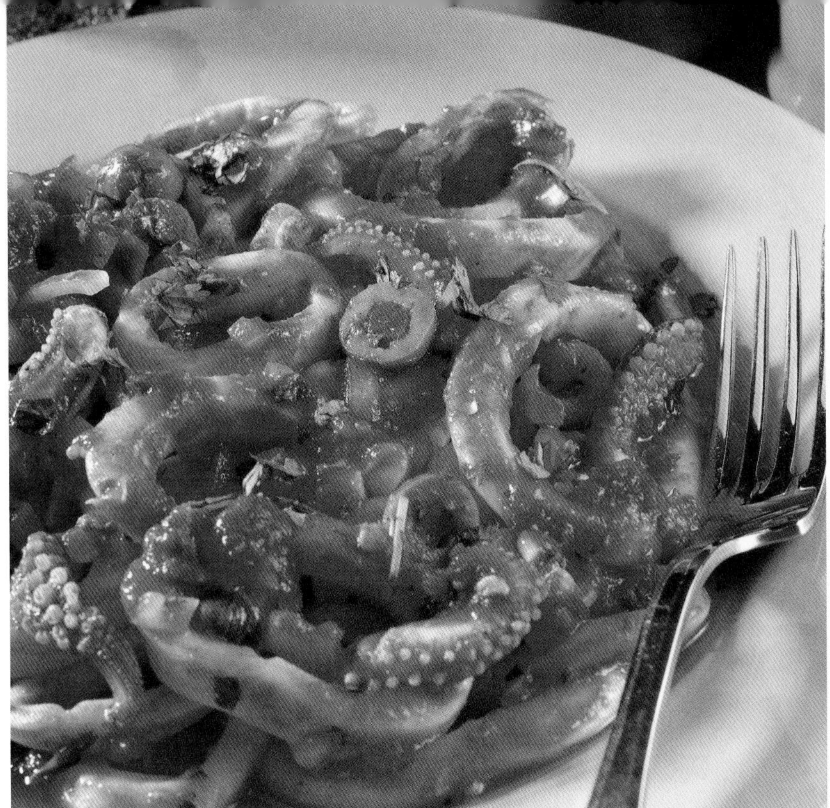

This flavoursome squid dish from Vera Cruz in Mexico would be good with warmed flour tortillas, for do-it-yourself tacos.

Simmered Squid

1 Heat the oil in a pan and lightly fry the squid until it turns opaque. Season with salt and pepper and remove from the pan with a draining spoon.

2 Add the onion and garlic to the remaining oil in the pan and cook until softened. Stir in the tomatoes, chilli, herbs, cinnamon, allspice, sugar and olives. Cover and cook over a medium-low heat for 5–10 minutes until the mixture thickens slightly. Uncover the pan and cook for a further 5 minutes to concentrate the flavours and reduce the liquid.

3 Stir in the reserved squid and any of the juices that have gathered. Add the capers and heat through.

4 Adjust the seasoning if necessary, then serve immediately, garnished with fresh coriander.

SERVES 4

3 tbsp extra virgin olive oil
900 g/2 lb cleaned squid, cut into rings and tentacles
1 onion, chopped
3 garlic cloves, chopped
400 g/14 oz canned chopped tomatoes
½–1 fresh mild green chilli, deseeded and chopped
1 tbsp finely chopped fresh parsley
¼ tsp chopped fresh thyme
¼ tsp chopped fresh oregano
¼ tsp chopped fresh marjoram
pinch of ground cinnamon
pinch of ground allspice
pinch of sugar
15–20 pimiento-stuffed green olives, sliced
1 tbsp capers
salt and pepper
1 tbsp chopped fresh coriander, to garnish

NUTRITION

Calories *307*; Sugars *6 g*; Protein *36 g*; Carbohydrate *10 g*; Fat *14 g*; Saturates *2 g*

easy

10 mins

20 mins

This is a modern version of the classic dish, using smoked salmon as well as fresh salmon and lots of fresh herbs – perfect for a dinner party.

A Modern Kedgeree

SERVES 4

- 2 tbsp butter
- 1 tbsp olive oil
- 1 onion, chopped finely
- 1 garlic clove, chopped finely
- 175 g/6 oz long-grain rice
- 400 ml/14 fl oz fish stock
- 175 g/6 oz salmon fillet, skinned and chopped
- 85 g/3 oz smoked salmon, chopped
- 2 tbsp double cream
- 2 tbsp chopped fresh dill
- 3 spring onions, chopped finely
- salt and pepper

to garnish

- sprigs of fresh dill
- lemon slices

1 Melt the butter with the oil in a large saucepan. Add the onion and cook over a low heat for 10 minutes until softened, but not coloured. Add the garlic and cook for a further 30 seconds.

2 Add the rice and cook for 2–3 minutes, stirring constantly, until transparent. Add the fish stock and stir well. Bring to the boil, cover and simmer very gently for 10 minutes.

3 Add the salmon fillet and the smoked salmon and stir well, adding a little more stock or water if the mixture seems dry. Cook for a further 6–8 minutes until the fish and rice are tender and all the stock is absorbed.

4 Turn off the heat and stir in the cream, chopped dill and spring onions. Season to taste with salt and pepper and serve immediately, garnished with sprigs of fresh dill and slices of lemon.

NUTRITION

Calories *370*; Sugars *3 g*; Protein *10 g*; Carbohydrate *39 g*; Fat *190 g*; Saturates *9 g*

easy

10 mins

35 mins

COOK'S TIP

Use smoked salmon trimmings for a budget dish.

An unusual and striking dish with fresh prawns and asparagus is very simple to prepare and ideal for impromptu supper parties.

Prawn *and* Asparagus Risotto

1 Bring the vegetable stock to the boil in a large pan. Add the asparagus and cook for 3 minutes until just tender. Strain, reserving the stock, and refresh the asparagus under cold running water. Drain and set aside.

2 Heat the oil in a large, heavy-based frying pan. Add the onion and cook over a low heat, stirring occasionally, for 5 minutes until softened. Add the garlic and cook for a further 30 seconds. Add the rice and cook, stirring constantly for about 1–2 minutes until coated with the oil and slightly translucent.

3 Keep the stock on a low heat. Increase the heat under the frying pan to medium and begin adding the stock, a ladleful at a time, stirring well between additions. Continue until almost all the stock has been absorbed. This should take 20–25 minutes.

4 Add the prawns and asparagus with the last ladleful of stock and cook for a further 5 minutes until the prawns and rice are tender and the stock has been absorbed. Remove from the heat.

5 Stir in the olive paste, basil and seasoning and set aside for 1 minute. Serve immediately, garnished with Parmesan shavings.

SERVES 4

1.2 litres/2 pints vegetable stock
375 g/12 oz asparagus, cut into 5-cm/2-inch lengths
2 tbsp olive oil
1 onion, chopped finely
1 garlic clove, chopped finely
375 g/12 oz arborio rice
450 g/1 lb raw tiger prawns, peeled and deveined
2 tbsp olive paste or tapénade
2 tbsp chopped fresh basil
salt and pepper
Parmesan cheese shavings, to garnish

NUTRITION
Calories *566*; Sugars *4 g*; Protein *30 g*; Carbohydrate *86 g*; Fat *14 g*; Saturates *2 g*

moderate
10 mins
40 mins

Fusilli, corkscrew-shaped pasta, is the best shape to use for this recipe because the creamy sauce is absorbed in the twists.

Pasta *with* Tuna *and* Lemon

SERVES 4

60 g/2 oz butter, diced
300 ml/10 fl oz double cream
4 tbsp lemon juice
1 tbsp grated lemon rind
½ tsp anchovy essence
400 g/14 oz dried fusilli
200 g/7 oz canned tuna in olive oil, drained and flaked
salt and pepper

to garnish

2 tbsp finely chopped fresh parsley
grated lemon rind

1 Bring a large saucepan of lightly salted water to the boil. Melt the butter in a large frying pan. Stir in the double cream and lemon juice and leave to simmer, stirring, for about 2 minutes until slightly thickened.

2 Stir in the lemon rind and anchovy essence. Meanwhile, cook the pasta for 10–12 minutes or according to the instructions on the packet until tender, but still firm to the bite. Drain well.

3 Add the sauce to the pasta and toss until well coated. Add the tuna and gently toss until well blended but not too broken up.

4 Season to taste with salt and pepper. Transfer to a platter and garnish with the parsley and lemon rind. Grind over some pepper and serve at once.

NUTRITION

Calories *892*; Sugars *5 g*; Protein *27 g*; Carbohydrate *78 g*; Fat *55 g*; Saturates *32 g*

easy

10 mins

15 mins

COOK'S TIP

For a vegetarian version, omit the tuna and anchovy essence. Add 150 g/5 oz stoned olives instead. For extra 'kick' add a pinch of chilli flakes to the sauce instead of the anchovy essence.

Mussels cooked in beer, tomatoes and Mexican spices are great summertime fare.

Mussels Cooked *with* Lager

1 Scrub the mussels under cold running water to remove any mud. Using a sharp knife, cut away the feathery 'beards' from the shells. Discard any open mussels that do not shut when tapped sharply with a knife. Rinse again under cold running water.

2 Place the lager, onions, garlic, chilli and tomatoes in a heavy-based pan. Bring to the boil.

3 Add the mussels and cook, covered, over a medium-high heat for about 10 minutes until the shells open. Discard any mussels that do not open.

4 Ladle into individual bowls and serve sprinkled with fresh coriander.

SERVES 4

1.5 kg/3 lb 5 oz live mussels
450 ml/16 fl oz lager
2 onions, chopped
5 garlic cloves, chopped coarsely
1 fresh green chilli, such as jalapeño or serrano, deseeded and sliced thinly
175 g/6 oz fresh tomatoes, diced, or canned chopped
2–3 tbsp chopped fresh coriander

NUTRITION

Calories *144*; Sugars *8 g*; Protein *13 g*; Carbohydrate *12 g*; Fat *2 g*; Saturates *0.25 g*

easy

35 mins

15 mins

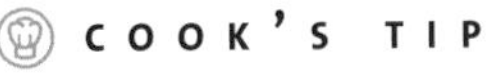

COOK'S TIP

Add the kernels of 2 corn cobs to the lager mixture at Step 2. A pinch of sugar might be needed to bring out the sweetness of the corn.

These delicious large mussels are served hot with a tasty tomato and vegetable sauce. Mop up the delicious sauce with some crusty bread.

Provençale-Style Mussels

SERVES 4

1 tbsp olive oil
1 large onion, chopped finely
1 garlic clove, chopped finely
1 small red pepper, deseeded and chopped finely
1 fresh rosemary sprig
2 bay leaves
400 g/14 oz canned chopped tomatoes
150 ml/5 fl oz/$^2/_3$ cup white wine
1 courgette, diced finely
2 tbsp tomato purée
1 tsp caster sugar
50 g/1$^3/_4$ oz stoned black olives in brine, drained and chopped
675 g/1½ lb cooked New Zealand mussels in their shells
1 tsp grated orange rind
salt and pepper
crusty bread, to serve
2 tbsp chopped fresh parsley, to garnish

1 Heat the olive oil in a large saucepan and gently fry the chopped onion, garlic and pepper for 3–4 minutes until just softened.

2 Add the rosemary and bay leaves to the saucepan with the tomatoes and 100 ml/3½ fl oz of the wine. Season to taste, then bring to the boil and simmer for 15 minutes.

3 Stir in the courgette, tomato purée, sugar and olives. Simmer for 10 minutes.

4 Meanwhile, bring a pan of water to the boil. Arrange the mussels in a steamer or a large sieve and place over the water. Sprinkle with the remaining wine and the orange rind. Cover and steam until the mussels open (discard any that remain closed).

5 Remove the mussels with a slotted spoon and arrange on a serving plate. Discard the herbs and spoon the sauce over the mussels. Garnish with chopped parsley and serve with crusty bread.

NUTRITION

Calories *253*; Sugars *8 g*; Protein *31 g*; Carbohydrate *9 g*; Fat *8 g*; Saturates *1 g*

challenging

5 mins

50 mins

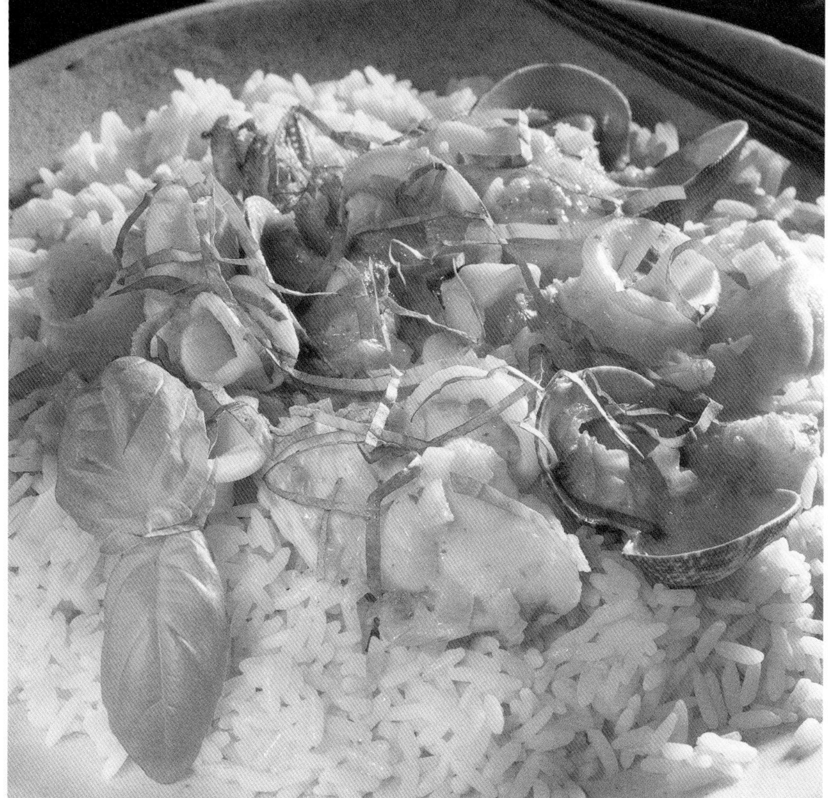

The fish in this fragrant, curry-like stew can be varied according to taste or availability, but do choose ones that stay firm when cooked.

Spicy Thai Seafood Stew

1 Cut the squid body cavities into thick rings and cut the fish fillet into bite-sized chunks.

2 Heat the oil in a large frying pan or wok and stir-fry the shallots, garlic and curry paste for 1–2 minutes. Add the lemon grass and shrimp paste, stir in the coconut milk and bring to the boil.

3 Reduce the heat to low. When the liquid is simmering gently, add the white fish chunks, squid rings and prawns. Stir and then simmer for 2 minutes.

4 Add the clams and simmer for a further minute until the clams open. Discard any clams that do not open.

5 Scatter the shredded basil leaves over the stew and serve immediately, garnished with whole basil leaves and spooned over boiled rice.

SERVES 4

200 g/7 oz prepared squid
500 g/1 lb 2 oz firm white fish fillet, preferably monkfish or halibut
1 tbsp sunflower oil
4 shallots, chopped finely
2 garlic cloves, chopped finely
2 tbsp Thai green curry paste
2 small lemon grass stalks, chopped finely
1 tsp shrimp paste
500 ml/18 fl oz coconut milk
200 g/7 oz raw tiger prawns, peeled and deveined
12 live clams, scrubbed
8 fresh basil leaves, shredded finely, plus extra to garnish
boiled rice, to serve

NUTRITION

Calories *267*; Sugars *7 g*; Protein *42 g*; Carbohydrate *9 g*; Fat *7 g*; Saturates *1 g*

moderate
5 mins
10 mins

COOK'S TIP

If you prefer, fresh mussels in their shells can be used instead of clams – add them at Step 4 and follow the recipe.

This pale green curry paste can be used as the basis for all sorts of Thai dishes. It is also delicious with chicken and beef.

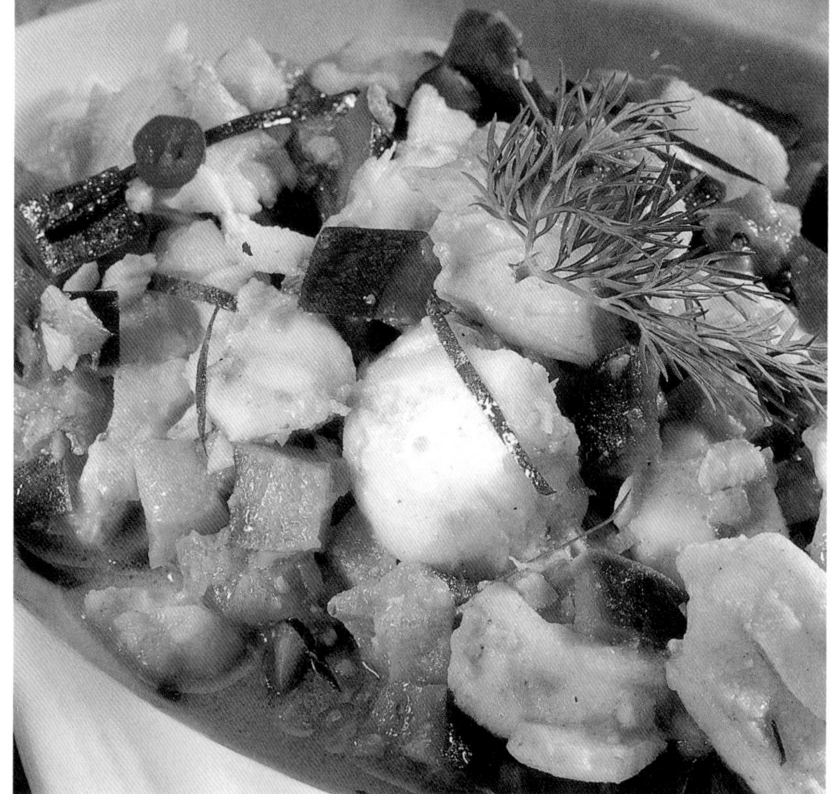

Thai Green Fish Curry

SERVES 4

2 tbsp vegetable oil
1 garlic clove, chopped
1 small aubergine, diced
125 ml/4 fl oz coconut cream
2 tbsp Thai fish sauce
1 tsp sugar
225 g/8 oz firm white fish, cut into pieces, such as cod, haddock or halibut
125 ml/4 fl oz fish stock
2 kaffir lime leaves, shredded finely
about 15 leaves Thai basil, or ordinary basil
plain boiled rice or noodles, to serve

green curry paste

5 fresh green chillies, deseeded and chopped
2 tsp chopped lemon grass
1 large shallot, chopped
2 garlic cloves, chopped
1 tsp grated fresh root ginger or galangal
2 sprigs of fresh coriander, chopped
½ tsp ground coriander
¼ tsp ground cumin
1 kaffir lime leaf, chopped finely
½ tsp salt

NUTRITION

Calories *217*; Sugars *3 g*; Protein *12 g*; Carbohydrate *5 g*; Fat *17 g*; Saturates *10 g*

easy

15 mins
15 mins

1 Make the curry paste. Put all the ingredients into a blender or spice grinder and blend to a smooth paste, adding a little water if necessary. Alternatively, pound together all the ingredients, using a mortar and pestle, until smooth. Set the curry paste aside.

2 Heat the oil in a frying pan or wok until almost smoking. Add the garlic and fry until golden. Add the curry paste and stir-fry for a few seconds before adding the aubergine. Stir-fry for about 4–5 minutes until softened.

3 Add the coconut cream. Bring to the boil and stir until the cream thickens and curdles slightly. Add the fish sauce and sugar and stir into the mixture.

4 Add the fish pieces and stock. Simmer, stirring occasionally, for 3–4 minutes until the fish is just tender. Add the lime leaves and basil, and then cook for a further minute.

5 Transfer to a warmed serving dish and serve with boiled rice or noodles.

Goan cuisine is famous for seafood and vindaloo dishes, which tend to be very hot. This recipe is a mild curry, but very flavoursome.

Goan Fish Curry

1 Put the fish on a plate and drizzle the vinegar over it. Combine half the salt and half the turmeric and sprinkle evenly over the fish. Cover and set aside for 20 minutes.

2 Heat the oil in a heavy-based frying pan and add the garlic. Brown slightly, then add the onion and cook, stirring occasionally, for 3–4 minutes until soft, but not browned. Add the ground coriander and stir for 1 minute.

3 Mix the remaining turmeric, cayenne and paprika with about 2 tablespoons water to make a paste. Add to the pan and cook over a low heat for 1–2 minutes.

4 Stir the tamarind pulp and boiling water. When thickened and the pulp has come away from the seeds, rub through a sieve. Discard the seeds.

5 Add the coconut, warm water and tamarind paste to the pan and stir until the coconut has dissolved. Add the fish and any juices on the plate and simmer gently for 4–5 minutes until the sauce has thickened and the fish is just tender. Serve on a bed of plain boiled rice.

SERVES 4

750 g/1 lb 10 oz monkfish fillet, cut into chunks
1 tbsp cider vinegar
1 tsp salt
1 tsp ground turmeric
3 tbsp vegetable oil
2 garlic cloves, crushed
1 small onion, chopped finely
2 tsp ground coriander
1 tsp cayenne pepper
2 tsp paprika
2 tbsp tamarind pulp plus 2 tbsp boiling water (see Step 4)
85 g/3 oz creamed coconut, cut into pieces
300 ml/ 10 fl oz warm water
plain boiled rice, to serve

NUTRITION

Calories *302*; Sugars *7 g*; Protein *31 g*; Carbohydrate *8 g*; Fat *17 g*; Saturates *7 g*

easy

 30 mins

 15 mins

Jambalaya is a dish of Cajun origin. There are as many versions of this dish as there are people who cook it. Here is a straightforward one.

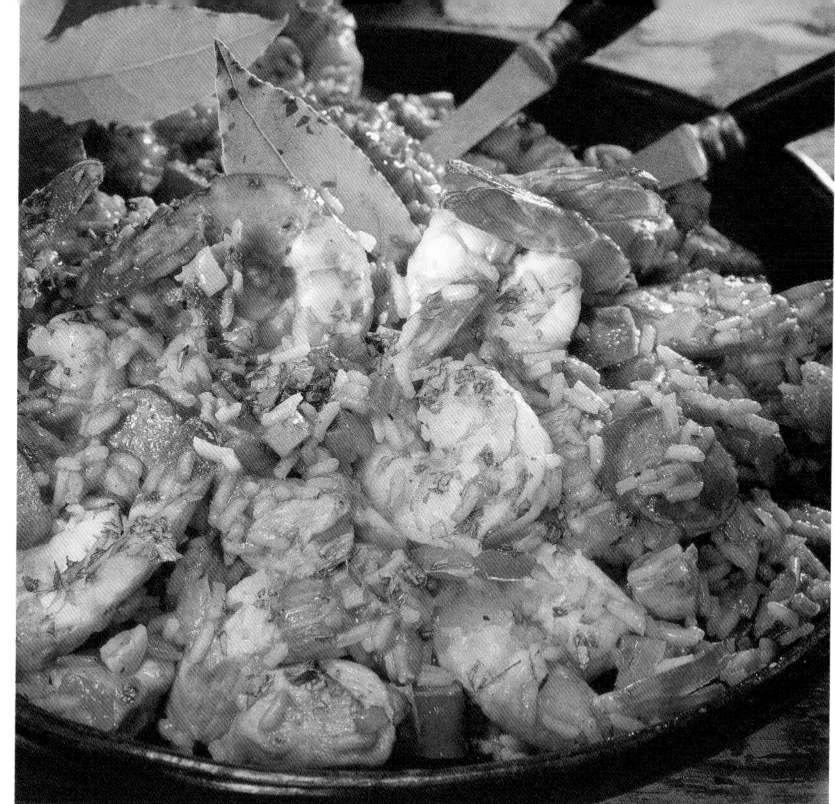

Jambalaya

SERVES 4

- 2 tbsp vegetable oil
- 2 onions, chopped roughly
- 1 green pepper, deseeded and chopped roughly
- 2 celery sticks, chopped roughly
- 3 garlic cloves, chopped finely
- 2 tsp paprika
- 300 g/10½ oz skinless, boneless chicken breasts, chopped
- 100 g/3½ oz kabanos sausages, chopped
- 3 tomatoes, peeled and chopped
- 450 g/1 lb long-grain rice
- 850 ml/1½ pint hot chicken or fish stock
- 1 tsp dried oregano
- 2 bay leaves
- 12 large prawn tails
- 4 spring onions, chopped finely
- 2 tbsp chopped fresh parsley
- salt and pepper
- salad, to serve

1. Heat the vegetable oil in a large frying pan and add the onions, pepper, celery and garlic. Cook over a low heat, stirring occasionally, for about 8–10 minutes until all the vegetables have softened. Add the paprika and cook for a further 30 seconds. Add the chicken and sausages and cook for 8–10 minutes until lightly browned. Add the tomatoes and cook for 2–3 minutes until collapsed.
2. Add the rice to the pan and stir well. Pour in the hot stock and stir in the oregano and bay leaves. Cover and simmer for 10 minutes over a very low heat.
3. Add the prawns and stir well. Cover again and cook for a further 6–8 minutes until the rice is tender and the prawns are cooked through.
4. Stir in the spring onions and parsley and season to taste. Serve with salad.

NUTRITION

Calories *283*; Sugars *8 g*; Protein *30 g*; Carbohydrate *12 g*; Fat *14 g*; Saturates *3 g*

easy

10 mins

45 mins

COOK'S TIP

Jambalaya is a versatile dish which has some basic ingredients – onions, green peppers, celery, rice and seasonings – to which you can add whatever else you may have to hand.

This robust stew is full of Mediterranean flavours. If you do not want to prepare the fish yourself, ask your local fishmonger to do it for you.

Italian Fish Stew

SERVES 4

- 2 tbsp olive oil
- 2 red onions, chopped finely
- 1 garlic clove, crushed
- 2 courgettes, sliced
- 400 g/14 oz canned chopped tomatoes
- 850 ml/1½ pints fish or vegetable stock
- 85 g/3 oz dried pasta shapes
- 350 g/12 oz firm white fish, such as cod, haddock or hake
- 1 tbsp chopped fresh basil or oregano or 1 tsp dried oregano
- 1 tsp grated lemon rind
- 1 tbsp cornflour
- 1 tbsp water
- salt and pepper
- sprigs of fresh basil or oregano, to garnish

1. Heat the oil in a large pan. Add the onions and garlic and cook over a low heat, stirring occasionally, for about 5 minutes until softened. Add the courgettes and cook, stirring frequently, for 2–3 minutes.
2. Add the tomatoes and stock to the pan and bring to the boil. Add the pasta, bring back to the boil, reduce the heat and cover. Simmer for 5 minutes.
3. Skin and bone the fish, then cut it into chunks. Add to the pan with the basil or oregano and lemon rind and simmer gently for 5 minutes until the fish is opaque and flakes easily (take care not to overcook it) and the pasta is tender, but still firm to the bite.
4. Blend the cornflour with the water to a smooth paste and stir into the stew. Cook gently for 2 minutes, stirring constantly, until thickened. Season with salt and pepper to taste.
5. Ladle the stew into 4 warmed soup bowls. Garnish with basil or oregano sprigs and serve immediately.

NUTRITION

Calories *236*; Sugars *4 g*; Protein *20 g*; Carbohydrate *25 g*; Fat *7 g*; Saturates *1 g*

moderate

5–10 mins

25 mins

This is a rich French stew of fish and vegetables, flavoured with saffron and herbs. The fish and vegetables, and the soup, are served separately.

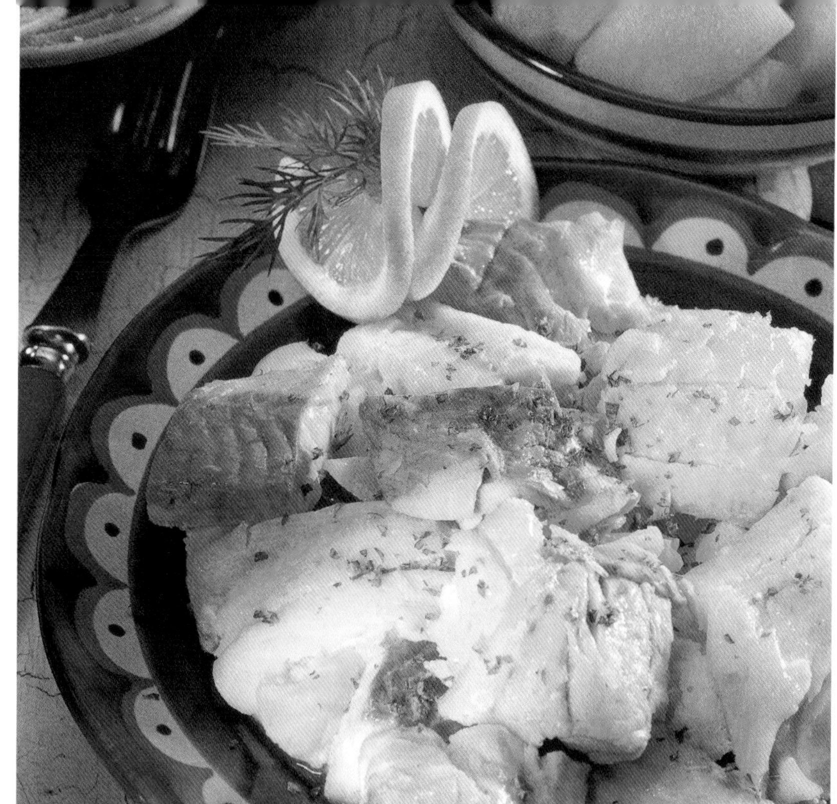

Cotriade

SERVES 4

large pinch of saffron
600 ml/1 pint hot fish stock
1 tbsp olive oil
2 tbsp butter
1 onion, sliced
2 garlic cloves, chopped
1 leek, sliced
1 small fennel bulb, sliced thinly
450 g/1 lb potatoes, cut into chunks
150 ml/5 fl oz dry white wine
1 tbsp fresh thyme leaves
2 bay leaves
4 ripe tomatoes, peeled and chopped
2 lb mixed fish fillets, such as haddock, hake, mackerel, red or grey mullet, chopped roughly
2 tbsp chopped fresh parsley
salt and pepper
crusty bread, to serve

1 Using a mortar and pestle, crush the saffron and add it to the fish stock. Stir the mixture and set aside to infuse for at least 10 minutes.

2 Heat the oil and butter together in a large, heavy-based saucepan. Add the onion and cook over a low heat, stirring occasionally, for 4–5 minutes until softened. Add the garlic, leek, fennel and potatoes. Cover and cook for a further 10–15 minutes until the vegetables are softened.

3 Add the white wine and simmer rapidly for 3–4 minutes until reduced by about half. Add the thyme, bay leaves and tomatoes and stir well. Add the saffron-infused fish stock. Bring to the boil, cover and simmer over a low heat for about 15 minutes until all the vegetables are tender.

4 Add the fish, return to the boil and simmer for a further 3–4 minutes until all the fish is tender. Add the parsley and season to taste. Using a slotted spoon, transfer the fish and vegetables to a warmed serving dish. Serve the soup with plenty of crusty bread.

NUTRITION
Calories *81*; Sugars *1 g*; Protein *7.4 g*; Carbohydrate *4 g*; Fat *4 g*; Saturates *1 g*

easy
 15 mins
 45 mins

COOK'S TIP

Once the fish and vegetables have been cooked, you could process the soup in a food processor or blender and sieve it to give a smooth fish soup.

As with many traditional French fish stews and soups, the fish and soup are served separately with a strongly flavoured sauce passed around to accompany it.

Bouillabaisse

1 To begin, make the red pepper and saffron sauce. Brush the red pepper quarters with a little of the olive oil. Place under a preheated hot grill , cook for 5–6 minutes on each side until charred and tender. Remove from the heat and place in a plastic bag until cool enough to handle. Peel the skins away.

2 Place the pepper pieces into a food processor with the egg yolk, saffron, chilli flakes, lemon juice and seasoning and process until smooth. Begin adding the remaining olive oil, drop by drop, until the mixture begins to thicken. Continue adding the olive oil in a steady stream until it is all incorporated and the mixture is thick. Add a little hot water if it seems too thick.

3 In a large pan, heat the olive oil, add the onions, leek, garlic and fennel and cook for 10–15 minutes until softened and starting to colour. Add the tomatoes, thyme, orange rind and seasoning and fry for a further 5 minutes until the tomatoes have collapsed.

4 Add the fish stock and bring to the boil. Simmer gently for 10 minutes until all the vegetables are tender. Add the fish and return to the boil. Simmer gently for 10 minutes until all the fish is tender.

5 When the soup is ready, toast the bread on both sides. Using a slotted spoon, divide the fish between serving plates. Add some of the soup to moisten the stew and serve with the bread. Pass around the red pepper and saffron sauce to accompany. Serve the remaining soup separately.

SERVES **6 – 8**

5 tbsp olive oil
2 large onions, chopped finely
1 leek, chopped finely
4 garlic cloves, crushed
½ small fennel bulb, chopped finely
5 ripe tomatoes, skinned and chopped
1 fresh thyme sprig
2 strips orange rind
1.75 litres/3 pints hot fish stock
2 kg/4 lb 8oz mixed fish, such as John Dory, sea bass, bream, red mullet, cod, skate, chopped roughly ; soft shell crabs, raw prawns, langoustines (shellfish left whole)
12–18 thick slices French bread
salt and pepper

saffron sauce

1 red pepper, deseeded and quartered
150 ml/5 fl oz light olive oil
1 egg yolk
large pinch of saffron
pinch of chilli flakes
lemon juice, to taste

NUTRITION

Calories *844*; Sugars *10 g*; Protein *69 g*; Carbohydrate *49 g*; Fat *43 g*; Saturates *6 g*

moderate

 45 mins

 45 mins

This is a rich and flavoursome stew of slowly cooked squid, in a sauce of tomatoes and red wine. The squid becomes very tender.

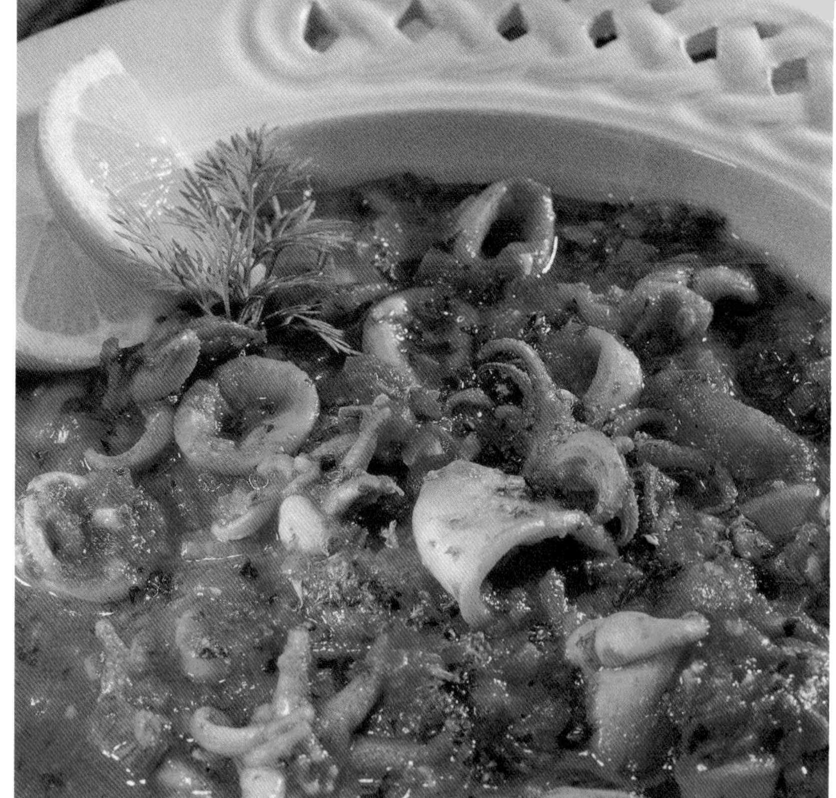

Squid Stew

SERVES 4

750 g/1 lb 10 oz squid
3 tbsp olive oil
1 onion, chopped
3 garlic cloves, chopped finely
1 tsp fresh thyme leaves
400 g/14 oz canned chopped tomatoes
150 ml/5 fl oz red wine
300 ml/10 fl oz water
1 tbsp chopped fresh parsley
salt and pepper

1 To prepare whole squid, hold the body firmly and grasp the tentacles just inside the body. Pull firmly to remove the innards. Find the transparent 'quill' and remove. Grasp the wings on the outside of the body and pull to remove the outer skin. Trim the tentacles just below the beak and reserve. Wash the body and tentacles under cold running water. Slice the body into rings. Drain well on kitchen paper.

2 Heat the oil in a large, flameproof casserole. Add the prepared squid and cook over a medium heat, stirring occasionally, until lightly browned.

3 Reduce the heat and add the onion, garlic and thyme. Cook for a further 5 minutes until softened.

4 Stir in the tomatoes, red wine and water. Bring to the boil and cook in a preheated oven, 140°C/275°F/Gas Mark 1, for 2 hours. Stir in the parsley and season to taste. Serve immediately.

NUTRITION
Calories *284*; Sugars *5 g*; Protein *31 g*; Carbohydrate *9 g*; Fat *12 g*; Saturates *2 g*

easy
20 mins
2 hrs 15 mins

COOK'S TIP

This recipe can be used as the basis for a more substantial fish stew. Before adding the parsley, add extra seafood such as scallops, pieces of fish fillet and large prawns. Cook for a further 2 minutes.

Fideua is a pasta dish which can be found south of Valencia, in western Spain. It is very like a paella but is made with very fine pasta.

Fideua

1 Heat the oil in a large frying pan or paella pan. Add the onion and cook over a low heat for 5 minutes until softened. Add the garlic and cook for a further 30 seconds. Add the saffron and paprika and stir well. Add the tomatoes and cook for a further 2–3 minutes until they have collapsed.

2 Add the vermicelli and stir well. Add the wine to the pan and boil rapidly until it has been absorbed.

3 Add the fish stock, prawns, mussels, squid and clams. Stir and return to a low simmer for 10 minutes until the prawns and squid are cooked through and the mussels and clams have opened. Discard any that remain shut. The stock should be almost completely absorbed.

4 Add the parsley and season to taste with salt and pepper. Serve immediately in warmed bowls, with lemon wedges.

SERVES 6

3 tbsp olive oil
1 large onion, chopped
2 garlic cloves, chopped finely
pinch of saffron, crushed
½ tsp paprika
3 tomatoes, peeled, deseeded and chopped
350 g/12 oz egg vermicelli, broken roughly into 5-cm/2-inch lengths
150 ml/5 fl oz white wine
300 ml/10 fl oz fish stock
12 large raw prawns
18 live mussels, scrubbed and bearded
350 g/12 oz cleaned squid, cut into rings
18 large clams, scrubbed
2 tbsp chopped fresh parsley
salt and pepper
lemon wedges, to serve

COOK'S TIP

Use any combination of seafood. Try langoustines, prawns and monkfish.

NUTRITION

Calories *373*; Sugars *4 g*; Protein *23 g*; Carbohydrate *52 g*; Fat *8 g*; Saturates *1 g*

moderate
10 mins
20 mins

Using curry paste in this recipe makes it quick and easy to prepare. It makes an ideal family supper.

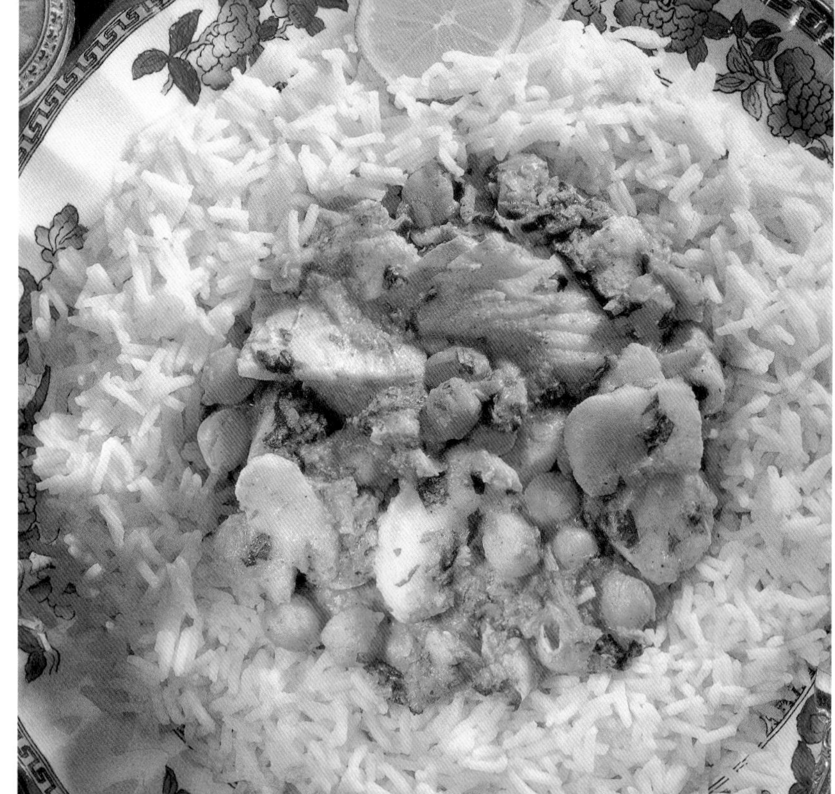

Coriander Cod Curry

SERVES 4

- 1 tbsp vegetable oil
- 1 small onion, chopped
- 2 garlic cloves, chopped
- 2.5-cm/1-inch piece of fresh root ginger, chopped roughly
- 2 large ripe tomatoes, peeled and chopped roughly
- 150 ml/5 fl oz fish stock
- 1 tbsp medium curry paste
- 1 tsp ground coriander
- 400 g/14 oz canned chickpeas, drained and rinsed
- 750 g/1 lb 10 oz cod fillet, cut into large chunks
- 4 tbsp chopped fresh coriander
- 4 tbsp thick yogurt
- salt and pepper
- steamed basmati rice, to serve

1. Heat the oil in a large pan and add the onion, garlic and ginger. Cook over a low heat for 4–5 minutes until softened. Remove from the heat. Put the onion mixture into a food processor or blender with the tomatoes and fish stock and process until smooth.
2. Return to the pan with the curry paste, ground coriander and chickpeas. Mix together well, then simmer gently for 15 minutes until thickened.
3. Add the pieces of fish and return to a simmer. Cook for 5 minutes until the fish is just tender. Remove from the heat and set aside for 2–3 minutes.
4. Stir in the coriander and yogurt. Season and serve with basmati rice.

NUTRITION

Calories *310*; Sugars *4 g*; Protein *42 g*; Carbohydrate *19 g*; Fat *8 g*; Saturates *1 g*

easy

10 mins

25 mins

COOK'S TIP

Instead of cod, make this curry using raw prawns and omit the chickpeas.

Like all Thai curries, this one has as its base a paste of chillies and spices and a sauce of coconut milk.

Red Prawn Curry

1 Make the red curry paste. Put all the ingredients in a blender or spice grinder and blend to a smooth paste, adding a little water if necessary. Alternatively, pound together using a mortar and pestle until smooth. Set aside.

2 Heat the oil in a wok or frying pan until almost smoking. Add the chopped garlic and fry until golden. Add 1 tablespoon of the curry paste and cook, stirring constantly, for a further minute. Add half the coconut milk, the fish sauce and the sugar. Stir well until the mixture has thickened slightly.

3 Add the prawns and simmer for 3–4 minutes until they change colour. Add the remaining coconut milk, the lime leaves and fresh red chilli. Cook for a further 2–3 minutes until the prawns are just tender.

4 Add the basil leaves and stir until wilted. Transfer to a warmed serving dish and serve immediately.

SERVES 4

- 2 tbsp vegetable oil
- 1 garlic clove, chopped finely
- 1 tbsp red curry paste (see below)
- 200 ml/7 fl oz coconut milk
- 2 tbsp Thai fish sauce
- 1 tsp sugar
- 12 large raw prawns, deveined
- 2 kaffir lime leaves, shredded finely
- 1 small fresh red chilli, deseeded and sliced thinly
- 10 leaves Thai basil, or ordinary basil

red curry paste

- 3 dried long red chillies
- ½ tsp ground coriander
- ¼ tsp ground cumin
- ½ tsp ground black pepper
- 2 garlic cloves, chopped
- 2 lemon grass stalks, chopped
- 1 kaffir lime leaf, chopped finely
- 1 tsp grated fresh root ginger or galangal
- 1 tsp shrimp paste (optional)
- ½ tsp salt

NUTRITION

Calories *149*; Sugars *4 g*; Protein *15 g*; Carbohydrate *6 g*; Fat *7 g*; Saturates *1 g*

easy

 15 mins

 10 mins

A rich dish of layers of pasta, with seafood and mushrooms in a tomato sauce, topped with béchamel sauce and baked until golden.

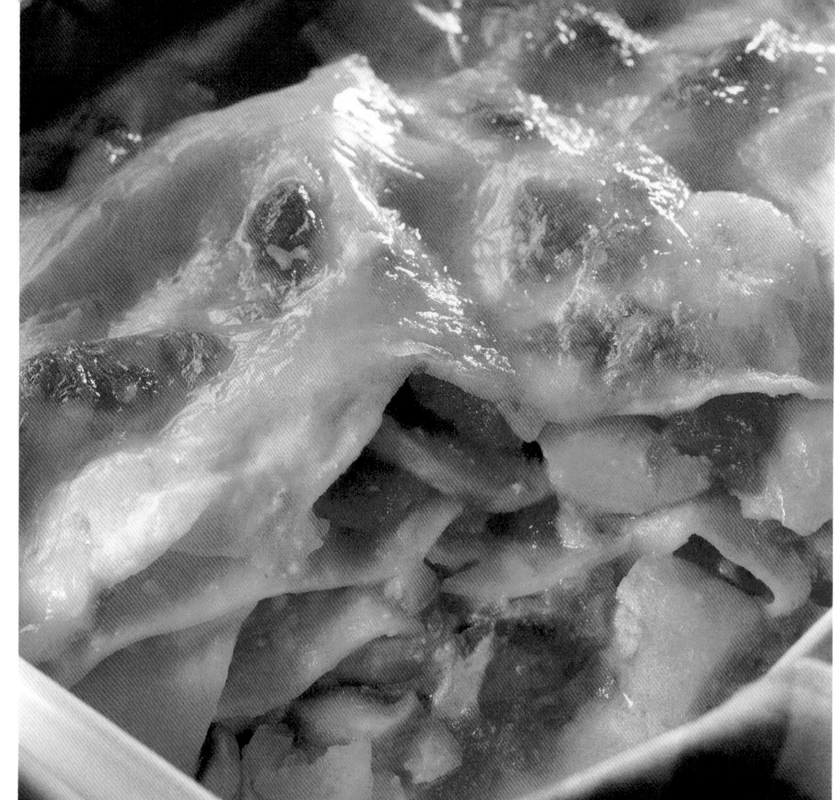

Seafood Lasagne

SERVES 4

- 50 g/1½ oz butter
- 40 g/1¼ oz flour
- 1 tsp mustard powder
- 600 ml/1 pint milk
- 2 tbsp olive oil
- 1 onion, chopped
- 2 garlic cloves, chopped finely
- 1 tbsp fresh thyme leaves
- 450 g/1 lb mixed mushrooms, sliced
- 150 ml/5 fl oz white wine
- 400 g/14 oz canned chopped tomatoes
- 450 g/1 lb mixed skinless white fish fillets, cubed
- 225 g/8 oz fresh scallops, trimmed
- 4–6 sheets fresh lasagne
- 225 g/8 oz mozzarella, drained and chopped
- salt and pepper

1 Melt the butter in a saucepan. Add the flour and mustard powder and stir until smooth. Simmer gently for 2 minutes without colouring. Gradually add the milk, whisking until smooth. Bring to the boil and simmer for 2 minutes. Remove from the heat and set aside. Cover the surface of the sauce with cling film to prevent a skin forming.

2 Heat the oil in a frying pan and add the onion, garlic and thyme. Cook gently for 5 minutes until softened. Add the mushrooms and fry for a further 5 minutes until softened. Stir in the wine and boil rapidly until nearly evaporated. Stir in the tomatoes. Bring to the boil and simmer, covered, for 15 minutes. Season and set aside.

3 Lightly grease a lasagne dish. Spoon half the tomato sauce over the base of the dish and top with half the fish and scallops.

4 Layer half the lasagne over the fish, pour over half the white sauce, add half the mozzarella. Repeat these layers, finishing with the white sauce and mozzarella.

5 Bake in a preheated oven at 200°C/400°F/Gas Mark 6 for 35–40 minutes until bubbling and golden and the fish is cooked through. Remove from the oven and leave to stand on a heat resistant surface or mat for 10 minutes before serving.

NUTRITION

Calories *696*; Sugars *14 g*; Protein *58 g*; Carbohydrate *38 g*; Fat *33 g*; Saturates *3 g*

 easy

30 mins

1 hr 10 mins

You can use whatever combination of shellfish you like in this recipe – it is poached in a savoury stock and served with freshly cooked spaghetti.

Seafood Spaghetti

1 Heat the oil in a large saucepan and fry the onion with the lemon juice, garlic and celery for 3–4 minutes until just softened.

2 Pour in the stock and wine. Bring to the boil and add the tarragon and mussels. Cover and simmer for 5 minutes. Add the prawns, squid and crab claws to the pan, mix together and cook for 3–4 minutes until the mussels have opened, the prawns are pink and the squid is opaque. Discard the tarragon and any mussels that have not opened.

3 Meanwhile, cook the spaghetti in a saucepan of boiling water according to the instructions on the packet. Drain well.

4 Add the spaghetti to the shellfish mixture and toss together. Season with salt and pepper to taste.

5 Transfer to warm serving plates and spoon over the cooking juices. Serve garnished with freshly chopped tarragon.

SERVES 4

2 tsp olive oil
1 small red onion, chopped finely
1 tbsp lemon juice
1 garlic clove, crushed
2 sticks celery, chopped finely
150 ml/5 fl oz Fresh Fish Stock (see page 14)
150 ml/5 fl oz dry white wine
small bunch of fresh tarragon
450 g/1 lb fresh mussels, prepared
225 g/8 oz fresh prawns, peeled and deveined
225 g/8 oz baby squid, cleaned, trimmed and sliced into rings
8 small cooked crab claws, cracked and peeled
225 g/8 oz spaghetti
salt and pepper
2 tbsp chopped fresh tarragon, to garnish

NUTRITION

Calories *372*; Sugars *3 g*; Protein *33 g*; Carbohydrate *45 g*; Fat *5 g*; Saturates *1 g*

easy

20 mins

30 mins

COOK'S TIP

Crab claws contain lean crab meat. Ask your fishmonger to crack the claws for you, leaving the pincers intact, because the shell is very tough.

This is an attractive dish to serve as an accompaniment, especially at parties, and will also freeze well.

Prawns *with* Spinach

SERVES 4 – 6

225 g/8 oz frozen prawns
350 g/12 oz canned spinach purée or frozen spinach, thawed and chopped
2 tomatoes
150 ml/¼ pint oil
1/2 tsp mustard seeds
1/2 tsp onion seeds
1 tsp finely chopped fresh root ginger
1 tsp fresh garlic, crushed
1 tsp chilli powder
1 tsp salt

1 Place the prawns in a bowl of cold water and set aside to defrost thoroughly.

2 Drain the can of spinach purée, if using.

3 Using a sharp knife, cut the tomatoes into slices.

4 Heat the oil in a large frying pan. Add the mustard and onion seeds to the pan.

5 Reduce the heat and add the tomatoes, spinach, ginger, garlic, chilli powder and salt to the pan and stir-fry for about 5–7 minutes.

6 Drain the prawns thoroughly.

7 Add the prawns to the spinach mixture in the pan. Gently stir the prawn and spinach mixture until well combined, cover and leave to simmer over a low heat for about 7–10 minutes.

8 Transfer the prawns and spinach to a serving dish and serve hot.

NUTRITION

Calories *404*; Sugars *2 g*; Protein *13 g*; Carbohydrate *2 g*; Fat *39 g*; Saturates *5 g*

easy

30 mins
20 mins

COOK'S TIP

If using frozen spinach, it should be thawed and squeezed dry before using. You could use fresh spinach, if you prefer.

A *tagine* is a Moroccan cooking vessel consisting of an earthenware dish with a domed lid that has a steam hole in the top.

Moroccan Fish Tagine

1 Heat the olive oil in a large pan or flameproof casserole. Add the onion and cook gently, stirring occasionally, for 10 minutes without colouring until softened. Add the saffron, cinnamon, ground coriander, cumin and turmeric and cook for a further 30 seconds, stirring.

2 Add the chopped tomatoes and fish stock and stir well. Bring to the boil, cover and simmer for 15 minutes. Uncover and simmer for a further 20–35 minutes until thickened.

3 Cut each red mullet in half, then add the pieces to the pan, pushing them into the sauce. Simmer for a further 5–6 minutes until the fish is just cooked.

4 Carefully stir in the olives, preserved lemon and the chopped coriander. Season to taste and serve with couscous.

SERVES 4

2 tbsp olive oil
1 large onion, chopped finely
pinch of saffron strands
½ tsp ground cinnamon
1 tsp ground coriander
½ tsp ground cumin
½ tsp ground turmeric
200 g/7 oz canned chopped tomatoes
300 ml/10 fl oz fish stock
4 small red mullet, cleaned, boned and heads and tails removed
55 g/2 oz stoned green olives
1 tbsp chopped preserved lemon
3 tbsp fresh chopped fresh coriander
salt and pepper
couscous, to serve

NUTRITION

Calories *188*; Sugars *5 g*; Protein *17 g*; Carbohydrate *7 g*; Fat *11 g*; Saturates *1 g*

easy

10 mins

1 hr 15 mins

COOK'S TIP

To preserve lemons, take enough to fill a preserving jar. Quarter them lengthways without cutting right through. Pack with 55 g/2 oz sea salt per lemon. Add the juice of 1 more lemon and cover with water. Leave for 1 month.

This is an impressive-looking Catalan dish using two classic Spanish cooking methods – the *sofrito* and the *picada*.

Spanish Fish Stew

SERVES 4

5 tbsp olive oil
2 large onions, chopped finely
2 tomatoes, peeled, deseeded and diced
2 slices white bread, crusts removed
4 almonds, toasted
3 garlic cloves, chopped roughly
350 g/12 oz cooked lobster
200 g/7 oz cleaned squid
200 g/7 oz monkfish fillet
200 g/7 oz cod fillet, skinned
1 tbsp plain flour
6 large raw prawns
6 langoustines
18 live mussels, scrubbed, beards removed
8 large live clams, scrubbed
1 tbsp chopped fresh parsley
125 ml/4 fl oz brandy
salt and pepper

1 Heat 3 tablespoons of the oil and cook the onions gently for 10–15 minutes until lightly golden. Add the tomatoes and cook until they have disintegrated. Set aside.

2 Heat 1 tablespoon of the remaining oil and fry the slices of bread until crisp. Break into pieces and put into a mortar with the almonds and 2 garlic cloves. Pound to a fine paste. Alternatively, process in a food processor.

3 Split the lobster lengthways. Remove and discard the intestinal vein, the stomach sac and the spongy gills. Crack the claws and remove the meat. Take out the flesh from the tail and chop into large chunks. Slice the squid into rings.

4 Season the monkfish, cod and lobster and dust with flour. Heat a little of the remaining oil and separately brown the monkfish, cod, lobster, squid, prawns and langoustines. Arrange them in a flameproof casserole as they brown.

5 Add the mussels and clams and the remaining garlic and parsley. Set the pan over a low heat. Pour over the brandy and ignite. When the flames have died down, add the tomato mixture and just enough water to cover. Bring to the boil and simmer for 3–4 minutes until the mussels and clams have opened. Stir in the bread mixture and season. Simmer for a further 5 minutes and serve.

NUTRITION

Calories *346*; Sugars *4 g*; Protein *37 g*; Carbohydrate *11 g*; Fat *13 g*; Saturates *2 g*

 challenging

30 mins

1 hr

Based on a traditional Cuban recipe, this dish is similar to Spanish paella, but it has the added kick of dark rum.

Fish *and* Rice *with* Dark Rum

1 Place the cubes of fish in a bowl and add the cumin, oregano, lime juice, rum and sugar. Season to taste with salt and pepper. Mix thoroughly, cover with clingfilm and set aside to chill for 2 hours.

2 Meanwhile, place the garlic, onion and peppers in a large pan. Pour in the stock and stir in the rice. Bring to the boil, lower the heat cover and simmer for 15 minutes.

3 Gently stir in the fish and the marinade juices. Bring back to the boil and simmer, uncovered, stirring occasionally but taking care not to break up the fish, for about 10 minutes until the fish is cooked through and the rice is tender.

4 Season to taste with salt and pepper and transfer to a warmed serving plate. Garnish with fresh oregano and lime wedges and serve with crusty bread.

SERVES 4

450 g/1 lb firm white fish fillets (such as cod or monkfish), skinned and cut into 2.5-cm/1-inch cubes
2 tsp ground cumin
2 tsp dried oregano
2 tbsp lime juice
150 ml/5 fl oz dark rum
1 tbsp dark muscovado sugar
3 garlic cloves, chopped finely
1 large onion, chopped
1 each medium red pepper, green pepper, yellow pepper, deseeded and sliced into rings
1.2 litres/2 pints fish stock
350 g/12 oz long-grain rice
salt and pepper
crusty bread, to serve

to garnish
fresh oregano leaves
lime wedges

NUTRITION

Calories *547*; Sugars *9 g*; Protein *27 g*; Carbohydrate *85 g*; Fat *4 g*; Saturates *1 g*

moderate
35 mins
2 hrs 15 mins

A different way to make the most of crab, this rich-tasting and colourful risotto is full of interesting flavours.

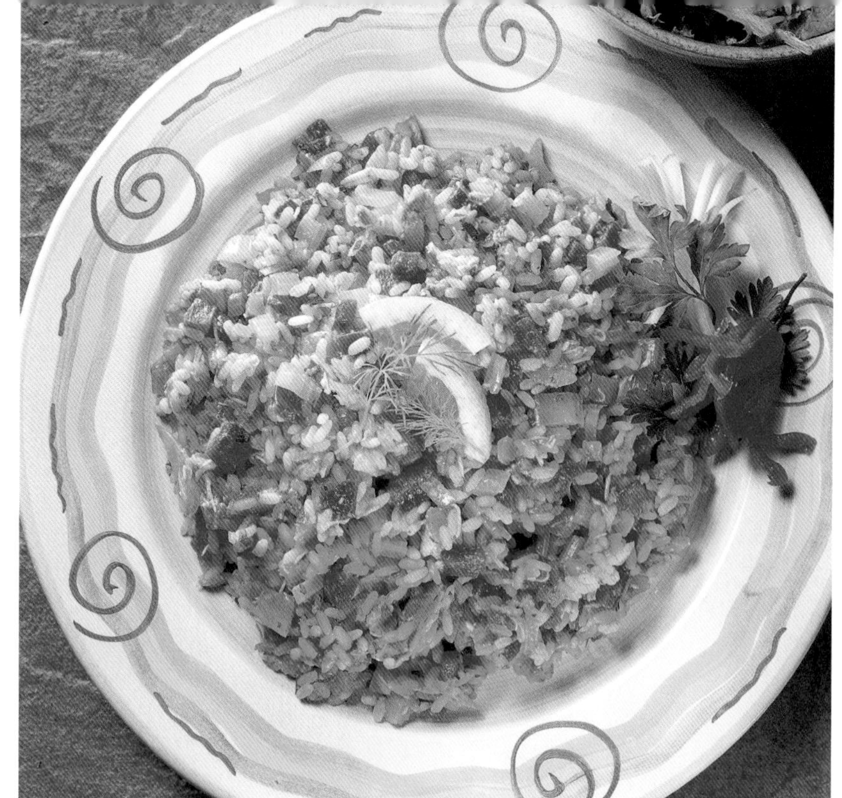

Crab Risotto

SERVES 4 – 6

2–3 large red peppers
3 tbsp olive oil
1 onion, chopped finely
1 small fennel bulb, chopped finely
2 celery sticks, chopped finely
¼–½ tsp cayenne pepper
350 g/12 oz arborio or carnaroli rice
800 g/1 lb 12 oz canned Italian peeled plum tomatoes, drained and chopped
50 ml/2 fl oz dry white vermouth (optional)
1.5 litres/2¾ pints fish or chicken stock, simmering
450 g/1 lb fresh cooked crab meat
50 ml/2 fl oz lemon juice
2–4 tbsp chopped fresh parsley or chervil
salt and pepper

1 Grill the peppers until the skins are charred. Transfer to a plastic bag and twist to seal. When cool enough to handle, peel off the charred skins, working over a bowl to catch the juices. Remove the cores and seeds. Chop the flesh and set aside, reserving the juices.

2 Heat the olive oil in a large heavy-based pan. Add the onion, fennel and celery and cook over a low heat, stirring occasionally, for 2–3 minutes until the vegetables are softened. Add the cayenne and rice and cook, stirring frequently, for about 2 minutes until the rice is translucent and well coated.

3 Stir in the chopped tomatoes and vermouth, if using. The liquid will bubble and steam rapidly. When the liquid is almost absorbed, add a ladleful (about 225 ml/8 fl oz) of the simmering stock. Cook, stirring constantly, until the liquid is completely absorbed.

4 Continue adding the stock, about half a ladleful at a time, allowing each addition to be absorbed before adding the next. This should take 20–25 minutes. The risotto should have a creamy consistency and the rice should be tender, but still firm to the bite.

5 Stir in the red peppers and reserved juices, the crab meat, lemon juice and parsley or chervil and heat. Season with salt and pepper to taste. Serve the risotto immediately.

NUTRITION

Calories *447*; Sugars *11 g*; Protein *22 g*; Carbohydrate *62 g*; Fat *13 g*; Saturates *2 g*

moderate
15 mins
50 mins

Although lobster is expensive, this dish is worth it. Keeping it simple allows the lobster flavour to come through.

Rich Lobster Risotto

1 Heat the oil and half the butter in a large heavy-based pan over a medium heat. Add the shallots and cook, stirring occasionally, for about 2 minutes until just beginning to soften. Add the rice and cayenne and cook, stirring frequently, for about 2 minutes until the rice is translucent and well coated with the oil and butter.

2 Pour in the vermouth; it will bubble and steam rapidly and evaporate almost immediately. Add a ladleful (about 225 ml/8 fl oz) of the simmering stock and cook, stirring constantly, until the stock is completely absorbed.

3 Continue adding the stock, about half a ladleful at a time, allowing each addition to be completely absorbed before adding the next – never allow the rice to cook 'dry'. This process should take about 20–25 minutes. The risotto should have a creamy consistency and the rice should be tender, but still firm to the bite.

4 Stir in the tomatoes and cream and cook for about 2 minutes.

5 Add the cooked lobster meat with the remaining butter and chervil and cook long enough to just heat the lobster meat gently. Serve immediately.

SERVES 4

1 tbsp vegetable oil
4 tbsp unsalted butter
2 shallots, chopped finely
300 g/10½ oz arborio or carnaroli rice
½ tsp cayenne pepper
85 ml/3 fl oz dry white vermouth
1.5 litres/2¾ pints shellfish, fish or chicken stock, simmering
225 g/8 oz cherry tomatoes, quartered and deseeded
2–3 tbsp double or whipping cream
450 g/1 lb cooked lobster meat, cut into coarse chunks
2 tbsp chopped fresh chervil or dill
salt and white pepper

NUTRITION

Calories *688*; Sugars *3 g*; Protein *32 g*; Carbohydrate *69 g*; Fat *31 g*; Saturates *16 g*

 moderate

 10 mins

25 mins

Here, fresh sardines are baked with eggs, herbs,and vegetables to form a dish rather like an elaborate omelette.

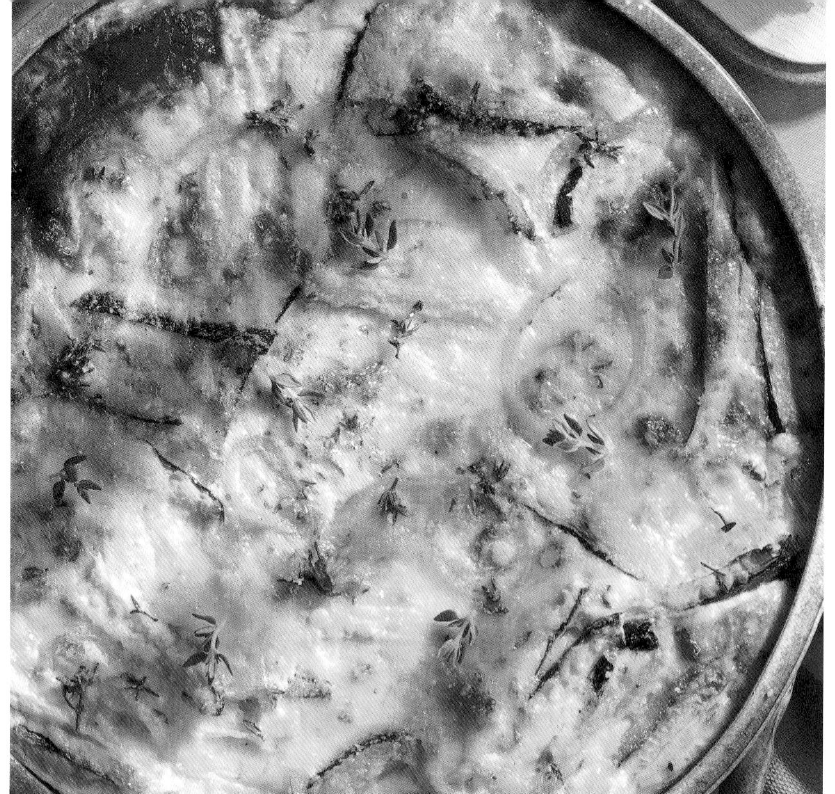

Fresh Baked Sardines

SERVES 4

2 tbsp olive oil
2 large onions, sliced into rings
3 garlic cloves, chopped
2 large courgettes, cut into sticks
3 tbsp fresh thyme, stalks removed
8 large sardine fillets
115 g/4 oz grated Parmesan cheese
4 eggs, beaten
300 ml/10 fl oz milk
salt and pepper

1 Heat 1 tablespoon of the olive oil in a frying pan. Add the onion rings and chopped garlic and fry over a low heat, stirring occasionally, for 2–3 minutes until soft and translucent.

2 Add the courgettes to the pan and cook, stirring occasionally, for about 5 minutes or until turning golden. Stir 2 tablespoons of the thyme leaves into the mixture and remove from the heat.

3 Place half the onions and courgettes in the base of a large ovenproof dish. Top with the sardine fillets and half the grated Parmesan cheese. Place the remaining onions and courgettes on top and sprinkle with the remaining thyme.

4 Mix the eggs and milk together in a bowl and season to taste with salt and pepper. Pour the mixture into the dish. Sprinkle the remaining Parmesan cheese over the top.

5 Bake in a preheated oven, 180°C/350°F/Gas Mark 4 for 20–25 minutes, or until golden and set. Serve the fresh baked sardines hot.

NUTRITION

Calories *690*; Sugars *12 g*; Protein *63 g*; Carbohydrate *17 g*; Fat *42 g*; Saturates *15 g*

 challenging

35 mins

20–25 mins

COOK'S TIP

If you cannot find sardines that are large enough to fillet, use small mackerel instead.

This is a dramatic-looking dish owing to the inclusion of the cuttlefish ink. Although typically Spanish, it is here teamed with polenta.

Cuttlefish *in their own* Ink

1 Cut off the cuttlefish tentacles in front of the eyes and remove the beak from the centre of the tentacles. Cut the head from the body and discard. Cut open the body section along the dark-coloured back. Remove the cuttle bone and the entrails, reserving the ink sac. Skin the body. Chop the flesh roughly and set aside. Split open the ink sac and dilute the ink in a little water. Set aside.

2 Heat the oil in a large pan and add the onion. Cook gently for 8–10 minutes until softened and golden. Add the garlic and cook for a further 30 seconds. Add the cuttlefish and cook for a further 5 minutes until starting to brown. Add the paprika and stir for 30 seconds before adding the tomatoes. Cook for 2–3 minutes until collapsed.

3 Add the red wine, fish stock and diluted ink and stir well. Bring to the boil and simmer gently, uncovered, for 25 minutes until the cuttlefish is tender and the sauce has thickened. Season to taste with salt and pepper.

4 Meanwhile, cook the polenta according to the packet instructions. When cooked, remove from the heat and stir in the parsley and seasoning.

5 Divide the polenta between plates and top with the cuttlefish and its sauce.

SERVES 4

450 g/1 lb small cuttlefish or squid, with their ink sacs
4 tbsp olive oil
1 small onion, chopped finely
2 garlic cloves, chopped finely
1 tsp paprika
175 g/6 oz ripe tomatoes, peeled, deseeded and chopped
150 ml/5 fl oz red wine
150 ml/5 fl oz fish stock
225 g/8 oz instant polenta
3 tbsp chopped fresh flat-leaved parsley
salt and pepper

NUTRITION

Calories *430*; Sugars *2 g*; Protein *24 g*; Carbohydrate *44 g*; Fat *14 g*; Saturates *2 g*

 challenging

15 mins

45 mins

Index

I

J

K

L

M

N

O

P

Q

R